D0547325

SHOW ME
THE
MONEY

SHOW ME THE MONEY

HOW TO FIND THE CASH TO GET YOUR BUSINESS OFF THE GROUND

ALAN BARRELL, DAVID GILL & MARTIN RIGBY

First published 2013 by Elliott and Thompson Limited
27 John Street, London WC1N 2BX
www.eandtbooks.com

ISBN: 978-1-908739-10-0

Text © Alan Barrell, David Gill and Martin Rigby 2013

The Authors have asserted their right under the Copyright, Designs and Patents
Act, 1988, to be identified as Authors of this Work.

All rights reserved. No part of this publication may be reproduced,
stored in or introduced into a retrieval system, or transmitted, in any form,
or by any means (electronic, mechanical, photocopying, recording or
otherwise) without the prior written permission of the publisher.
Any person who does any unauthorized act in relation to this
publication may be liable to criminal prosecution and
civil claims for damages.

Fictional company names have been used in some examples
and case studies. Any similarity to existing company
names is purely coincidental.

9 8 7 6 5 4 3 2 1

A catalogue record for this book is available from the British Library.

Typeset by Envy Design Ltd

Figures designed by Louis Mackay

Printed by TJ International Ltd

CONTENTS

ACKNOWLEDGEMENTS

A work of this nature results from the steady accumulation of information and insight over many years from many people. Individually and collectively, we have had the privilege of 'learning by doing' with cohorts of students at numerous universities, scores of tenants at the St John's Innovation Centre and hundreds of prospective investee firms at pitch panels and across the table in investment meetings.

Singling out individuals by name is daunting given the range of assistance we have received over the years, but it would be remiss of us not to mention the highly committed team who helped deliver the Understanding Finance for Business programme at St John's Innovation Centre in recent years: Paul Anson, Kate Atkins, Marcie Bell, David Byford, Andrea Cockerton, Peter Cowley, Huw Edwards, John Goodger, Richard Moseley, Hugh Parnell, Alex Smeets, Miranda Weston Smith and Bob Westrip.

As for our more particular acknowledgements:

Alan would like to thank Gonçalo de Vasconcelos and Barry James for their contributions on crowd-funding; Jonathan Milner and Pilgrim Beart for adding authenticity through their respective case studies; and colleagues at the Centre for Entrepreneurial Learning, Judge Business School, who over the years have provided some of the wisdom it has been a privilege to acquire and share.

For enlightening discussions at the Access to Finance Expert

Group since the financial crash, **David** would specially like to thank Ray Perman, Gordon Murray and Richard Roberts. Jonathan Walker (Stanford Sloan '05) and Kurt Stammberger (Stanford Sloan '05) provided considerable insight into how start-ups work in Silicon Valley and how venture funds value their investments. David is also indebted to his colleagues at St John's for tolerating the effect that writing this book had on his previously serene disposition.

Martin would like to thank Andrew Burke, Steffi Hussels and Julie Silvester for helping him shape key ideas about growing and funding entrepreneurial businesses as well as his co-founders at Psonar, Ray Anderson and Richard Urwin, for the opportunity to put them into practice. Last but not least he'd like to thank Kate Baxendale, his partner, for putting up with his spending too much time in front of computers.

Finally, we are all grateful to Olivia Bays at Elliott & Thompson for her almost forgiving attitude to our approach to deadlines, borrowed from the late Douglas Adams: 'I love deadlines. I like the whooshing sound they make as they fly by.'

INTRODUCTION

Never waste the opportunity offered by a good crisis.
– Niccolò Machiavelli

What this book covers

Show Me The Money is about enabling you, the entrepreneur, to understand smart money and the people who provide it so that you can access the right type of funding for your venture as easily as possible. You can think of this book as a companion volume to *The Smart Entrepreneur: How to build for a successful business*[1] (*TSE*, for short). *TSE* covers dealing with the broad range of management issues facing entrepreneurs; *Show Me The Money* focuses on raising and managing money for entrepreneurial – often younger and smaller – ventures.

Much of the world, developed or developing, has woken up over the past 30 years to the expanding potential of entrepreneurship. Not just economic potential either: simplified refrigerators and creative uses of mobile phones are empowering farmers and fishermen in India[2] just as new tools enabling analysis of the components of living cells at the molecular level are changing healthcare.[3] However, it is a

---

1 Bart Clarysse and Sabrina Kiefer (London: Elliott & Thompson, 2011).
2 See, for instance: Navi Radjou, Jaideep Prabhu and Simone Ahuja, *Jugaad Innovation: Think frugal, be flexible, generate breakthrough growth* (San Francisco: Jossey-Bass, 2012); Vijay Godindarajan and Chris Trimble, *Reverse Innovation* (Boston: HBR Press, 2012); and C. Prahalad, *The Fortune at the Bottom of the Pyramid* (Cranbury, NJ: Pearson Education, 2009).
3 See www.abcamplc.com.

bittersweet irony that, at least until the opportunity created by the 2007–08 financial crisis, provision of finance during this quiet social and economic revolution had barely moved on from the 1970s.

Over the previous two decades, banks deluded themselves and policymakers alike that an embarrassment of riches lay in selling each other jumbled-up second-hand mortgages rather than undertaking the harder graft of supporting growth firms through industry knowledge and relationship management. Considerable truth underpins the jibe from Paul Volcker, former chairman of the US Federal Reserve (or central bank), that 'the ATM was the only financial innovation he can think of that has improved society'.[4] Fortunately, this is now changing, with the financial crisis leading to a resurgence of interest in investments made by business angels, rapid growth in crowd-funding, the creation for the first time in a generation of a handful of new banks, renewed interest in corporate venturing and a new approach by government to financial regulation and industrial policy, including the reintroduction of grants to support key sectors.

In this section of *Show Me The Money*, we aim to achieve three goals:

- **Content:** In addition to giving you an overview of the whole project, to provide you with an insight into who we, the authors, are – our experience and approach. We also set out as crisply as we can what we understand entrepreneurship to mean.
- **Framework:** To give you a mental map of the current funding scene, including important trends, what works and what doesn't, and which type of funding is most suitable for your venture as it moves through different stages of development. This area is moving faster than at any time in recent memory.
- **How to:** Finally, to set out a succinct version of the key 'dos and don'ts' that are explored in more detail in later chapters. One of the authors was a troop commander in the British Army, and over the years we have come to see the virtues of the Army instruction method: 'tell 'em what you're going to tell 'em, tell 'em, then tell 'em what you've told 'em'.

---

4 *Wall Street Journal*, 19 December 2009.

Context: something about us

In one way or another all three of us have been involved in entrepreneurship in general and funding new ventures in particular for many years. We have all run companies and managed venture funds. And we have all dedicated much of our own time to helping the rising generation of entrepreneurs understand how to build a business case and raise smart money. It is on this accumulated experience of lecturing on business models, raising and managing money, judging business plan competitions and mentoring start-ups that we have drawn in putting this book together.

Our goal has been to distil and simplify the lessons we have learned thanks to the commitment of the entrepreneurs we have worked with over the past 30 years. Learning in this context is a hands-on experience and we do not pretend that using this book will be a complete substitute for your finding out for yourself through immersion, trial and error. But we do hope that it will enable you to accelerate your journey to the end result of raising capital for new ventures.

All three of us are based in Cambridge. Cambridge is a fascinating place to be in terms of entrepreneurship. Though its population is only about 115,000, in less than 50 years the city has gone from being a small, remote Fenland market town known mostly for its medieval university to become

Europe's most successful technology cluster, having produced ten companies valued at more than $1 billion, and two valued at more than $10 billion. In total, Cambridge has over 1,525 high-tech companies, employing more than 53,000 people. In 2011, these companies had a combined turnover of over £11.8bn.

With SVC2UK research revealing that only half the number of companies scale-up in the UK compared to the US, Cambridge has led the way in creating and scaling high-tech companies. Two companies with market capitalisation of over $10bn, Arm and Autonomy, have been built in Cambridge, along with a further ten with market cap of over $1bn – Abcam, AVEVA, CAT, Chiroscience,

CSR, Domino, Ionica, Marshall, Solexa, and Virata. In total at least £50bn of market capitalisation has been generated by the Cambridge cluster.[5]

In planning this book, we had concerns that our combined experience would be overly weighted to the 'Silicon Fen' environment; that we would be a touch parochial. However, as the project unfolded we came to the view that being grounded as practitioners in one of the most vibrant entrepreneurial communities in Europe added specificity and colour to the numerous examples we give based on personal involvement. It helps that Cambridge has become a magnet for entrepreneurs and policymakers from around the world. Staying close to home became one of the easiest ways of becoming cosmopolitan. In addition to frequent interactions with overseas entrepreneurs on our home turf, Alan in particular is much in demand as a speaker and adviser on entrepreneurship and smart funding in countries as far afield as China, Finland and Brazil.

We have striven to make the style of this book both informative and informal. While we aim to convey as much of the critical detail as necessary at each stage, *Show Me The Money* is emphatically not designed to emulate the impenetrable style of the foot-thick tomes on finance you'll be sold if you undertake an MBA or similar course. Accessibility and memorability are key.

Second, all three of us have noted with regret the extent to which the world of entrepreneurship is being invaded by that bane of business life, the self-styled guru. Quite probably you will find your email inbox being filled with spam inviting you to attend a one-day (or one-week) seminar run by showmen with chutzpah to match their glossy credentials, relieving you of a large fee in exchange for simplistic but cleverly-packaged nostrums purporting to solve all your management problems. We earnestly hope that this book never misleads you in this way. Running a business is a complex, inchoate process for which one-

---

5 http://blog.duedil.com/post/37782025436/cambridge-europes-most-successful-tech-cluster [posted December 2012]. Note that one of the current authors, Alan Barrell, was CEO of Domino. SVC2UK is an organisation headed by some of the founders of LinkedIn to bring leading Silicon Valley investors and entrepreneurs to the UK each year: www.svc2uk.com.

size-fits-all remedies simply do not apply. While we strive for clarity, we can't pretend that solutions are always simple.

Next, we hope we respect your intelligence. A depressing number of business books add a caveat to every assertion or example as if the authors had a compliance officer sitting next to them and insisting on inserting words such as 'illustrative only', 'take professional advice' or – the worst – 'on the one hand … but on the other'. We know that you know that already, and we hope that makes this book more punchy.

Finally, all of us have spent too long in the entrepreneurial finance game not to call a spade a spade: if we think that something is a waste of time or misleading or inappropriate for 'gazelle' firms (those that at least double in size every three years) such as yours, we'll let you know.

More context: what is entrepreneurship?

At one point, his interviewer asked the question that is on all our minds: 'Should wise people have known better?' Of course, they should have, Buffett replied, but there's a 'natural progression' to how good new ideas go wrong. He called this progression the 'three I's.' First come the innovators, who see opportunities that others don't. Then come the imitators, who copy what the innovators have done. And then come the idiots, whose avarice undoes the very innovations they are trying to use to get rich.[6]

While we refer you to *The Smart Entrepreneur* for a full discussion of what entrepreneurs do in practice, it will help give context to the rest of this book if we provide you with a flavour up front of our understanding of what entrepreneurship really is and some of the crucial ways in which it differs from other forms of business management.[7]

Analyses of entrepreneurship have identified several different roles and key characteristics over the past 200 years. A survey by Amar

---

6 Bill Taylor, 'Wisdom of Warren Buffett: On innovators, imitators, and idiots', HBR Blog Network, 9 October 2008: http://blogs.hbr.org/taylor/2008/10/wisdom_of_warren_buffet_on_imi.html.

7 This section draws heavily on some of our previous work: David Gill, Tim Minshall, Craig Pickering and Martin Rigby, *Funding Technology: Britain forty years on* (Cambridge: University of Cambridge Institute for Manufacturing, 2007), p. 16. Available at: www.etcapital.com/britain.pdf.

Bhidé[8] sets out a framework first proposed by Humberto Barreto[9]: 'Barreto classifies the roles played by the entrepreneur in the history of economic thought into the four categories of co-ordination, arbitrage, innovation and uncertainty bearing.'[10]

On this analysis, the **co-ordination role** of the entrepreneur was identified by Jean-Baptiste Say (1767–1832), whose *Treatise on Political Economy* (1803) Napoleon sought to have amended to conform to the protectionism of the wartime economy. Say identified the entrepreneur as 'the link of communication' between the 'various classes of producers' and between the producer and the consumer.

Say and Richard Cantillon (*c.* 1680–1734) saw the **risk-bearing role** of the entrepreneur as vital, and Say considered it the fourth factor of production along with land, labour and capital. Producers such as farmers would pay fixed costs for inputs such as seeds or labour but would not have a committed price for their harvest; neither, in due course, would the middlemen, the wholesalers or the retailers: 'Cantillon suggested that entrepreneurs performed the vital economic function of committing to buy inputs without knowing how much customers would pay for their end products.'[11]

As for the distinction between risk and **uncertainty-bearing**, the American economist Frank Knight (1885–1972), one of the founders of the 'Chicago School', distinguished between risk (which is insurable) and uncertainty (which is not). Risks are recurring events and can be laid off through insurance; uncertainties the entrepreneur must bear him or herself. The magnitude of the uncertainties will explain the long-run profitability of an industry in which entrepreneurs are free to enter and leave, or at least exit with low costs.

The 'Austrian School' does not see the entrepreneur as a risk-bearer. Joseph Schumpeter (1883–1950) famously saw the entrepreneur as an **innovator**, leading the way in the creation of new industries through a process of 'creative destruction' and motivated by the 'dream and the will to found a private kingdom'. He argued that: 'Risk

---

8 *The Origin and Evolution of New Businesses* (New York: Oxford University Press, 2000).
9 http://www.depauw.edu/news-media/latest-news/details/24722/.
10 Bhidé, p. 6.
11 Ibid.

obviously always falls on the owner of the means of production or of the money-capital which was paid for them, hence never on the entrepreneur as such.'[12]

Beneath this high-level vision, other members of the Austrian School, such as Israel Kirzner (b. 1930) and Friedrich Hayek (1899–1992), identified the **arbitrage-role** of the entrepreneur. In a socialist or centralised economy, bureaucrats or policymakers have no incentive to find out prices driven by supply and demand, but in a market economy entrepreneurs are driven by the profit motive to sell products at higher prices than they paid for them. The entrepreneur moves markets towards equilibrium through profit arbitrage.

You may be thinking that it is impossible for entrepreneurs to maintain all four roles simultaneously. After all, if Schumpeter is right, then, because innovators sweep away the old guard, they are not risk-bearers and Cantillon is wrong. More realistically, entrepreneurship represents a range of skills and attributes, with different ones being deployed depending on circumstances. The underlying pattern comprises a combination of:

- Enlarging the *available* pie – co-ordinators, risk-bearers and arbitrageurs all do that even when they do not create new products.
- Being more comfortable than average in working with uncertainty, and finding ways of converting uncertainty into manageable risk, one step at a time.
- Being motivated by an element of vision (the impact that innovation can have: 'look how many people are using my software!') as well as profit – though in the commercial sphere profit remains a driver; in our experience many of the most successful entrepreneurs suffer from the benign egoism of wanting to leave the world a better a place at the same time.

Perhaps the key difference between entrepreneurs and managers in more established firms or industries is the use of innovation to

---

12 Joseph A. Schumpeter, *Business Cycles: A theoretical, historical, and statistical analysis of the capitalist process* (New York and Maidenhead: McGraw-Hill, 1939).

Figure 1. Net lending by UK banks to the commercial sector, 2011–2012

Derived from *Trends in Lending: July 2012*, Bank of England.
Data source: www.bankofengland.co.uk

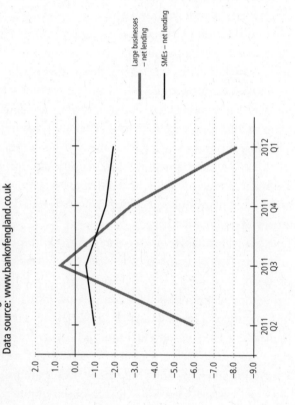

enlarge the overall pie. There is a world of difference between the creative approach of the true innovator and the rent-seeking or paper-shuffling view that Paul Volcker found among the pseudo-engineers of financial markets:

> I found myself sitting next to one of the inventors of financial engineering. I didn't know him, but I knew who he was and that he had won a Nobel Prize, and I nudged him and asked what all the financial engineering does for the economy and what it does for productivity.
>
> Much to my surprise, he leaned over and whispered in my ear that it does nothing – and this was from a leader in the world of financial engineering. I asked him what it did do, and he said that it moves around the rents in the financial system – and besides, it's a lot of intellectual fun.[13]

Readers, your country needs you: a lot of intellectual fun (and the trousering of riches beyond avarice by a tiny minority) has led to a long-term slump in the economy and in business lending (see Figure 1), out of which only real entrepreneurs can lead the world: 'They were careless people, Tom and Daisy – they smashed up things and creatures and then retreated back into their money or their vast carelessness, or whatever it was that kept them together, and let other people clean up the mess they had made.'[14]

Framework: today's financial and investment climate

Time spent in reconnaissance is seldom wasted.
– Sir MacPherson Robertson (1860–1945)

In the 'Trends in venture capital' section below, we discuss building your database of investors to approach, making sure you understand the criteria that a given fund or angel syndicate will likely apply –

---

13 Paul Volcker, cited in the *Wall Street Journal*, 14 December 2009. Not that entrepreneurs are opposed to intellectual fun. Rent-seeking is defined by economists as: 'an attempt to obtain economic rent by manipulating the social or political environment in which economic activities occur, rather than by creating new wealth. One example is spending money on political lobbying in order to be given a share of wealth that has already been created.' Available at: http://en.wikipedia.org/wiki/Economic_rent.
14 F. Scott Fitzgerald, *The Great Gatsby* (New York: Charles Scribner's Sons, 1925), Chapter 9.

what other investments have they made recently, how much will they invest, how long is their timeline, and so on. In the next few pages, we widen the perspective a little to survey the state of the overall market: looking at the bigger picture, what are the key trends you need to know about as they impact on the behaviour of individual investors?

It's only a partial exaggeration to say that 'all politics is local', and similar considerations apply to entrepreneurial investments. Because being embedded in a particular milieu is usually critical for success (domain expertise, knowing who to consult or recruit, from whom to cadge a favour, where to find a grant, and so on) and because start-up investing is often a hands-on activity (much more than simply reading quarterly management accounts is required), it's rare for investors in the entrepreneurial space to operate much across borders. Our comments are accordingly heavily biased in favour of the UK, but we do refer to other countries where appropriate.

The geography of finance

[T]here are known knowns; there are things we know that we know. There are known unknowns; that is to say there are things that, we now know we don't know. But there are also unknown unknowns – there are things we do not know we don't know. (Donald Rumsfeld, then US Secretary of Defense, February 2002)[15]

First, it will be crucial for you to understand where you fit in the overall funding landscape. Figure 2 sets out in pictorial form a conceptual framework that lies behind much of the strategy proposed in this book. Put simply, the better you understand which stage you fit in along the horizontal axis (from pre-seed to sustained growth), the better you'll be able to target investors operating at your stage of development, know what their key concerns are and present your case in a way that addresses their needs in a funding proposal.

Second, over time, as your business grows and benefits from steady growth, a broad range of products, brand recognition and management experience, your funding need may go up in terms of the quantum

---

15 www.youtube.com/watch?v=GiPe1OiKQuk.

Figure 2. Risk finance ladder up the funding landscape
ECFs = Enterprise Capital Funds (see below, page 17)

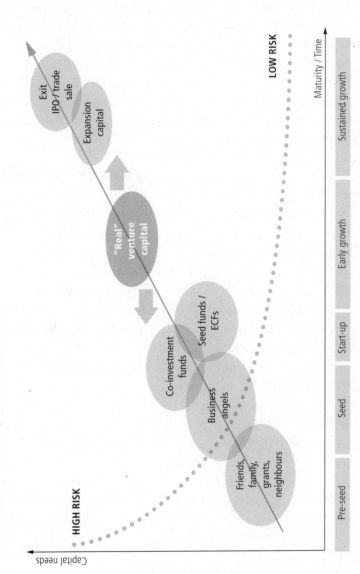

sought from third parties, but the level of risk you represent should go down – you will have moved from the 'unknown unknowns' of the seed stage (when you cannot identify or quantify all the data you need to make an informed decision) to the 'known knowns' of the bank funding stage, when you have years of empirical data to inform your decisions about which products to launch in which markets at what price.[16]

Third, you will see on our funding map that many of the bubbles representing different types of finance overlap or at least intersect well. Imagine these as stepping-stones across the lake you need to traverse. With some of these clusters of stones, you'd have a reasonably easy, anxiety-free stroll. But in the middle of your journey you'll likely be looking for ways to help you across the deep, dark section of the lake: for many years now, in most of Europe there has been a growing absence of 'stepping-stones' to prevent growth firms falling in the water mid-journey.

For reasons discussed in more detail below, finding what we have called 'real venture capital' to see you over the early-growth phase has become increasingly difficult. Part of the purpose of this book is to help you identify ways around seemingly insuperable difficulties.

Meanwhile, as a make-sense test, you may wish to consider Figure 3. As a proportion of total business finance, new equity, 'family friends and fools' and grants are used by under a quarter of all firms. Think of yourself as one of the select few.

Before and after the booms

The phrase 'This time is different' has been described as the most expensive four words in the English language.[17] At least once a generation, with increasing frequency, markets succumb to irrational exuberance, delude themselves that principles of valuation have been reinvented, then bid prices up to vertiginous levels – only to look shocked and aggrieved when the pendulum swings hard the other

---

16 For a more sceptical view of the computability of probabilities and the disproportionate effect of hard-to-predict events in financial markets especially, see Nassim Nicolas Taleb, *The Black Swan* (London: Penguin, 2008).

17 See Carmen M. Reinhart and Kenneth Rogoff, *This Time is Different: Eight centuries of financial folly* (Princeton, NJ: Princeton University Press, 2009).

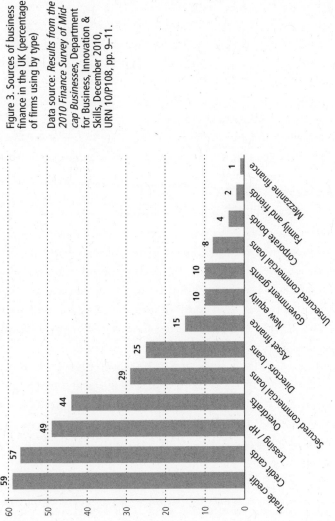

Figure 3. Sources of business finance in the UK (percentage of firms using by type)

Data source: *Results from the 2010 Finance Survey of Mid-cap Businesses*, Department for Business, Innovation & Skills, December 2010, URN 10/P108, pp. 9–11.

way.[18] In the past 15 years, this has happened twice in ways that still impact on entrepreneurial finance:

1. First, the dotcom boom and bust. From about 1997 many investors became over-excited about the potential of the internet to transform how consumers and corporations alike would do business. By March 2001, early-stage firms that had been listed on the NASDAQ – the favourite stock market for 'tech stocks' – saw their valuations tumble, and with that the entire investment chain back down the line from venture funds to angels to family and friends unravelled.[19] After perhaps two or three years in the doldrums, markets rebounded with yet more vigour, so that:

2. More recently, a much wider financial crash started in August 2007 – as billions of dollars of securities backed by sub-prime mortgages could no longer confidently be valued – reached a crescendo with the implosion on 15 September 2008 of the major investment bank, Lehman Brothers. For a week or two, the survival of the banking system was in the balance.[20] Since then, most forms of financial investment, and indeed economic activity in general, have been subdued in developed countries.[21]

The upshot is that, since late 2008, most forms of funding for small- to medium-sized enterprises have been tougher to access than they were in the five years or so of the noughties boom. But that does not mean from your perspective as an entrepreneur seeking funding that you should be downbeat; it does mean,

---

18 For a pacy introduction to how frequently in modern times 'second round' rather than pioneer innovators and investors have been the ones to profit from this cyclicality, see Alisdair Nairn, *Engines that Move Markets: Technology investing from railroads to the internet and beyond* (Chichester: Wiley, 2002).

19 Contrasting accounts of the dotcom episode can be found in: John Cassidy, *Dot.Con – the Greatest Story Ever Sold* (London: Allen Lane, 2002); and Rory Cellan-Jones, *Dot.Bomb: The rise and fall of dot.com Britain* (London: Aurum, 2001).

20 Alistair Darling, *Back from the Brink* (London: Atlantic Books, 2011), Chapter 6.

21 The one industry the crash has stimulated is books about itself. Identifying the best in this broad category is a challenge, but see: *Fool's Gold: How unrestrained greed corrupted a dream, shattered global markets and unleashed a catastrophe* by *Financial Times* journalist Gillian Tett (London: Abacus, 2010); *The Big Short: Inside the doomsday machine* by former Salomon Brothers bond dealer Michael Lewis (London: Penguin, 2011); and *How Do We Fix This Mess?* by the BBC's Robert Peston (London: Hodder & Stoughton, 2012).

however, that you need to be better informed, better prepared, more persistent and more realistic. Think of these pages as your time spent on general reconnaissance.

Trends in venture capital

Even before the crash, availability of real risk capital – investment at the pre-profit, often pre-revenue stage – was becoming scarcer. Each year, the British Venture Capital Association (BVCA) publishes a review of its members' activities, analysed in a variety of ways, including how much investment has been made at different deal stages, from smaller venture transactions to larger rounds involving substantial, established businesses undergoing a re-organisation, for instance by means of a management buy-out (MBO) or management buy-in (MBI).

Since larger transactions require more money, it is not surprising that as a category MBOs receive greater funding than venture deals, but the scale of the difference and the virtual collapse of the venture sector in institutional fund-management terms is remarkable. To see what this means in practice, consider Figure 4, which sets out trends in investment by BVCA members – mostly institutional fund managers. In 2011, the latest year for which data is available, £347 million was invested in early-stage/venture rounds compared to £2950 million in MBOs/MBIs – a ratio of 1:8.5. That the ratio of early- to late-stage deals in 2007 just before the crash was even higher, at 1:17 (£434 million versus £7520 million), only serves to show the extent to which the boom was out of control. And without investment at early stages, it is difficult to see where the pipeline of new businesses – the potential MBOs of the next decade – will come from.[22]

Why is venture the perennial poor relation, out of favour in institutional circles? A major part of the answer is track-record. Taken from the perspective of long-term returns, 'venture' and another key category 'technology' regularly underperform other stages and sub-categories: returns in the buy-out market have been around 15 per

---

22 *BVCA Private Equity and Venture Capital Report on Investment Activity 2011.* Available at: http://admin. bvca.co.uk/library/documents/RIA_2011.pdf.

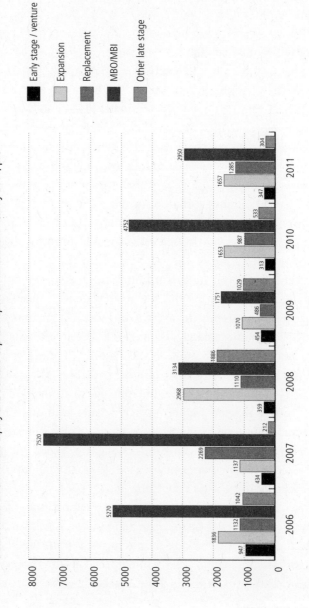

Figure 4. BVCA member investments by stage, December 2011

Data source: BVCA Private Equity and Venture Capital Report on Investment Activity 2011, p. 3

cent IRR over ten years, but returns on venture and technology have been either side of zero[23] – as we can see from Figure 5.

Considerable recent research suggests that the venture and technology categories are not inherently bad bets – even if they may present higher levels of uncertainty than later-stage or more generalist investments. Factors identified as improving the chances of venture funds include:

- A flow of good quality deals
- Broad geographic coverage
- Larger fund size
- The ability to make follow-on investments
- The ability to exit investments on a timely basis

Policy lessons have since been implemented:

Many past UK interventions have fallen foul of a few common problems: trying to achieve too many goals; being sub-scale; limiting the pool of potential investments; and having unrealistic time horizons. However, recent government schemes (i.e. ECFs) have avoided many of these pitfalls and are aiming to make use of the best of private sector experience and establish a credible policy in the area.[24]

Another key concern was 'thin markets':

where limited numbers of investors and entrepreneurial growth firms within the economy have difficulty finding and contracting with each other at reasonable costs. Thick markets, characterised by high levels of repeated interaction between venture capital (VC) and high-growth firms, are needed to build human capital in the sector and provide a large enough market for an ecosystem of high

---

23 *BVCA Private Equity and Venture Capital Performance Measurement Survey 2011*. Available at: http://admin.bvca.co.uk/library/documents/Performance_Measurement_Survey_2011.pdf.
24 Josh Lerner, Yannis Pierrakis, Liam Collins and Albert Bravo Biosca, *Atlantic Drift: Venture capital performance in the UK and the US* (London: NESTA, June 2011), p. 29. ECFs (Enterprise Capital Funds) are venture funds backed by the UK government and are designed to help fill the 'equity gap' by up to £2 million per investment.

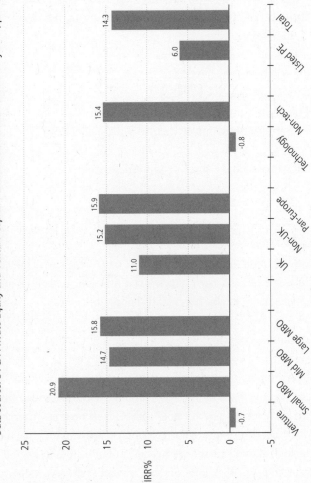

Figure 5. BVCA long-run returns by stage and subcategory, December 2011
Data source: *BVCA Private Equity and Venture Capital Performance Measurement Survey 2011*, p. 5

quality advisers to develop specialising in supporting early-stage VC investment.[25]

Risk alone was far from being the main cause of the low returns; poor fund design, very small fund size and the loss of human capital were at least as much to blame. In addition, the UK had until recently insufficient supporting 'soft' infrastructure and other sources of risk funding to leverage what little venture capital was available:

> The lack of other sources of funding for early stage companies is recognised as one of the underlying reasons for poor UK and European early stage technology VC performance…. If we continue in the UK to expect VC firms to bear the brunt of financing early stage science and technology companies which are not 'venture ready', we will only help them deliver returns which turn off their own investors and reduce the level of genuine private sector venture capital which is available in the UK.[26]

So what is venture capital?

'When I use a word,' Humpty Dumpty said, in rather a scornful tone, 'it means just what I choose it to mean – neither more nor less.'
– Lewis Carroll, *Through the Looking Glass* (1872)

In Chapter 6, we dive a lot deeper into how venture funding operates and what investors are looking for. At this point, though, it is important to bring some clarity to a phrase whose numerous meanings can at times seem contradictory.

'Venture capital' is sometimes used to include all forms of equity funding other than shares in publicly-traded companies. As such,

---

25 www.nesta.org.uk/library/documents/Thin-Markets-v9.pdf. For international comparisons, see also Josh Lerner, *Boulevard of Broken Dreams* (Princeton, NJ: Princeton University Press, 2009).
26 D. Connell, *'Secrets' of the World's Largest Seed Capital Fund: How the United States government uses its SBIR programme and procurement budgets to support small technology firms* (Cambridge: University of Cambridge Centre for Business Research, 2006), p. 38.

it would include small/early-stage deals as well as large/later-stage transactions. When used in this way, 'venture capital' includes 'private equity'.

But at other times, the term 'venture capital' is used specifically in contrast to 'private equity'. Though both types of funding tend to use similar instruments and metrics (such as ratchets and internal rates of return, both of which are discussed in more detail in Chapter 6) and the investment firms running venture and private equity funds tend to belong to the same trade bodies (such as the European Venture Capital Association[27] or the British Venture Capital Association[28]), the dynamics of the companies in which they each invest are fundamentally different.

Put simply, because later-stage private equity is given to companies with a track-record of selling a range of products or services over several years, an established management team, a market reputation and probably some tangible assets to provide security, private equity transactions benefit from having many more 'known knowns' to be modelled and tweaked than do venture deals.

Activity has congregated at the private equity rather than the venture stage of the market for a number of reasons:

- The rewards in percentage terms (often ± 2% management fee and 20% carried interest or profit share) will be similar across fund sizes and types of investment, but in cash terms the rewards to managers running larger funds investing in bigger deals will be markedly larger.
- Later-stage deals represent manageable, quantifiable risk, with considerable prior trading data for transactions such as management buy-outs, whereas early-stage firms with little or no trading data include unquantifiable uncertainties.
- Early-stage transactions may require longer to reach a suitable exit point than the typical eight- to ten-year life of a limited partnership fund.
- Above all, in the boom days up until 2007, late-stage deals were leveraged by excessive and underpriced debt (see below).

---

27 http://evca.eu.
28 www.bvca.co.uk.

In summary, the term 'venture capital' is context-dependent, somewhat like the phrase 'common law', which may be used broadly to mean the opposite of 'civil law' or narrowly to mean 'law which is not statute but judge-based'. Or, for that matter, colloquially to mean custom and usage: your 'common-law husband', for instance. That said, the British Venture Capital Association in its periodic reviews of the market uses the following definitions of investment stages:

Seed: Financing that allows a business concept to be developed, perhaps involving the production of a business plan, prototypes and additional research, prior to bringing a product to market and commencing large-scale manufacturing.

Start-up: Financing provided to companies for use in product development and initial marketing. Companies may be in the process of being set up or may have been in business for a short time but have not yet sold their product commercially.

Other early stage: Financing provided to companies that have completed the product development stage and require further funds to initiate commercial manufacturing and sales. They may not yet be generating profits.

Late-stage venture: Financing provided to companies that have reached a fairly stable growth rate; that is, not growing as fast as the rates attained in the early stage. These companies may or may not be profitable, but are more likely to be than in previous stages of development.

Expansion: Sometimes known as 'development' or 'growth' capital, provided for the growth and expansion of an operating company which is trading profitably. Capital may be used to finance increased production capacity, market or product development, and/or to provide additional working capital.

Bridge financing: Financing made available to a company in the period of transition from being privately owned to being publicly quoted.

Replacement capital: Minority stake purchase from another private equity investment organisation or from another shareholder or shareholders.

Refinancing bank debt: Funds provided to enable a company to repay existing bank debt.

PIPE: Private investment in public companies (minority stake only).

Rescue/turnaround: Financing made available to existing businesses which have experienced trading difficulties, with a view to re-establishing prosperity.

Management buy-out (MBO): Funds provided to enable current operating management and investors to acquire an existing product line or business. Institutional buy-outs (IBOs), leveraged buy-outs (LBOs) and other types of similar financing are included under MBOs.

Management buy-in (MBI): Funds provided to enable an external manager or group of managers to buy into a company.

Public to private: Purchase of quoted shares with the purpose of de-listing the company.

Secondary buy-out: Purchase of a company from another private equity investment organisation.[29]

When you look at the definitions of PIPE (or, for that matter, public-to-private), you may wonder just how 'private' private equity really is.

THE 'MAGIC' OF LEVERAGE

A fundamental difference between venture and private equity transactions is that with assets to be used as security – or in good times, cash flows to lend against – private equity deals usually benefit from significant amounts of debt funding (or 'leverage') to enhance the returns provided to the equity investors.[30] A strong argument can be made that, during the boom years, too much leverage was provided to the private equity sector, but by the end of 2012 leverage was if anything back above its pre-crash highs: the *Wall Street Journal* reported that over the previous six months, 'the average amount of debt that [private equity firms] raise has been about 5.5 times a company's earnings, just above the 2006 average of 5.4 times'.[31]

---

29 http://admin.bvca.co.uk/library/documents/RIA_2011.pdf, p. 15.
30 For a penetrating overview of the misuse of leverage and tax breaks by private equity practitioners, see Robert Peston, *Who Runs Britain?* (London: Hodder & Stoughton, 2008), pp. 28–67.
31 www.businessinsider.com/private-equity-leverage-almost-at-2006-2012-12.

For the transformative impact of leverage from the point of view of equity investors – at least in benign economic times – consider the equity return in the following example:

- You run Flipassets LLP, a private equity fund
- Your fund invests £100 million to buy NaffHotels PLC
- Its total market capitalisation was £900 million, so you borrowed an additional £800M
- The total return on the deal when you sold NaffHotels to DossHouse PLC was 5%
- But you were only paying 3% all-in on the bank debt
- So the total *net* return to you, the equity investor, is calculated as follows:

(a) Profit from investment = Investment * Return on investment
    = £900m * 5% = £45m

(b) Interest on debt = Debt * Cost of debt
    = £800m * 3% = £24m

(c) Net profit to the fund = Profit from investment – Interest on debt
    = £45m – £24m = £21m

(d) Return on equity as % = Net profit / Total equity * 100
    = £21m/£100m*100
    = 21%

In other words, leverage of 9:1 has multiplied your equity return by 4!

What is filling the gap? Business angels

To some extent, the gap in risk funding for high-potential firms has been met by business **angels**, many of whom have invested in multiple rounds and in increasing amounts. In aggregate, angels invest about three times as much in early-stage deals as do venture funds: 'Although there is no comprehensive survey of business angel activity available, an estimated 4,000 to 6,000 business angels were investing up to £1 billion annually by 2000.'[32]

32 Robert E. Wiltbank, *Siding with the Angels* (BBAA/NESTA, May 2009), p. 4. Available at: http://www.ukbusinessangelsassociation.org.uk/sites/default/files/media/files/bbaa_nesta_siding_with_the_angels.pdf.

Along with your own family and a few faithful friends (often referred to unfairly as 'fools'), business angels are likely to be among the most important of your allies at the outset of your entrepreneurial career, supplementing other sources of funding – such as grants – discussed in more detail in Chapter 5. So what is a business angel?

The term was adapted from the world of the theatre, where high-net-worth individuals with an interest in seeing a play produced would underwrite the costs of mounting the initial production, being repaid out of the box-office takings according to an agreed percentage.[33] No two business angels display the same characteristics, but the variety of motivations tends to be similar to that of the theatre funders: a mixture of the inherent interest of the proposal, financial return and wider benefits – whether societal (in the health sector, for instance) or personal (the opportunity to engage with a ground-breaking start-up, perhaps).

Because you don't need a special licence or other form of registration to be an angel in the same way that you would to work as a pilot or comply with VAT regulations, it is extraordinarily hard to provide a definition of 'angel' that will please all practitioners and allow for a comprehensive gathering of data (number of investments, sums involved, rates of return – if you can't measure it, can you manage it?). The closest we can find to an agreed description of a business angel is from the two leading academic authorities on the subject:

> an individual, acting alone or in a formal or informal syndicate, who invests his or her own money directly in an unquoted business in which there is no family connection and who, after making the investment, takes an active involvement in the business, for example as an adviser or member of the board of directors.[34]

The key points are that, though angels may hunt in packs or act as lone wolves for a variety of motives, what matters is that (unlike institutional

---

33 For a humorous insight into the world of theatre angels, see the classic 1968 film *The Producers*, directed by Mel Brooks.
34 C. Mason and R. Harrison, *Developing Time Series Data on the Size and Scope of the UK Business Angel Market* (London: BERR, 2008), p. 8.

funds) they invest their own money in non-family businesses and – crucially – provide the smarts along with the cash: involvement with planning as a non-executive director, for instance, and introductions to strategic customers, invaluable suppliers or vital new hires.

WHAT MAKES ANGELS TICK?

With the need to look after their existing portfolio and fewer positive exits such as trade sales, angels risk running out of fire power, especially where new proposals are concerned.[35] However, angels *are* still investing: *if you understand their motivation and work hard on presenting your case* (see Chapter 3), you'll greatly increase your chances of attracting the right angels.

So what makes angels tick? A revealing survey of 158 UK-based angel investors in late 2008, who between them had invested £134 million into 1,080 transactions, with 406 exits ('exit' meaning any termination of an investment: a venture going out of business, being acquired or going public) addressed the following key issues:

• What are the investment outcomes to business angel investing?
• What are the characteristics of UK business angel investors?
• What strategies and practices are related to improved investment outcomes?[36]

The results are most easily seen in graphic form; see Figure 6. First, the UK cohort showed that, in over half of all investments, angels lost money. The US experience was a little better, but not much – so you may ask why angels keep going.

The answer is in that 'long tail' to the right of the graph: in a significant minority of cases (more significant in the US than the UK), angels can make ten, thirty or even more times their original stake back. The survey showed that, on average, angels made a 22 per cent gross internal rate of return – higher even than professional funds investing in late-stage deals. Which leads to a revealing question:

---

35 C. Mason and R. Harrison, *Annual Report on the Business Angel Market in the United Kingdom: 2009/10* (London: BIS, 2011), p. 5.
36 Wiltbank, *Siding with the Angels*, p. 4.

Figure 6. Angel returns – UK versus US

Source: Robert E. Wiltbank, *Siding with the Angels* (BBAA/NESTA, May 2009)

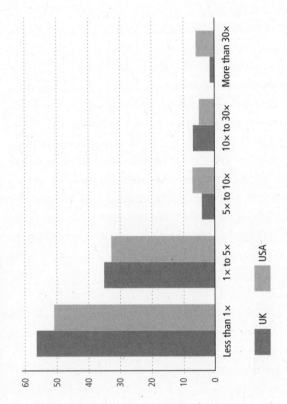

which factors are most likely to push angel deals into territory where the returns are many times the original stake?

The answers matter to you, the entrepreneur. Because most angel investments make use of tax-effective instruments (such as the Enterprise Investment Scheme – see Chapter 4) which favour the use of ordinary shares, angels own the same type of equity as you do as founders: when they do well, you do well.

Figure 7 highlights one of the factors clearly influencing success. Angels with relevant industry experience fared much better than those without the right commercial background. The latter lost money on more than half the deals they invested in, whereas those with useful (probably sectoral) experience to deploy made ten or thirty times their money out of nearly one in five of their ventures.

Another key driver is the extent to which investors researched proposals. We look at pre-investment scrutiny (called due diligence) in more detail in Chapter 4. It usually combines both commercial analysis (probing your business model, talking to your existing customers and getting to know you, the entrepreneur) with some enquiry into legal questions (ownership of patents, recasting of the articles of association). At the time, you may find such cross-examination disconcerting, even a cause for concern ('don't they trust me?'), but the evidence shows that angels who probed hardest obtained the best results, receiving more than their initial stake back in over half of all cases – and sometimes considerably more. (See Figure 8 for the full scale of the positive impact of due diligence.) By implication, when they succeed so will you.

The third key driver is the level of involvement angels have with your business post-investment. We think the survey results bear out common sense and long-term experience. On the one hand, if you have attracted an experienced angel with the business smarts to challenge your strategy and the ability to introduce you to potential key customers, you'd likely want to make use of her abilities in your venture. You do not want an entirely passive investor.

On the other hand, neither do you want someone whose investment is really a means of buying himself a job. There are always exceptions,

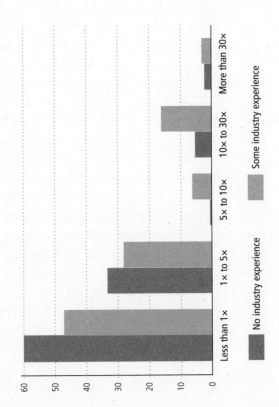

Figure 7. Impact of industry experience on angel returns

Source: Robert E. Wiltbank, *Siding with the Angels* (BBAA/NESTA, May 2009)

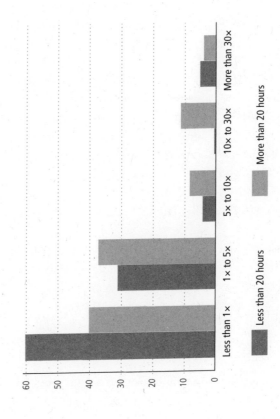

Figure 8. Impact of due diligence on angel returns

Source: Robert E. Wiltbank, *Siding with the Angels* (BBAA/NESTA, May 2009)

but it is unlikely that an individual putting in £150,000 in exchange for the salaried position of marketing director is quite the wizard he has made himself out to be. Many successful angels have a portfolio of a dozen or more investments (and need this variety because of the high mortality rate of individual companies). With a large portfolio, no angel can afford over the longer term to devote more than a few hours each week to any one investee company.

We know of investors who keep up with the executive management of their portfolio firms through booking weekly conference calls to supplement attendance at monthly board meetings. Other things being equal, this is probably about the right level of involvement you should be looking for from angels. It may well be that one of their number is singled out to represent the entire syndicate that committed funds to your venture, but generally board involvement is a positive factor in the success mix. Figure 9 shows that angels with board involvement did significantly better than those without. Angel investment, like entrepreneurship itself, is a contact sport.

BANKS, GRANTS … AND SOME NEW KIDS ON THE BLOCK

A friend of ours gave up a potentially stellar academic career at Oxford University to run his own tech start-up. When asked why, he answered laconically with a light bulb joke:

Q: How many Oxford dons does it take to change a light bulb?

A: Change? Change? Why would you want to change?

Until recently we would have felt the same about finance for entrepreneurs – that change never happens – but by the end of this section you may be more chipper about new developments.

What other sources of funding are available? **Banks** should not normally be seen as suitable sources of funding for new firms before they are shipping product and generating revenues. But once again it is important to note the impact of blockages in one part of the financial system on the rest of the economy: as banks cut back on lending to more established firms, these larger firms are unable to purchase goods and services from start-ups.

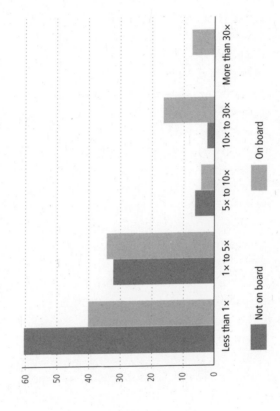

Figure 9. Impact of board involvement on angel returns

Source: Robert E. Wiltbank, *Siding with the Angels*
(BBAA/NESTA, May 2009)

The reductions in bank lending can be seen from Bank of England data set out in Figure 10: a severe decline in net lending (gross lending minus repayments) by UK banks to UK-based non-financial institutions in recent times. SMEs are defined as those with annual account turnover below £25 million.[37] The *rate* of decline in lending is easing (which is why the lines are now tipping modestly up and to the right) but because the lines in Figure 10 are still below the origin you can see immediately that the volume of net new lending quarter on quarter continues to contract.

We explore in more detail in Chapter 5 the criteria banks use when assessing loans, the variety of lending instruments available and how best to present your case once you do reach the point of generating income from sales.

If the existing commercial banks appear to be operating on a work-to-rule basis (and forthcoming international regulations known as Basel III will likely make unsecured lending to early-stage firms even harder), nevertheless as an entrepreneur looking to raise new funds you have numerous reasons to feel more cheerful now than you might have done a few years ago. The financial downturn has stimulated remarkable creativity by real entrepreneurs in the finance space. In no particular order, this creative patch has witnessed numerous relevant initiatives, which individually may seem marginal but that collectively have the power to increase the availability of risk funding at early stages:

- The emergence of **peer-to-peer** (P2P) investing coming up alongside peer-to-peer lending, which was already gaining ground before the downturn. No doubt more will need to happen before P2P investment becomes a regular sub-sector of the angel-related market – we suspect that mistakes and fraud (Warren Buffett's 'idiots' at work, again) will lead to greater regulation and possibly consolidation around a handful of leading platforms. But P2P investment and other crowd-sourcing arrangements are already enabling hundreds of additional, generally smaller, deals to be completed.

---

37 http://www.bankofengland.co.uk/publications/Pages/other/monetary/trendsinlendingdatasets2012.aspx.

Figure 10. Aggregate net lending to UK businesses, 2007–11

Data source: *Trends in Lending: July 2012*, Bank of England, p. 4

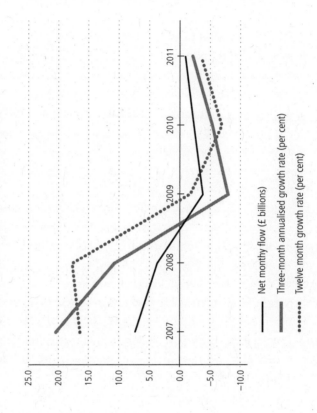

—— Net monthly flow (£ billions)

—— Three-month annualised growth rate (per cent)

••••• Twelve month growth rate (per cent)

- With second-generation platforms facilitating more passive investment in syndicates by less-experienced angels alongside practised 'lead' investors, P2P may lead to an increased pool of experience as well as cutting down radically on search, appraisal and other so-called 'shoe leather costs'. See the Syndicate Room case study below for more information.
- New banks are being launched for the first time in more than a century (after generations of banking consolidation; the four largest clearing banks in the UK account for over 80 per cent of all commercial bank accounts). Several new banks aim to focus on the business market; other previously small players are expanding, not least through the acquisition of branches from the 'big 4' (Barclays, HSBC, Lloyds and RBS, who together account for around 80 per cent of the UK market), which are being forced to divest assets because of competition regulation.
- Among the contender banks are:
  - Metro Bank,[38] founded in 2010, the first institution to receive a new 'high-street' banking licence in the UK for 150 years.
  - Triodos,[39] a co-operative founded in 1980 in the Netherlands to support ethical lending and now opening branches in at least four other European states.
  - Virgin Money,[40] which bought most of what was left of Northern Rock (the first major casualty of the 2007–08 financial crash) in 2012, having previously gained a banking licence through the purchase of the much-smaller Church House Trust.
  - Cambridge and Counties Bank,[41] another 2012 launch, and an unusual contender in that a local authority pension fund helped recapitalise an exiting lender with the aim of improving the supply of business finance (initially on a fully-secured basis).

---

38 www.metrobankonline.co.uk/.
39 www.triodos.co.uk.
40 www.virginmoney.com/worldwide/.
41 www.ccbank.co.uk.

- Santander,[42] a substantial Spanish bank dating back to the nineteenth century, entered the UK commercial market via the acquisition in 2010 of two former building societies (Abbey National and Alliance & Leicester) that succumbed to the financial crash.
- The Co-operative Bank[43] was due to acquire 600 branches from Lloyds Banking Group in 2013; these will now be rebranded 'TSB' and sold off via a stock-market listing.
- Handelsbanken[44] (the Swedish-based 'commerce bank') now has 140 branches in the UK. Each branch sets its own business plan and has responsibility for its own balance sheet – there is no separate 'bad loans' division as is common in the 'big 4' (usually given a euphemistic title such as 'lending services'). Sweden was ahead of its competitors in shaking up banking following a crash in the 1990s.
- Silicon Valley Bank,[45] a respected Californian player of 30 years standing, specialising in technology sectors, has expanded its operations outside the United States (Israel, China, India), and the first international, full service branch in London opened in 2012.

In an industry notoriously resistant to change, this number of developments in a short space of time represents little short of a quiet revolution, one which may soon accelerate: with the exception of Metro Bank, new players have had to think laterally to gain a banking licence, for instance through acquiring a smaller institution already authorised by the regulatory authorities, but at the time of writing, simpler regulations to facilitate the entry of new players were being consulted on.[46]

---

42 www.santander.co.uk.
43 www.co-operativebank.co.uk.
44 www.handelsbanken.co.uk.
45 www.svb.com.
46 http://news.sky.com/story/1033450/fsa-to-sweep-away-new-bank-barriers.

CASE STUDY
Syndicate Room: enlarging the angel pool[47]

A new model of finance is starting to emerge: syndicate funding. Think about it as the good old syndicate model adapted to new technology. Just like the old model, syndicate funding brings together a usually larger lead investor with smaller co-investors. However, instead of this process being cumbersome and, as a result, usually kept to a limited number of well-connected investors, this new model uses crowd-funding technology to allow a larger number of passive investors to co-invest with more active and experienced investors whom they may not ever even meet in person.

Television shows such as *Dragons' Den* and tax breaks such as EIS and SEIS tax relief have created an under-served market need; time-poor but cash-rich professionals have developed an appetite for investing in start-ups but they lack a robust way of doing so. For now, equity crowd-funding platforms do not provide enough trust and quality deal-flow for larger passive investors, business angel networks are not appropriate for these individuals and investment funds are not exciting enough to a younger, tech-savvy generation of cash-rich professionals.

The first company offering this model in the UK is Syndicate Room.[48] The company provides a regulated environment for these individuals to invest in early ventures as passive business angels. The principle behind it is simple. Many high-net-worth individuals have an appetite for investing in new ventures but are either not in a position to or have no desire to become active business angel themselves. Syndicate Room provides the means for such people to become passive business angels in new venture projects at the click of a button. The model unlocks a source of capital that so far has been unable to find its way into start-ups, using it to leverage active business angels' capital and allowing both parties to develop a portfolio risk management approach.

Syndicate Room is a regulated platform for sophisticated investors to co-invest alongside active business angels. Syndicate Room enables individual business angels and members of business angel networks to

47 We are grateful to Gonçalo de Vasconcelos of Syndicate Room for assistance in preparing this section.
48 www.syndicateroom.com. David Gill is a non-executive director of Syndicate Room Ltd.

leverage their investment by allowing informed individuals to co-invest as passive business angels. In turn, these individuals are able to invest in the same deals as active and well-connected business angels and take advantage of their EIS and SEIS tax allowances. Business angels avoid dilution of shareholding and control by formal venture capitalists and other investment funds.

Syndicate Room's target market comprises high-net-worth individuals who work full time and professionals earning over £100k/year, as well as retired high-net-worth individuals who are sophisticated enough to invest as passive investors, such as retired entrepreneurs, accountants and lawyers. Active business angels also use Syndicate Room to diversify their portfolio by investing as passive investors in other start-ups.

These individuals have historically shied away from this type of investment because of its capital requirements and lack of credible solutions. However, Syndicate Room resolves both these issues and government initiatives such as EIS and SEIS tax relief make this type of investment even more appetising. At the end of 2012 Syndicate Room and its co-founders Gonçalo de Vasconcelos and Yutaro Kojima won the 2012 Enterprise Fellowship Scheme.

As of early 2013, Syndicate Room was already partnering with most of the key business angel networks in the UK and is promising to become a key player in this market. As a result of investment deals always having lead investors investing their own capital, the valuation of the start-up is much more realistic and better for investors as it isn't merely set by the entrepreneur but it is the result of long negotiations between the lead investors and the entrepreneurs.

De Vasconcelos expects most deals to be in the range of £150,000 to £500,000, and that around 60 per cent of the capital invested will come from active business angels; the remaining 40 per cent will be sourced from passive business angels and will work as a 'sanity check' for lead investors. If 20 or 40 people think the investment deal is worth their capital, the lead investor can be confident that he is not missing any obvious threat to the new venture. View the arrangement as complementary due diligence without either party being liable to each other.

The main competitors to Syndicate Room are EIS and SEIS funds as these provide the tax advantage together with having a professional team choosing the deals on the customer's behalf. However, they take away control over the investments from the customer as well as the excitement of investing in start-ups.

De Vasconcelos highlighted that, 'for entrepreneurs SR's model has the advantage of gathering the best of both worlds: advice and guidance from experienced Business Angels and passive capital from an army of brand apostles. However, entrepreneurs are unlikely to get the same valuation as they might get from crowd-funding platforms as valuation will have to be negotiated with the lead investor or investors, rather than simply set by the entrepreneur.'

Finally, on the subject of recent developments in funding for small and medium-sized enterprises, an industry-led working group on alternative debt markets made ten recommendations to the UK government in March 2012, including initiatives to improve supply-chain finance as well as P2P and other options for mid-tier firms. It also alluded to the importance of having a national 'business bank' similar to the German Kreditanstalt für Wiederaufbau (KfW):

Our recommendations include proposals to create two new agencies and to unify existing Government interventions under a single brand. The combination [...] would create an entity which carries out many of the functions undertaken by state-owned business support agencies such as KfW in Germany [.... A] KfW-type structure would provide a mechanism to address the market failures impacting the supply as well as the demand barriers preventing businesses from accessing non-bank finance.[49]

Change is happening fast. Change for entrepreneurs means opportunity.[50]

---

49 The Breedon Review, p. 3. Available at: https://www.gov.uk/government/uploads/system/uploads/attachment_data/file/32230/12-668-boosting-finance-options-for-business.pdf.
50 For a review of changing attitudes to local quoted and longer-term investment, see Gervais Williams, *Slow Finance* (London: Bloomsbury, 2011).

How to defy the forces of destiny: dealing with funders

Be not afraid of greatness: some are born great, some achieve greatness and some have greatness thrust upon them.
– Shakespeare, *Twelfth Night* [51]

This section is about how to start putting together a coherent proposal – and in such a way that it fits with the market and investor expectations.

So far we have given you an overview of what *Show Me The Money* will cover and provided you with a conceptual framework for understanding the current market for money. We now turn to a short introduction on how to go about raising and managing funding as the last stage of providing you with a general map to the big picture, helping you (we hope) to see how debt and equity, in particular, differ. This synopsis will be expanded upon stage by stage in later chapters as different types of finance are explained in more detail.

Getting started: what is 'investment readiness'?

First up, we have to say to many of the teams we see that you won't get money just because you need it; you must be investment ready: needing money and being ready for investment are – alas – not necessarily the same thing. In putting your case, it helps if you can demonstrate at least a path to profitability in the short-to-medium term. Your projections must include convincing assumptions on which you have built your future revenues; an 'invention' or a 'good idea' of itself is only the seed of an ungerminated business.

Timing is of the essence. Consider the simplified graph in Figure 11. Your bargaining power will always be strongest when you have time on your side: think of seeking out funding before you need it in earnest. To close a debt deal will likely take weeks. Securing equity – especially when you are talking to investors who are not yet your shareholders – will probably take between six and twelve months from when you first hit the funding circuit. And if you are applying for a

---

51 Act II, Scene V.

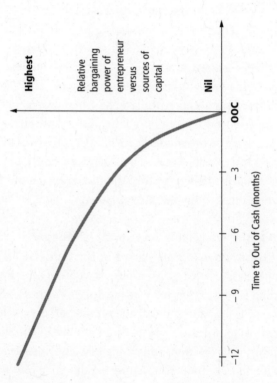

Figure 11. Bargaining power relative to remaining cash

grant, remember that deadlines tend to be cut and dried; miss one, and you may have to wait for the next call for proposals.

And looking for investment is inherently subject to Hofstadter's Law: 'It always takes longer than you expect, even when you take into account Hofstadter's Law.'[52]

Pitching to banks versus pitching to investors

By now, you will have realised that banks and investors such as venture funds provide different types of money for different stages of your business's evolution and categories of risk. These nuances also affect how to approach each source of money. As a simplification, think of banks as being most interested in looking at an individual transaction – how short term can the loan be, will it be self-liquidating, can you give security? Investors by contrast have a long-term stake in the whole company; they need to be intimate with your business model and comfortable that you, the founder, have what it takes to make the plan happen.

Table 1. What to include in different types of business plan

Business plans for banks	Business plans for equity providers
• Executive summary of 2 pages at most • Business background – products and market • Management team and experience • Competitive position • The peak requirement • Profit and loss account and cash flow – with assumptions • Evidence of ability to service (including repay!) all borrowings in the business and security available	• An *outstanding* 2–3 page executive summary • The market opportunity • Product/technology and competitive analysis • The business model • The management team • How the investor achieves an exit; indicative basis of valuation • Appendices for bigger items, including detailed financial and technical data (e.g. patents)

---

52 Douglas Hofstadter, *Gödel, Escher, Bach: An eternal golden braid* (London: Penguin, 2000), p. 152.

Putting this in practice, starting with the business plan you submit, the case to the bank will ordinarily be shorter and will concentrate on how the bank is secured and repaid. With the plan for investors, the result should be closer to 'putting an elevator pitch of the whole business on paper'. Table 1 contrasts business plans suitable for banks with those for equity providers.

More on what angels are looking for

In Chapter 2, we set out in detail what investors are looking for. For the purposes of this summary, we suggest you think of these six elements: team, product, market, sector, profits and exit:

- Investors back people, and to succeed your team will need a range of complementary abilities; if you know you have gaps in the team, suggest how you will fill them. Are you as people ready to take external investment?
- Equity is rare and it is rocket fuel. Do you really have exceptional growth prospects? Why is your chosen sector hot? Is your timing right or are you just a me-too outfit entering a market that is about to peak?
- Protecting your position is not just about intellectual property! Know-how, reputation, first-mover gains or being embedded in key networks matter at least as much.
- What stage are you at? If you can show that you are more than just an idea, that you have proven yourself and have some customers, the more convincing your case will be. Particularly if your offering is genuinely innovative, using Geoffrey Moore's classic diagram provided in Figure 12 may help you to understand where you are in the market evolution cycle – and to explain the case to your targeted investors. If you do have some customers, are they just the enthusiasts? If so, how will this current round of funding enable you to reach the majority of consumers?
- You must be able to explain your *business model*. Where do you fit in the value chain; how do you 'productise' your idea so that day in, day out you will make money?

- How convincingly can you value your business now and when investors exit? (Chapter 6 explores this issue in more detail.)
- What happens when you need more money? Angels in particular are leery of pitches such as: 'in two years' time we will seek £5 million from a venture fund'. This is because angels know that finding such funding is exceptionally difficult – they do not want their deal to become one of the 'living dead' – and even if venture monies are forthcoming, the angels risk being crushed down to a modest holding.

Figure 12. Geoffrey Moore's chasm for innovation firms [53]

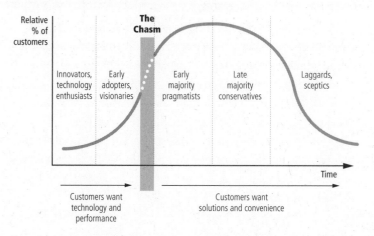

Remember that many countries provide special tax breaks for angels. If you can, make sure that the deal you are proposing complies with the rules to obtain such breaks. In the UK as many as three out of five angel deals use the Enterprise Investment Scheme (EIS) or Seed Enterprise Investment Scheme (SEIS).[54] While valuing a tax break accurately is a difficult task, knowing that she will receive 30 or even 50 per cent back from the government may tip the balance in persuading an angel investor to engage with proposals containing numerous unknown unknowns.

---

53 Geoffrey A. Moore, *Crossing the Chasm* (New York: HarperCollins, 1991).
54 www.hmrc.gov.uk/eis/.

Once the deal is done

Once the deal is done, investors will want you to concentrate on delivering the plan. Above all, it helps to remember that post-investment, everybody is on the same side: don't treat your angels as the enemy or carry on as if you were still negotiating the deal. We have two general observations here. First, be aware of what can go wrong, so that you can deal with it. Second, your chances of making sure things do not go wrong will be greatly assisted with the right monitoring and reporting tools. Taking these in turn:

First, what can go wrong?

- Your plan may have been over-optimistic, so that you need to make radical adjustments to, or 'pivot', the entire concept (more on this in Chapter 3). Pivoting means it changes direction quickly while staying grounded in whatever you've learned; it is *not* jumping randomly from one plan to another.

- Some key issues were not disclosed. If this was a sin of commission – an active failure on your part – the relationship with your investors will likely be difficult to recover.

- Cash is not carefully managed. Most investors look very keenly at 'burn rate': with the money you have in the bank, how many weeks will you survive given your current expenditure? How can you eek out cash to make it last longer?

- You experience delays finding customers. Are these just delays or will the dogs never eat your recipe of dog food? Is it the recipe, or the packaging, or the distribution channels? Are you due yet another pivot?

- Your teams don't settle into clear roles. This often most affects those teams that started out as a band of friends, with no one prepared to step up and take charge as CEO. Issues can also arise as a result of integrating new hires.

- Complex deals can create conflicts. We explore in Chapter 4 why investors use instruments such as ratchets, but the less your interests and theirs are aligned and the more complicated it is to say what success looks like, the less likely it is that you will hit your targets.

Second, your investors will likely present you with the format in which they wish to receive regular financial information. Whether or not they do so, we suggest that for your own ability to measure and manage the business you start straightaway with two key financial tools: a cash flow forecast and basic management accounts.[55]

The **cash flow forecast** can generally be prepared monthly (we have worked with businesses in dire circumstances where weekly was required) and set out on a rolling basis, looking perhaps three months ahead to see how your performance is working out against plan. To be fully effective, it should provide an analysis of variance and show how you can control your burn rate. This will help you identify pinch-points – and above all know when you are out of cash.

Management accounts typically include:
- A profit and loss statement or P&L, which differs from the cash flow mainly because of timing differences (including accruals and work in progress) and non-cash items, such as depreciation of tangible assets or amortisation of debt.
- A balance sheet, enabling you and your investors to understand your asset position at a given time.

Ideally, both the cash flow and the management accounts will be produced within one week of the month end. This will enable you to identify problems early – and avoid some of the issues we discussed under what can go wrong, above.

And finally: money is power and cash is king
We have a colleague who spends most of his time mentoring growth firms, after perhaps a total of 40 years working on 'both sides of the balance sheet'. From him we borrow the words he usually uses in taking to task new teams that have ambition but still lack financial focus: 'Turnover is vanity, profit is sanity and cash is reality.'

---

55 See Karen Berman and Joe Knight, *Financial Intelligence for Entrepreneurs: What you really need to know about the numbers* (Boston, MA: HBS Press, 2008).

And now, let's look in more detail at how to drive from vanity to reality.

Summary
- You *must* understand what different types of funding providers are looking for. Until cash flows from sales, try equity or grants. You cannot approach a bank when you have no cash flow, or an investor unless you are likely to be an exceptional performer.
- Preparation is key – you cannot bowl up to an investor meeting without a shrewd idea of the questions you will face, and how to answer them convincingly.
- Ask someone you know well – and who knows you but is not directly involved in the business – to take an objective look at your proposal before you start seeking finance. Your slightly irritating, nerdy and pedantic friend really comes into her own here in giving you a tough time before you go 'live'.
- It is *always* easier to raise money when you don't need it: negotiate facilities when the need is not immediate. It may be best not to use cash for purchases if you can enter into leasing or similar arrangements.
- Raising money *always* takes longer than you anticipate, so plan accordingly.
- You will rarely get all the money you require to begin with.
- You nearly always underestimate how much you will need.
- Getting your sums wrong does not inspire confidence: the bases on which projections are prepared are a matter of judgement, but make sure basic calculation errors do not creep into your financials.

The box below summarises some of the new developments to consider in relation to international aspects of financing businesses. The principles we set out in *Show Me The Money* can be applied anywhere, but some special considerations must be taken into account when working in international markets, especially those in developing countries and emerging markets. Some of the more creative forms of finance described below were still developing as this book was being written. The summary information provided here and in the short pieces on crowd-funding (see Chapter 5) and the Syndicate Room case study (above) are intended to point you towards further information or advice if the information seems appropriate to a specific place or set of circumstances.

Internationalisation, new technologies, emerging markets and alternative sources of finance: latest developments

As the future unfolds and progress in the age of new technology accelerates, businesses will become increasingly international. Indeed, we already hear the description 'born global' being applied in business circles around the world. Not only has distance, as a concept, been changed by communications technology forever in our daily lives, as well as in our imagination, but companies in many parts of the world not before considered centres of new business development are springing up, replicating the latest business models from elsewhere and inventing new ones. In China, India, other parts of Asia, Africa and South America, the 'digital divide' is being narrowed. We hear now of 'Chilicon Valley', for example.

According to data published by the Organisation for Economic Co-operation and Development (OECD), in terms of gross domestic product (GDP) most growth comes from new companies. The second international conference of 'Start Up Nations', held in Ottawa in 2012, was attended by delegates from 20 countries, including the UK, Canada, Chile, Lithuania and Malaysia, to name but a few.

In universities around the world, student enterprise societies are now highly active and organisations such as the National Association of College and University Entrepreneurs (NACUE) in the UK and the International Consortium of University Entrepreneurs (iCUE) are well-organised and provide educational and management advice and support to University Enterprise Societies, which are now being established in many universities worldwide. More university spin-outs and start-ups requiring finance are emerging. Most recently we have seen the emergence of another organisation in this domain with similar goals – Start Up Generation. It is literally being formed as we write.

Emerging markets are now generating much more of the world's growth than mature markets, many of which are in recession. Emerging markets are giving birth to their own funding institutions and, in some cases, getting government grants to support the formation of new companies, including university spin-outs and all manner of start-ups from elsewhere. This is the 'age of the entrepreneur'. Finding funding is a challenge for nations, provinces, companies, regions and individuals.

Emerging technologies – really innovative technologies – are especially challenging. Turning ideas into inventions, inventions into products and products into companies is complex and difficult. Funding is only one of the challenges – but a big one. Assessing a market for something entirely new that has never existed before provides a challenge for investors as well as entrepreneurs. Who could have predicted the success of Google, Facebook, Skype, LinkedIn and so on? Investors poured money into these companies – eventually, in some cases after great struggle and near disaster. So, we stress that for really new and emerging technologies very deep thinking and planning may be needed, and networking with those close to sources of adventurous private equity funding will be important.

While this book seeks to serve *everyone* interested in the subject of funding businesses, it is not possible to include details of all the national and international variants on subjects such as grant funding or to provide details other than references to useful websites and literature related to venture capital markets and industries in all countries.

There are very good sources of information on European Commission- and US-based grant schemes. In the UK and Europe, schemes inspired by the US Small Business Innovation Research (SBIR) programme are taking root and proving successful. Public funding for small businesses seeking to do business with governments (procurement-linked schemes) is receiving increased attention. The success of UK schemes such as the Small Business Research Initiative – funded with government money via the Technology Strategy Board – has stimulated a European Union objective to make available €7 billion over seven years for such programmes.

In Asia, government support for new business formation is already extensive. Grants can be extremely helpful in the very early stages of company funding. Grant application will always be specific to the criteria and rules of each particular scheme, although the principles involved in making a convincing case remain central to achieving success.

Wherever a company or entrepreneur is situated, we can say that the basics, the fundamentals, we deal with in *Show Me The Money* will hold true. Having a clear business model, a good notion of cash flow, evidence of an addressable market and a good competitive position, together with a truly professional and convincing approach to presentation pitched in line with the known criteria of investors, are all vital. Our work with and in countries such as China and India shows that the models we use in the classroom related to entrepreneurial finance work well across borders and cultures.

Knowledge of the local funding market is essential. However, we have also seen numerous examples of companies in one country obtaining financing from a distant source. For companies with global potential, global sources of finance exist. The US remains a major source of equity financing for companies from far afield.

The Chinese venture capital industry is beginning to invest outside China and putting increasing amounts of money into Chinese companies with international potential. Chinese and Indian investors are seeking investments around the world. Israel has attracted large amounts of US venture money as it has developed an exceptional cluster of new companies.

One of the case studies featured in the book – Cambridge Healthcare Ltd – sourced its first significant venture capital from Luxembourg and Malaysia. There are other examples. Investing in companies with global potential has extended across borders. Investment capital looks for the best deals to support and earn from.

As we write, innovative developments continue as the digital age progresses. 'Crowd-funding' has attracted a lot of attention recently. This type of funding enables significant numbers of individuals to invest small amounts (as little as £1,000) in companies and not-for-profit organisations. The many small amounts can accumulate to make a substantial investment. Careful co-ordination of these many small investments is necessary and companies are springing up to manage such crowd-funding. In a sense, crowd-funding is the awakening of 'sleeping capital'. And there is much sleeping capital – or uninvested capital – available within the asset bases of high-net-worth individuals. This sleeping capital can be attracted to sit alongside investments made by business angels as serious 'top-ups' to the amounts the angels themselves can afford to risk. The case study on Syndicate Room and the information on crowd-funding in Chapter 5 explore these exciting developments further. As we write, one entrepreneur has raised £2.5 million to develop a new version of a computer game, with 25,000 individuals each providing small amounts to make up the total. The rationale here is that the investors are actually making an advance purchase of the computer game they want to play, not investing primarily for a financial return. Different crowd-funding investors will have different motivations.

The angels manage the investment processes professionally and the less-involved providers can observe the results of spreading their available cash within a wider portfolio of interesting companies/organisations. Syndicate Room (described earlier in this chapter) operates a matchmaking scheme connecting the sleeping capital of private investors with the activities of business angels. By validating the investment potential of those seeking funding the company thus provides a flow of quality assessed investment opportunities to investor groups.

When seeking finance for a company there is no substitute – anywhere in the world – for in-depth knowledge and research to find the most likely sources. A wealth of information exists online and you can seek advice from experts, mentors, adviser financial institutions and government-based support agencies as well as locate details of funds, grants, loan prospects and other sources from all over the world.

We have no space here to explore other alternative sources of finance in more detail. There is significant literature on microfinance – the lending of small amounts of money to poor borrowers in emerging markets to enable low-level but important economic development, often in rural areas. Grameenbank, founded by Mohammed Younis, who was awarded a Nobel Prize, and Grameenphone, started in Bangladesh by Iqubal Quadir, are good examples. Other developments such as peer-to-peer lending, thus avoiding banks, and Vodafone's Money Transfer scheme, or M-PESA as it's more commonly known, which enables money transfers and loans via SMS messages using low-cost mobile telephones, are becoming more widely applied in the developing world. Alternative finance is a subject worthy of a complete book, but the scenario is changing rapidly.

CHAPTER 1

FIRST PRINCIPLES – AND ASSESSING YOUR VIABILITY

Overview

Yogi Berra, the famous Italian-American baseball coach, reportedly said, 'If you don't know where you're going, you might end up somewhere else' – which is a rather colourful way of emphasising the need for a plan and planning. We cover in detail how to develop a business plan in Chapter 3, but here let's assume you are right at the beginning of your entrepreneurial journey. You may just be thinking about starting an enterprise (and the word is used advisedly since this book seeks to help those working in the not-for-profit sectors as well as those setting up commercial operations).

If you have a business already, this is a good time to check on the stage it has reached and to reconsider its structure and positioning. Everyone reading this book is likely to want to explore how to finance an enterprise, especially from start-up or in the early stages. And so we start with some searching questions intended to expose how serious you are and how far your thought processes and planning, and indeed actions, have brought you. Starting an enterprise is exciting and challenging. Recollections of giving up all other means of gainful employment and earnings to start over again with no capital and no income – but already facing costs – remain etched on our minds as we write. It's not for the faint-hearted, for sure! But we assume that the faint-hearted aren't reading this book.

The entrepreneurial journey will have begun with dreams, a vision, innovative ideas, hopefully passion followed by much consideration, probably discussion with trusted friends, family and mentors, and a sense of restlessness and frustration that things may not have come together in a sufficiently clear form – in the mind or in recorded notes – to make a start possible. So many questions unanswered; so much to find out and learn. There may be more than one of you; you may be a duo or a team already. No matter – the principle of first things first will serve you well.

Here, then, we explore the fundamentals, the basics. For some already 'on the road', this part may seem like a checklist to merely scan. It could still be useful. For those either contemplating or right at the beginning, here are some simple but critical matters to think about and get right from day one. These details apply to all enterprises. Many companies have found themselves on the brink of success only to be delayed, or even damaged, by having to fix something crucial but fundamental, which should have been sorted out at the start. While it is true that some of these fundamental details are unexciting, boring even, the eventual soundness and security of your business may depend on them.

If you haven't started, do you have a plan?

Since starting an enterprise is a big step to take, having a clear set of ideas about what you intend and whether there is a market for your product or service seems a vital first step. Here is a simple test to help you assess the clarity of your thinking on the enterprise you have in mind. See if you can clearly and succinctly describe your business under the following headings (which will prove very useful later, too, when we discuss how best to present a business to investors):

- **What is your *vision* for the enterprise?** This is the big picture, showing what your enterprise will achieve and the difference it will make. An example might be: 'To lead the revolution in 3D digital modelling' (this is a real example, that of Cambridge Innovision, a company founded some years ago).
- **What is your *purpose*?** In summary, what will you do or provide? For the company using the vision statement above, its

purpose or mission was: 'Through products and services [to] become the supplier of choice enabling museums, art galleries and industrial clients to excel in presenting exhibits and products in unique 3D format online and worldwide.'

- **Does a *market* exist and can you access it?** The vision and purpose may sound electric! But is there really a market and where is it? How big is it? Is anyone else serving it? At this stage in planning the enterprise, details and precise numbers may not be known. But there will be a need to justify starting a business with some definite evidence that there is a market of sufficient substance to be exploited. Routes to that market also need to be understood at this stage, at least in outline.

- **Will you face *competition*?** Competition need not deter you – but the plan, if you start the business, will need to explore it in detail. And if you face a lot of competition, you will need to think seriously about whether to go ahead and invest as another player in a busy market. That will engage you in thinking about why you may be different and what advantages your products and services may offer.

- **Can you clearly define your *product* and/or *service*?** Do you have a very clear idea of what you want to offer? Is it more than an idea; have you tested the concept or proved the principle? Do you have a mock up, a bench model or a prototype? Have you written down a service description a prospective customer might understand? If the product is not yet designed, you need to consider the likely scope and scale of the work needed to get that done and the attendant investment needed to do it. Are there similar products/services already available in the market?

- **Have you formulated a *plan*?** Have you put together a plan yet? Maybe not but now is the time to begin considering how a plan will emerge and who you may need to help develop it over time.

- **Do you need to involve other *people*?** Who, in addition to yourself, will need to be involved? Will it be just you at the start? What initial organisation will be required? What skills, knowledge and talents? If you need other people, are they already available? If not, will they be easy or difficult to find and attract? Do you have a mental vision of a developing organisation? The structure of your enterprise will be determined in part by whether you have directors, how many more you might plan for in the future and how the sharing of ownership will be decided.

- **Do you need physical *premises*?** Not all companies need physical premises; some will be starting from home and some will be forever virtual.

- **How will you *finance* your enterprise?** This book is all about raising money for enterprises, but have you done preliminary work on what it will take to get the operation literally off the ground? Will you and associates be funding the very early stages? Will you be working part or full time? Have you worked out roughly how much the business might need to get it through year one? Are you secure for a defined period of time without outside funding? The simple step of opening a bank account may not be as straightforward as you might think unless you have good answers to simple questions about those early months of operating a business.

- **What potential *risks* may your enterprise face?** This issue will certainly arise in interactions with potential investors. You must take a rigorous approach to evaluating all aspects of your planned actions and the likelihood of success.

- **What are your longer-term *intentions* and personal *objectives*?** Is the enterprise being started as a lifelong business venture, something you will always want to own and operate? Or is the main intention to make a very good profit and return in a specific timeframe and then to exit the business in due course? Why are you doing this? Perhaps you want to make a difference to the lives of others, to improve healthcare or to alleviate poverty. Maybe you just want to make a fortune. Possibly you have an inclusive set of motives to make money, create wealth and improve the environment – only you, the founder, can know. But your motivations are key and will determine in large part issues of funding and raising finance. Investors will be highly interested in what is motivating those seeking finance. And investors include, as subsequent chapters will explore, not only equity and loan investors but those administering grants and research money.

Having worked through this exercise you may now wish to confer with and consult partners, colleagues, associates and advisers. This may be a good and useful next step. Possibly, however, you now feel more fired up than ever; you're ready to go! The next section explores the basics to be considered in setting up the enterprise and urges attention to detail in building basic structures and systems from day one.

Getting the basics right from the start: company formation and establishment

Anyone can start a company at minimal cost. It can be done online. However, we advise you to seek professional help unless you are a professional on aspects of company formation yourself. You can locate the necessary service providers virtually anywhere. Since this book deals with funding businesses, it is assumed that your enterprise will be formed in a way compliant with law (English law in most cases) and we recommend that you appoint a lawyer with suitable experience and qualifications.

This process of itself is very important and the advice of wise counsellors with direct knowledge and experience of individuals and firms available to help would be a great first step. Depending upon the type of business, legal advisers and services can be specialised and some may simply be not qualified for a particular company or market situation. For example, if a company's most important asset is likely to be intellectual property a law firm with appropriate expertise will be needed. In some cases a firm of specialist patent attorneys may be engaged in addition to a general services law firm. Some lawyers and law firms have no expertise in technology businesses, some specialise in the sector.

Some law firms have expertise related to service sector businesses; others specialise in information technology/digital age businesses. If you expect your company to have substantial business overseas, a law firm with knowledge of international business and international offices or associates will be essential. It is always possible to start with a small local firm and develop and change as the business grows. But it is important to make the selection taking account of the points emphasised here. Apart from accounting and financial services and banking, which we will come to later, the best possible legal advice is the most critical professional service your business requires.

WHAT KIND OF COMPANY OR ENTERPRISE DO YOU WANT TO SET UP?

When starting a business, there are choices to be made. In this book we use the term 'enterprise' in its broadest sense because some readers will be seeking to start a not-for-profit organisation while others want to plunge into the great commercial world. When setting up a commercial enterprise, you can:
- Be a sole trader
- Form a partnership
- Set up a limited company

Although they exist, we have not included other variants, and it seems likely that any company seeking to raise money as a sole trader will attract interest only from family and friends (and maybe fools); in these circumstances the kinds of investment-readiness preparation this book seeks to encourage and support would not be necessary.

Partnerships do exist in large numbers and some have been known to raise outside capital. But in general, other than the kinds of limited liability partnerships formed by legal firms and other professional service organisations, the partnership approach is unlikely to be favoured by grant givers and equity investors. If fundraising by a partnership is undertaken, all the principles referred to in this book will apply equally, as would also be the case with a limited company.

For companies or enterprises setting up in the not-for-profit sector, the company limited by guarantee is the favoured approach, although recently the community interest company (CIC) has gained in popularity and numbers, providing as it does some flexibility in share ownership. Forming a charity is a highly specialised process and should be undertaken only with the advice and engagement of a law firm with specific knowledge and experience.

Indeed, as already emphasised, lawyers and law firms offering proven knowledge and experience of the form of company and its sectoral interests should be sought out and consulted as far as possible. Legal fees can be significant and early-stage companies may feel the need to resort to 'affordable legal advice'. Experience tells us that legal advice and services is not one of those areas where cost cutting is wise.

For the purposes of the remainder of this chapter we are assuming that the entrepreneur/s will choose the limited company route for a commercial operation and either the company limited by guarantee or community interest company in the not-for-profit sector. In all cases the procedures for starting up and registration will be similar and the necessary documentation will be provided by legal advisers.

There are also companies specialising in company secretarial services that can do all the work needed. It's best to check the professional competence of these firms by seeking testimonials from previous clients. If you decide to go it alone to start your company, you can complete the entire process online, including registering the business with Companies House. Go to www.companieshouse.gov.uk.

CONSIDERING NAMES

When you decide to register your company, clearly it must have a name. Preliminaries will include checking the availability of any names you're considering; this is a quick and easy process at www.companieshouse.gov.uk or www.duport.co.uk. The naming issue and registration of the name is essentially the same whatever the company type selected. Product names likewise need to be registered and, like designs, can be protected.

Trade marks can be valuable intellectual property. Website domain names have become highly tradable too; some people have made a business out of registering and owning domain names and selling them on, sometimes at astonishingly high prices. This is the age of brands and high-impact domain names relate to branding trends and values. When registering the company, it is likely to be most effective to cover all the naming and web domain issues at the same time, if possible.

Names are important. It is worth taking the time to consult as widely as possible with people whose views might be valuable before making a final decision. It is important to be distinctive and for the name to be closely associated with the business and products. Obscure and over-lengthy names are likely to confuse.

DIRECTORS AND DIRECTORSHIPS

Directors will need to be appointed for limited companies, companies limited by guarantee and community interest companies. One director is the minimum. In charitable organisations trustees are appointed to a trustee board. Company directors do not automatically become employees, although individuals can be both and, in the case of founder directors who are 'doing the business', this is invariably the case. Those engaged directly will be executives.

Other appointed directors may be termed 'non-executive'. The roles and responsibilities of directors and the non-executive and executive roles and responsibilities are discussed in more detail in Chapter 7. One fact to keep in mind is that *all* directors have clearly defined legal responsibilities, whether executive or not. And for all approaching company formation and directorship for the first time, it is very important to understand the key legalities, accountabilities to all shareholders and issues of good company governance.

There are many books and courses dealing with company directorship, and new directors would be wise to ensure they explore and understand their responsibilities. One key responsibility in law for company directors is to ensure that the company at all times is financially viable and solvent.

OWNERSHIP AND EQUITY ALLOCATION

You will need to make a decision, following professional advice, regarding how much share capital to issue at the point of founding the company. In most cases only a proportion of the shares created will be issued to founding directors – usually at a nominal price. Many founding partners of companies take an equal share at foundation stage, but there are no rules about this. Others investing at this start-up stage will usually acquire a minority share holding. The advice of wise mentors and your legal team should be sought and heeded. Decisions taken at this early stage and turned into the first shareholder agreements can be very difficult to undo and unravel later when circumstances and sentiments about investments and ownership may have changed.

It is often the case that family members and friends offer or seek to invest at start-up or soon after. This can be very helpful for the company with world-changing ideas and no money. However, we strongly advise you to start with clear, professional and written shareholder agreements to enable subsequent inward investment without undue complications. The most helpful and seemingly manageable old aunt with cash to spare may be a great source of capital and declare that she will never interfere in your business; however, she may not be so fit and well or indeed sound of mind a relatively short time later when more capital is needed and new investors are ready to engage.

Likewise, 'friends' do not always remain so and disagreements and disputes can arise. Taking money in without having properly constructed shareholder agreements is dangerous and not good business practice.

OTHER BORING ESSENTIALS

Entrepreneurs need to be creative and innovative. Entrepreneurs are often not interested in administration and have little or no time for 'boring details'. Seldom is the entrepreneur an accountant (although some accountants are entrepreneurial). However, once a business is formed and starts any kind of activity –and the first actions of a company often involve spending money – having properly constructed management accounts in place should be considered a prerequisite. Some entrepreneurs manage all this by themselves; generally, however, expert advice and help are needed.

In most instances a competent bookkeeping or accounting company can establish the accounting system and procedures; many companies outsource this service at relatively modest cost. Having structured accounts and the means to handle simple 'in and out transactions' will set the business off on a professional footing and make subsequent transactions easier. When setting up an account, the bank will probably demand that management accounts are available for examination. The bank will definitely want to see evidence of ongoing good management and accounting practice, whether or not any loan finance is under discussion. And choosing a bank is no trivial matter, either. In some instances, you may not even have a choice. One of us helped a very young entrepreneur to set up a retail wine business by personally underwriting and guaranteeing an account with his own bank; the entrepreneuer was unable to access one on his own.

Having a choice of bank is a better option, and in these days of computer-based banking it is too easy to overlook the value of a supportive bank manager to work with. Such professionals do still exist; accounting firms can often provide insights and advice on choice of bank.

Choosing an accountancy firm is also an issue for an early-stage company. Here again, seek the advice of others already past this stage. Among the considerations to deal with will be whether to register immediately for value added tax (VAT). New companies that plan a long-term future generally do so. One immediate benefit is being able to claim VAT returns on purchases of equipment and other expenditures. Although VAT registration is not mandatory until a company has revenues of £79,000 or more, we advise registering the limited company soon after formation.

Once a company is formed it will be subject to compliance with the Companies Act, which entails the production and submission of annual accounts to Companies House and other obligations. Directors will also have clear legal responsibilities, as previously discussed. Companies must trade only as 'going concerns', and one of the key legal responsibilities of directors is to ensure and declare that the company is at all times financially viable. Directors permitting a company to continue trading when insolvent are liable to risk being barred from company directorship for periods of time.

THE BUSINESS MODEL AND BUSINESS PLAN

Business planning is covered in detail in Chapter 3. It is mentioned here to reinforce the importance of developing from your answers to the questions posed above, a coherent and financially supportable business model that responds to the essential demand: 'Show me the money!' Bankers as well as investors will want to see a model that shows clearly the flow of revenues as well as costs. The emergence of ever more digital and web-based companies makes this a particularly important issue. The 'make it, sell it, collect the money and pay the bills' model is easy to understand. The complexity and variety of revenue streams in many current web-based models, for example, can be confusing in the extreme.

The issues mentioned above need very careful thought and close attention when drawing up the business model to present to investors. Beyond the basic model, the detailed business plan will need to give clear substance to a financial model which investors can understand and find credible. Detailed work on the business plan for some entrepreneurs falls into the category of 'boring detail'. The mechanics of building the business plan can be handled by the finance manager or accountant. But the critical inputs must come from the entrepreneur who will be committing to delivering the planned results. If the revenue model is complex, involving revenues from a variety of sources such as membership subscriptions, sales of products and services, advertising and licensing (which can be the case with many web-based businesses these days), schematic representation of revenue flows and not just numbers can be helpful in discussing where the money comes from and ensuring investors feel confident that the model is sound.

If you have already started, are there special or other considerations?
For those already up and running but still at an early stage, the first
sections of this chapter should have provided a useful checklist to give
you a sense of whether you have a clear vision, purpose and plan –
even if only in outline. It should also provide a useful means to check
if all the basics have been put in place and stimulate actions to reach
that point if there are gaps.

Having a clearly expressed record of what you have achieved so far
can be a very helpful way of capturing key information from which
to develop the next phase of the plan. If you have won an award or
successfully completed a product trial or prototype, add the details
to the material you will present to investors when seeking finance.
Any press coverage of positive note will also be worth collecting and
collating. All positive third-party comments and testimonials will
be useful.

Having worked through the early part of this chapter, unless you
managed to tick all the boxes, this could be a good time to reconsider
and reconfigure your plan, the approach and aspects of the detail.
For some companies this might mean quite radical re-thinking and
change. Business plans are not static – markets change, economic
conditions change, product development and customer research
and reactions lead to new and improved ideas. Flexibility is key. And
a rapid response to new and unexpected opportunities can lead to
unexpected and exceptional early success.

An excellent case is that of Domino Printing Sciences plc, now
a highly successful international company manufacturing and
marketing sophisticated ink jet printing equipment and consumables.
It has a market capitalisation today of $1 billion. Founded in 1979 by a
Cambridge engineering graduate, Graeme Minto, Domino was a truly
entrepreneurial start-up. ICI had supported a project to develop an
industrial colour ink jet printer through a contract with the company
Cambridge Consultants Limited. Minto had been the project manager
for Cambridge Consultants for more than five years. Suddenly, ICI
decided to cease investing in the project. For Minto, this could have
meant the end of his job.

But by this time he could see a market and an opportunity for a variable information printing system which need not be full colour but could start life monochrome. With courage and an obvious passion for the technology he had been developing, he negotiated a licence agreement to use the technology, took a second mortgage on his house to raise the money needed to start a company and set out to develop high-speed variable information printing systems for the printing and graphic arts industries. His first customer was a printing company.

But soon after the formation of Domino, then struggling with all the challenges of start up, effectively out of the blue government agencies in the US and Europe passed new legislation mandating that selective variable information be displayed on a wide variety of food and pharmaceutical products. Information such as best before date, batch number and expiry date, which we all now take for granted as part of the guarantee of safe food and effective drugs, never before demanded, became essential if manufacturers were to comply.

In the pharmaceutical sector the demands were driven by notable disasters when contaminated batches of products were distributed and resulted in patient deaths; there was no means of identifying and recalling unused amounts of the contaminated batches. A huge new global market had opened up effectively unannounced. And Graeme Minto, of agile mind and entrepreneurial spirit, responded without delay. Products and support mechanisms and organisations were rapidly put in place and the business grew by leaps and bounds in Europe and the US, not in the market originally targeted, the printing industry, but in the much larger fast-moving consumer goods packaging industries.

In 1985, six years after its birth and having by that time attracted venture capital investment, Domino went to the London Stock Exchange with a public offering of shares. It was by then profitable and growing dramatically, and the issue was oversubscribed 43 times. Subsequently more money was raised through rights issues to make acquisitions and extend the product line as Domino became and remained number one in its market. It is still the leader today, employing more than three thousand people, with a number of international subsidiaries and with more than 90 per cent of its business now taking place outside the UK, in more than 100 countries.

Domino Printing Sciences plc is an excellent example of the enormous value that can result from responding flexibly to emerging market opportunity. In recent times we have seen moves towards Open Innovation. Large companies in particular are seeking to remain competitive and to sustain growth through an open-minded approach to what is going on in technology development and markets. Historically, until the last two decades, companies often acted protectively and sought not to co-operate widely with others seen as potential competitors. The 'fully-integrated company' was a paradigm that dominated the pre-World Wide Web and digital revolution world. Now, with ever-increasing access to knowledge, the realisation that no company can embrace all the knowledge, skills and experience it needs, and the acknowledgement that innovation is the life blood of positive change, development and survival, Open Innovation has become a widespread concept and practice.[56]

Open innovation in an age of very rapid technological development and change makes possible effective synergystic alliances between companies, especially large multinationals and early-stage innovative companies, to join forces and accelerate the introduction of new products in response to market opportunity. Young companies seeking rapid and international growth have all the more reason to ensure they have excellent market intelligence and the flexibility of mindset to respond to unexpected technology and market developments.

For those already in business and for those getting started and making the first successful steps, the journey should be considered one of clear initial purpose and focus, but one in which the road map is constantly revisited and under review.

---

56 For readers interested in exploring Open Innovation further, see the work of Henry Chesbrough and colleagues, working in the US. Particularly recommended is: H. Chesbrough and W. Vanhaverbeke, *Open Innovation: A new paradigm in industrial innovation* (Oxford: Oxford University Press, 2006). Also illuminating is 'How to implement open innovation', a paper available in PDF format from the Institute of Manufacturing, Cambridge (go to www.ifm.eng.cam.ac.uk/uploads/resources/reports/OI_Report.pdf).

About organisations and organisational development

Thus far we have not discussed organisation in any detail. A start-up may be one or two people initially. Cambridge Healthcare Ltd, described earlier, started life and ran for more than a year with one full-time employee, the founder Dawson King and a part-time non-executive director. Cambridge Healthcare, with no dedicated premises, developed and launched its first product within six months of formation. It raised £200,000 of equity investment at the outset from business angels and a year or so later a further £1 million from two venture firms.

From the outset it did have most of the necessary boring details like management accounts in place, and strict financial control was exercised. Following the latest fundraising, a board and advisory board are being formed, the founder is acting as both CEO and chief technical officer and more software developers are being hired. In other words, an organisation is being formed to take the company into the next stage of its development. Cambridge Healthcare is not a particularly exceptional example of a start-up case these days.

Organisation and people development are key issues to be planned and dealt with in any company. In the start-up there will be many unanswered questions. Remaining flexible is important. But investors will expect to see and hear about organisational plans, and there is a clear need to have in view an emerging organisational structure which is much more than an organogram setting out the hierarchy among people and functions in the company. Each company will have specific requirements for bringing particular kinds of qualified people and possibly trainees on board. The organisational plan will proceed within a timetable of planned progress, so will need to be flexible.

The number of employees planned for will be reflected in the costs laid out in the business plan. Outside contracted specialists may be used in the early stages of company development. These will need to be specified in the organisational plan. A three-year business plan will need to foresee how the organisational capabilities and structure are expected to develop. This will include planned development of the board and the introduction of non-executive directors, not just executives and other employees.

It is important to keep in mind an outline plan for organisation and people development which embraces options that depend upon developing circumstances and is described clearly enough to discuss with prospective investors. Within this, questions concerning the eventual and developing roles of founders will need to be confronted. In many instances the founder becomes the first chief executive or managing director, essentially by default. In many technology-based companies the founder may be very technically skilled but have little or no management experience. The development of the organisation may require the introduction of an experienced chief executive. This sometimes proves difficult for the founder and is a matter requiring very sensitive and careful handling. In such cases the presence of an experienced chairperson or non-executive director can prove invaluable.

As companies pass into and through the phases of development shown in Figure 13, the requirements for varying and new skills, talents and experience usually change. The management team at start-up can of necessity look very different two or three years into development of the company. There is no single model which could possibly cover all eventualities. But the principle of constant review and revision leading to constructive change and development needs to be applied. Matters of performance and performance assessment and review and dealing with poor or non-performance are not subjects for this book but need to be kept in mind as factors which will play a part in developing functional and responsive organisations, as will issues of remuneration and incentives.

Investment readiness checklist: 'Show me the traction'

The detailed preparation for fundraising is covered in subsequent chapters. Here, we have concentrated on fundamentals. It may be some time before some entrepreneurs and companies reach the point of contemplating serious attempts to raise serious money. The checklist to confirm readiness to confront investors with a proposition should

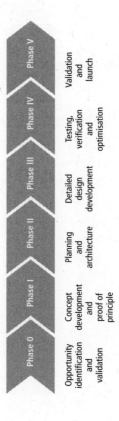

Figure 13. The phases of product development

Phase 0	Phase I	Phase II	Phase III	Phase IV	Phase V
Opportunity identification and validation	Concept development and proof of principle	Planning and architecture	Detailed design development	Testing, verification and optimisation	Validation and launch

be studied with care at the end of the final chapter. It is included here so that you can keep it in mind while working through the rest of the chapters as a constant reminder of the end point we seek to arrive at with confidence to go forth and demand: 'Show me the money'.

- Are all the basics in place for you to claim you have a truly established company or enterprise, is it legally registered, is intellectual property protected, are basic accounting structures in place?
- Do you have a clear record of what you have achieved so far?
- Can you express, with passion, your *vision* for the business? Will it excite and engage others?
- Do you have a clear *purpose* and *plan* expressed in suitable detail in the business model and financial plan – or are you confident that these items will be prepared before you approach investors?
- Is your timetable of milestones to be achieved realistic and has it been tested by reference to independent advisers?
- Can you validate and justify claims you make about the *market*?
- Do you have the outline of an organisation development plan?
- Will you be able to answer questions about risks when investors ask?
- Have you assembled or are you assembling a list of frequently asked questions (FAQs) and model answers?
- Do you have, or plan to have, a very well-structured approach to researching and approaching those investors most likely to 'show you the money'?
- Do you really believe and do your valued advisers confirm that you are truly a candidate for outside investment?

Now is the time to move on and explore the market for money and sources of the finance you need and to begin to consider in detail how you can position your proposition to win favour in a highly competitive environment.

The case study below details the highs and lows experienced by Abcam plc's founder, Jonathan Milner, in his quest for capital and ultimately the company's survival.

CASE STUDY
Interview with an entrepreneur
Alan Barrell talks to Jonathan Milner of Abcam plc

Abcam was founded in 1998 by Jonathan Milner PhD, who is still CEO and very engaged in the business. It has become a world leader in provision for online purchase of sophisticated biological reagents used in medical research and the technical support needed by users. Jonathan was a PhD candidate working in cancer research and was frustrated by the lack of a regular supply of the reagents he needed. Abcam was set up to fill this serious gap in supply and demand.

Abcam eventually floated on the Alternative Investment Market in London and is currently valued at a market capitalisation of $1 billion. It employs 2,000 people and has offices in the UK (Cambridge and Bristol), the US (Oregon, San Francisco and Cambridge, MA), China (Hong Kong and Hangzhou) and Japan (Tokyo). It sells into 140 countries. Abcam is a great example of a company born of entrepreneurial intent and spirit. Financing was not a 'doddle', as the interview with the founder shows. Alan Barrell, himself an entrepreneur having been involved with a number of technology-based start-up and high-growth businesses, when running a venture fund, did *not* choose to invest in Abcam. Not one of his better decisions, as history shows … but life is like that.

ALAN: Where did the initial start-up money come from?
JONATHAN: *When I first discussed the idea for Abcam in 1998 with David Cleevely (founder of Analysys – a leading European telecommunications consultancy), he asked me if I had any money. I said no but I would see what I could do. I went away and after convincing my wife it was a really good idea we re-mortgaged our house to raise £11k. David put in £4K and got 40%; I put in £11K and got 60%.*

Was the company profitable from the outset?
No, it was not profitable until 2002, although we ran it extremely lean and managed our cash flow very well, helped by boot-strapping and

doing custom projects for our scientist customers. I took a salary cut from my post doc salary, which was about £21k, down to £18K; money was extremely tight. Having an excellent finance director in the company early on (Eddie Copeland joined us in 2000) was a critical factor. Finally we became profitable in 2002.

Where did the first 'outside money' come from and at what stage/age?

Subsequently, David networked with what was then the fledgling pre-Cambridge angels and we raised about another £200k in 2000. Also Analysys provided £250K in web development; although I hadn't read the small print and they could invoice that at any time (instead of converting to equity), which two of them did, forcing the company potentially into liquidation. Just two investors were behind this mainly, complete bastards not to be named here, not David. In the end David stepped in and used his pension fund in order to buy out the Analysys shares. As for the two who caused the crisis; well, if they had stayed invested, then they would now be worth millions, ha ha ha! There is a God after all ... draw your own conclusions.

Can you say how subsequent funding was obtained and when customers became the main source of income?

So altogether we got the company going for around a £500K investment if you include the web development equity. Then we broke even in 2001 and reported a profit in 2002; it was a great feeling.

How much equity have the founding owners retained?

David has pretty much sold all of his shares but I still own around 15% of Abcam plc.

Can you tell me about moments of crisis, financial fragility and risk that will forever be in your mind?

Definitely. The situation with Analysys. Also in the beginning buying stock and not being able to sell it; that was a hard business lesson to learn. Inventory eats cash!

What is the most important piece of advice you would offer to today's entrepreneurs about finding and dealing with finance?

Always read the small print (as I said before). Make sure you have enough in the coffers to see you through the bad times; if you are up against it, then money becomes very expensive as the funders can ask any terms they want from the desperate. Cash is king, remember, and as a rule of thumb you will probably need twice as much and things will take twice as long as your initial business plan suggests.

What are your views on venture finance – good, bad or ugly?

We didn't use venture finance for Abcam but I have had experience of it in other companies. What any company needs to realise when taking on venture financing is that often the aspirations of the founders do not match with those of the VCs, and normally this is due to the VCs wanting an exit and return on their investment earlier than the founders, who are still emotionally attached to their business and their baby. This can cause some quite ugly arguments in the boardroom.

Jonathan's views are his own and not attributable to his company or any others. We thank him for his openness and candour.

CHAPTER 2

MORE PRELIMINARIES: 'THE MARKET FOR MONEY'

For the importance of money essentially flows from its being a link between the present and the future.
– John Maynard Keynes

Overview

Understanding the priorities (and prejudices) of bankers and investors, as well as the different types of business finance available, is key to being successful in trying to raise money.

This section covers:
- The different types of business finance that are available
- The objectives of the people and institutions that manage money
- Deciding which kind of funder is the best fit with the business
- How to approach funders most effectively

Fundraising can be a time-consuming and frustrating business. It takes considerable effort to prepare an effective business plan and presentation (see Chapter 3 on preparing for fundraising), and even more time making approaches to banks and investors or pitching at conferences or meetings of business angel groups. Just as it makes sense to thoroughly research a market before launching a new product, it is equally important to understand the 'market for money'.

Equity versus loan finance

There are two main ways to raise external finance:
- By borrowing money to be repaid over time in return for interest (loan finance).
- By selling a stake in the ownership of the business (equity).

The most important distinction in business finance is that between equity and loan, not only because the cost of each can be radically different, but also because of the fundamentally different nature of the relationship between the provider of the finance and the business after the money has been committed.

The relationship between the business and a lender is similar to that with any supplier – even if the lender may have more extensive rights than other suppliers if the business fails to pay interest or make repayments. In contrast, an equity investor becomes a shareholder, that is, a part owner of the business, with all the rights that come with ownership, including a say in matters such as who runs the business, whether and how it can raise more money and, ultimately, whether or not to sell the business.

★ KEY CONCEPT

LENDERS REMAIN SUPPLIERS	EQUITY INVESTORS BECOME PART OWNERS

While there are many variations on these two basic ways of raising money, all commercial finance products can be distilled down to being loans or equity – although the frontier between the two categories is not always clear (for grants, see Chapter 5). Nonetheless, it is worth being clear about the basic characteristics of both lending and equity, not least because the approach and decision making of investors or lenders will be influenced by the type of finance being sought.

Table 2. Debts vs. equity: basic differences

Equity	Loan finance
Money invested for a share of ownership	Money borrowed that is repayable
Permanent capital	Temporary capital
Wholly at risk	Normally secured on the assets of the business
Shareholders' return via dividends, sale of shares or sale of the whole business	Lenders' return by repayment of principal (money lent) and interest

Loan finance

Characteristics

The main characteristic of loan finance is that there is a contractual obligation on the part of the borrower to pay interest and to repay the principal (that is, the sum borrowed) on or by a given date.

In addition, most lenders to private companies will almost certainly have specific rights above those of a normal creditor to enable recovery of interest or principal in the event of default (that is, failure by the borrower to pay the full amount due, either of interest or principal, on a given date).

Types of loan finance

Standard forms of lending include:

- **Term loans**   which have a fixed life and repayment schedule.
- **Mortgage loans**   which are loans secured against property.
- **Overdrafts**   which are a flexible form of finance where the borrower can draw down and repay funds at will within agreed limits.
- **Operational finance:**
  - **Leasing**   where an asset is borrowed and interest paid against its capital value less tax allowances; and factoring, where the debts owed to a business are assigned to a finance house, which lends against the value of those debts.

– **Invoice discounting and factoring**   where the lender advances a variable amount of finance related to all or some of the outstanding debt owed by customers.

These products are explained further below and in Chapter 5.

More esoteric loans include loan stock and company bonds and other products that may have unusual repayment rights or rights to interest and that may have special rights, such as conversion into shares, and may not be secured against the assets of the business.

Loan terms

REPAYMENT

Loans can be repaid in several ways. The principal can be repaid in a single tranche at the end of the life of the loan. This is called a 'bullet' repayment and is, for example, the method used in an endowment mortgage home loan. Alternatively, the principal can be repaid over the life of the loan in equal payments, with separate interest payments (which used to be common for commercial term loans). In most cases where banks are lending to SMEs, repayment and interest is paid in equal combined payments over the life of the loan, each payment comprising mainly interest at the outset of the loan period but increasingly principal as the end of the term is reached.

INTEREST

The return for a lender is interest payable periodically (usually monthly, quarterly, bi-annually or annually) at a rate or a margin fixed at the outset of the loan agreement. If the interest is at a fixed rate, then this is expressed as a percentage of the capital borrowed (for example, 12 per cent is £12 interest payable annually per £100 borrowed). If the interest is variable, then it is usually expressed as a percentage margin over one of the standard base rates, such as finance house base rate (for leasing or lease purchase – see the 'Operational finance' section, later in this chapter), three-month LIBOR (for lending by City institutions) or bank base rate (for loans from the clearing banks).

SECURITY AND DEFAULT

Since the only return to a lender is interest, beyond repayment of the money borrowed (the 'principal'), the loss of all or part of the principal can have a significant, detrimental impact on the economics of lending.

★ EXAMPLE
Why banks can't fund losses out of interest

As an example of this challenge in action, say a bank lends money charging an interest rate of 10% per annum. The bank has to finance that loan, either by taking deposits or by raising money on the wholesale markets. Depositors or wholesale lenders may receive interest of 7.5% per annum, leaving the bank with a margin of 2.5%, out of which it needs to meet the costs of running its lending business as well as covering any losses. Let's assume that a further 0.5% of the annual interest on all the bank's loans is the cost of making and administering those loans. Under this scenario, if a business borrower was to fail, having borrowed £100,000, and the bank lost all the principal, it would have to lend 50 times that amount, or a further £5,000,000, to recover the lost £100,000 within a year.

For this reason, every banker is looking for security, that is, the right to be repaid from the proceeds of liquidating (selling for cash) some of the assets (such as property) owned by the borrower. To make this work, a lender will usually seek some specific rights to recover the outstanding debt in the event of default. These rights may appear in the loan agreement or in a specific agreement relating to the security itself, such as a mortgage.

FIXED CHARGES

Where these rights, in the form of a charge, relate to a particular asset or assets, the charge is termed a 'fixed' charge. Generally, these charges give the lender priority in the recovery of loan and unpaid interest, but limited to the cash that can be raised by liquidating the assets charged, over the unsecured creditors. The most common example of

SHOW ME THE MONEY

a fixed charge is a domestic mortgage, which secures the loan made to a homeowner on a house or flat, usually where the loan has been used to purchase that property. A less obvious fixed charge is one over book debts, that is, the money owed to a business by its customers. Only a bank or an invoice discounter (see the 'Operational finance' section, later in this chapter) can have a valid fixed charge over book debts.

FLOATING CHARGES

Additionally, the company can grant a charge against its assets in general, called a floating charge, which, while it gives priority to the lender over most unsecured creditors, ranks after the preferential creditors (creditors ranking ahead of others when realisations are achieved from assets not covered by a fixed charge – mainly wages and pension contributions); since 15 September 2003, HMRC[57] is no longer a preferential creditor in respect of tax, including VAT and PAYE).

REGISTRATION OF CHARGES

The lender must register these charges with Companies House in the case of charges on business assets, and additionally with the Land Registry in the case of charges on property (i.e. buildings and land). Registration enables subsequent lenders or other creditors to establish whether there are uncharged assets in the business available for them to seek fixed charges over, or to take a general view of the quality and solvency of the business.

BANK DEBENTURES

Most banks will require borrowers to enter into a standard security agreement, usually referred to as a debenture, which formalises their claim to a fixed charge over book debts and a floating charge over all other assets, and specifies the rights the bank has to act in the event that the borrower fails to pay interest, or make repayments, when they are due.

---

57 Or its predecessors: Inland Revenue, HM Customs & Excise and the Department of Social Security in respect of National Insurance contributions.

APPOINTMENT OF A RECEIVER

In the case of a default, particularly when it becomes clear that the borrower can no longer service the debt, the lender who has a charge on the borrower's assets will usually have the ultimate right to appoint a receiver to recover the outstanding debt from the sale of those assets.

Operational finance

Operational finance is a term used to describe financing that is related to the assets used in the business. These assets may be plant and equipment, for which the operational finance product could be leasing or hire purchase, or they may be financial assets, such as valid invoices issued, for which the operational finance product might be factoring or invoice discounting.

PROVIDERS

The clearing banks all have operational finance subsidiaries and there are a number of independent providers. The UK trade bodies for operational finance are:

- *Asset Based Finance Association*   which is focused on working capital finance (see below). ABFA maintains a directory of members and has a useful tool on its website[58] to let borrowers identify providers for the financing they are seeking.
- *Finance and Leasing Association*   which is focused on fixed asset finance (see below) and also maintains a directory of members on its website.[59]

---

58 www.abfa.org.uk.
59 www.fla.org.uk.

TYPES OF OPERATIONAL FINANCE

The principal types of operational finance are described in Table 3.

Table 3. Types of operational finance

Fixed asset finance	The purchase of a fixed asset can be financed by a **lease**, secured on the asset itself by a legal charge, where the borrower makes regular payments to the finance house of principal and interest until the amount advanced under the lease is repaid. Ownership of the fixed asset is retained by the finance house until the end of the term of the lease, when the asset may be bought by the borrower or sold on the open market.
	Alternatively, a fixed asset can be financed through a **hire purchase** contract, where ownership of the asset lies with the borrower but the finance house has rights to repossess the asset in the event of default.
Working capital finance	**Factoring** is the original variant of working capital finance, where a business assigns its sales invoices to a finance house, which lends a proportion of the face value of each invoice until the debtor pays. When the debtor pays, the business receives the balance of the invoice value, less interest and charges. The finance house administers the sales ledger, collecting the debts and chasing debtors.
	Invoice discounting is a variant whereby the business continues to administer its own sales ledger but is otherwise essentially the same as factoring. Debtors are made aware that the invoices have been assigned to the finance house. In **confidential invoice discounting**, the debtor is unaware of the assignment of the debt to the finance house and deals with the business as though the debt were unassigned.
Trade finance	Trade finance covers a wide range of financing products, including the provision of letters of credit, export credit insurance and international factoring. It is most often required in trade relating to physical goods, including capital goods, components and raw or partially-processed materials.
	This a complex and fast-changing area of business, which is beyond the scope of this book.

★ BACKGROUND

Why the banks push customers towards operational finance

In a recent opinion piece in the *Financial Times*,[60] Jonathan Ford lamented the loss of the traditional bank manager as caricatured so brilliantly in the form of Captain Mainwaring, hero of the BBC's *Dad's Army*. The essence of Ford's argument is that boring bankers rooted in their communities made sound judgements about their customers based on local knowledge and mutual dependence.

In reality, a combination of competitive pressure and poor performance by UK retail banks has led to cost-cutting and a significant de-skilling of branch-level bank employees. This, in turn, has led to the banks looking to automate and streamline lending to business customers – especially in trying to ensure that lending is matched to available security as closely as possible.

The easiest way to do this is to substitute operational finance, where the amount lent is tied directly to the available assets and cash flows, for overdrafts or even term loans. This reduces the scope for human error in lending decisions by bank staff.

However, the mechanical relationship between cash advanced to a business and the assets the business has available to secure that lending, which is a basic characteristic of factoring or invoice discounting, can cause financing to dry up when the need for it is greatest. Put simply, when a business is growing it generates more invoices to discount and therefore can borrow more. When trading gets tough and sales fall, fewer invoices are generated so the business can borrow less – precisely at the time when there is likely to be most pressure on its cash flow.

Equity

Characteristics

Equity finance is money or other investment (including investment of tangible or intangible assets, such as patents or other intellectual property, or investment of services) provided by an investor in

---

60 1 July 2012.

return for a share of the ownership of the business. The word 'equity' implies three things:

1. That the investor shares in all the profits of the business, including the proceeds of any sale of the whole or part of the business, without limitation.
2. That the investor accepts the risk of losing all or part of the investment in return for that unlimited share in the profits.
3. That the investor has some say in the direction of the business – especially in appointing the directors who are responsible for its day-to-day management and in agreeing to any increase in the share capital (since that potentially reduces the proportionate ownership of existing shareholders) and other similar matters.

★ KEY CONCEPT

The key attribute of equity shares is that they entitle the holder to a return beyond a pre-determined dividend (similar to interest) and/or a pre-determined repayment of capital.

Types of equity

This section assumes that the investor is investing in a company, rather than a partnership.[61]

ORDINARY SHARES

Equity investors acquire shares in a company in return for making an investment, which may be cash or the provision of other value. Although shares can carry a wide range of different rights, and have names to match, the standard share is called an *ordinary share*. The rights accruing to ordinary shares, like all shares, are determined by a combination of legislation (particularly the Companies Act 2006) and the articles of association – which is the basic governance document of a UK limited company. The articles cannot remove rights specified by legislation.

---

61 In the US and UK there are forms of partnership whereby a 'sleeping' partner can invest equity finance in the business, such as the UK Limited Partnership regulated under the Limited Partnerships Act 1907, but these are outside the scope of this book.

PAR VALUE AND SHARE PREMIUM

Ordinary shares, like all shares, have a par value – theoretically the value of the company at incorporation divided by the number of shares then issued. Shares can be issued part-paid,[62] or can be issued at any price above the par value, with the difference between the par value and the issue price being the 'share premium'.

RIGHTS ACCRUING TO ORDINARY SHARES

Although ordinary shares can have whatever rights are determined by the company's articles (subject to the requirements of legislation), they usually carry the following basic rights:

- The holder can vote at general meetings of the company (usually on the basis of one vote per share held).
- The holder has the right to receive any dividend that the directors declare payable (expressed as x pence per share).
- The holder will receive a share of the proceeds of the assets of the company on sale or liquidation determined by their proportion of total shares held (but which may be subject to the holder's own, or other shareholders', preference rights).

The amount that an individual shareholder gets from the payment of a dividend or a distribution of capital is determined by the proportion of the total ordinary shareholding held.

★ **EXAMPLE**
Calculating a dividend or return of capital on ordinary shares
A shareholder owns 250 £1 ordinary shares in a company with a total issued share capital of 1,000 £1 ordinary shares. This shareholder owns 25% of the company's equity. When a dividend is declared the shareholder is entitled to receive 25% of the total dividends declared on the ordinary shares.

Similarly, if and when the company is liquidated solvently,[63] the

---

62 In the event of the insolvent liquidation of a company, the liquidator can call on the holders of part-paid shares to pay the difference, per share, between the amount already paid and the par value.
63 That is, its total assets exceed its total liabilities.

shareholder will receive 25% of the liquidation proceeds, after payment of all the creditors and meeting the costs of the liquidation. If the company's total assets are less than its total liabilities when it is liquidated, then the shareholders will receive no return (the company was insolvent). It is perfectly possible that the total proceeds exceed the total liabilities but don't exceed the aggregate amount invested by the shareholders – the return to each shareholder will be determined by the proportion of the issued ordinary share capital held by that person.

However, special classes of shares can have rights to dividend or return of capital that rank ahead of ordinary shares (see the Summary Terminology of Investment below).

PRE-EMPTION AND OTHER RIGHTS

A shareholder may have the:

• right to participate in any issue of new shares
• right of first refusal when another shareholder sells existing shares

Both of these are proportionate to shareholding.

★ EXAMPLE
Exercising pre-emption rights in a new share issue
A company is raising £1,000,000 of capital by means of an issue of new shares priced at £10 per share. John Brown, an existing shareholder, owns 50,000 of the 500,000 shares in issue (i.e. 10%) before the fundraising. He will therefore be entitled to subscribe for 10% of the new shares or 10,000 shares (10% of 100,000). A fundraising like this, where pre-emption rights apply, is often called a 'rights issue'.

STANDARD SHAREHOLDERS' RIGHTS

Shareholders appoint the directors and auditors (or, more usually, approve their appointment) and must approve any amendment to the memorandum and articles of the company, its legal status or changes to its capital structure. Finally, they must approve any resolution to wind up the company. The resolutions affecting these changes require differing majorities of the shareholders entitled to vote dependent on the proposed change.

CLASS RIGHTS AND PREFERRED SHARES

It is possible, and quite common, for a company to have different classes of shares, giving the holders of shares of different classes different rights. In the case of investors, they may seek shares that have an enhanced right to a return of capital (called a liquidation preference) relative to ordinary shares, or which limit the ability of the company to do certain things (such as issue new shares or appoint directors) without the approval of the class. These shares are usually referred to as 'preferred ordinary shares' in the UK and 'preferred stock' in the US. Other matters that could be subject to class consents include acquiring, selling or mortgaging assets; fixing directors' salaries; determining a mandatory dividend policy; making acquisitions or selling the company.

Summary terminology of investment

Cumulative: dividends still continue to accrue even when the issuer fails to make timely payments

Preferred: shares with priority over common stock in payment of dividends and/or on a liquidation and/or in receiving a given multiple return of capital on a trade sale

Participating: the right to a specific dividend paid before dividends on common stock

Convertible: instrument that may convert into common stock to benefit from enhanced residual value on sale/disposal of the company

Redeemable: right (normally of the investor) to seek repayment often after specified time, such as five years; power to induce buy-back and/or convert equity to debt, giving influence to induce the company to arrange a liquidity event

Shares: equity; residual worth

Non-equity share capital

There are, however, several other categories of shares. These carry different, or additional, rights to ordinary shares and may, or may not, be equity. It is important to focus on this latter point: when is a share *equity*? As we discussed at the beginning of the chapter, it is sometimes difficult to draw the line between lending and equity, particularly when some shares are, effectively, lending. Section 548 of the Companies Act 2006 provides a useful definition of what is equity:

> In the Companies Acts 'equity share capital', in relation to a company, means its issued share capital excluding any part of that capital that, neither as respects dividends nor as respects capital, carries any right to participate beyond a specified amount in a distribution.

With this definition in mind, it is possible to categorise shares by their rights and decide if they do count as equity.

PREFERENCE SHARES

Most forms of non-equity share capital are referred to as 'preference shares' (note that this is not the same as 'preferred ordinary shares' in UK parlance or 'preferred stock' in US parlance). The premise behind a preference share is simple: it enjoys preference in the distribution of capital or income in return for giving up unrestricted participation in such distributions (that is, a surrender of upside in return for some degree of predictability). The predictability of a preference share usually includes its right to a fixed level of dividend, which the company is obliged to pay if it can legally do so, and its right to redemption at a specific date in the future. In this sense, preference shares are quite like debt.

However, preference shares are different to debt in one important regard: a company cannot legally pay a preference dividend or redeem a preference share if it does not have the distributable profits (or some other limited forms of reserves) to do so. Nor, unlike a lender, can the holder of preference shares sue the company for dividends or redemptions that are due but which the company is unable to pay because of insufficient reserves. To put it another way, a company is not insolvent merely because it cannot pay its preference share dividends or redeem preference shares on time – whereas it would be if it were payments or interest or repayments of debt that were outstanding.

USES OF PREFERENCE SHARES

There are two principal uses of preference shares:

- To structure a transaction in a way that gives greater predictability of return (either income or capital) – likely to be driven by an investor but less common than the use of preferred shares, which have some of the same attributes (see the 'Class rights and preferred shares' section earlier in this chapter).
- To adjust the effective price of a deal – which could be driven by either an investor or by founders.

Preference shares make more sense in mature businesses with predictable income but more limited capital upside than they do in early-stage investments, where the ability to pay dividends and redeem shares is far less certain, particularly in terms of timing.

Understanding investors: what are they looking for?

Investors' objectives

Most equity investors, especially in early-stage businesses, are looking to achieve a capital return on their investment. Potentially they may also be seeking a yield (i.e. dividends paid periodically).

RISK VERSUS REWARD

Ultimately the level of return that the investor is seeking is a function of the perceived risk in the transaction moderated by alternative risk/reward profiles that can be achieved in other available investments. Fundamentally, unlike a bank or other lender, an investor accepts the risk of losing the capital invested in a company's shares because of the potential for a return that will adequately compensate for the risk taken.

CAPITAL GAIN

Equity investors, including venture funds, assess the growth and profitability prospects of a business in which they are considering investing. While they may want to see an ability to pay dividends, they are more likely to be looking for the capacity to develop a trading record that could make it a candidate for sale or a flotation that could offer a substantial capital gain on their investment.

TIME TO EXIT

Many venture investors manage fixed life funds, which means that they need a realisation of their investments within a predictable timescale, rather than being able to hold shares for an unspecified period and take a dividend yield. Even angel investors are likely to be looking for some kind of capital exit within a finite period – in the UK, this is often as soon as possible after the shares have been held for the qualifying period under the Enterprise Investment Scheme.

★ KEY CONCEPT

Founders need to establish from the outset an investor's objective for an investment and whether that objective is compatible with their own aims for the business.

EVALUATION

All equity investors evaluate the risk and potential return of an investment they are considering making. Factors to be assessed include:

- management team and their track-record
- products or services and their market potential
- business model and its progress to date
- competitive position
- use of cash and cash generation relative to growth
- management's plans, forecasts and projections
- potential growth and profitability

Assessing these factors together allows an investor to calibrate the right terms for an investment which balance the level of risk proportionate to the expected return.

Looking at these evaluation factors in more detail:

- *Management*   Investors want to see a highly motivated management team that is showing personal and financial commitment to their business. The better the track-record of the team in the industry or product area, the better, but investors recognise that in early-stage businesses there is unlikely to be a complete management team covering all main functions. What they will want to evaluate is the ability of the founders/ management team to be persistent and have the capacity to sell the vision to key constituencies: customers, investors, employees, suppliers and partners. The investment process itself is an opportunity for the founders to demonstrate their ability to sell, their understanding of the market and the potential of their product, and their ability to respond to challenges and be adaptive as the business evolves.

- *Product/service and intellectual property*   Investors are attracted to products or services that offer a clear proposition to consumers with benefits that are immediately obvious and give clear competitive advantage. The logistics of sourcing or manufacturing and delivering the project need to be proven with effective quality control, and the business needs to demonstrate a capacity to innovate and evolve its products and services to maintain competitiveness.

   If the product or service is technology intensive, investors will want to understand the stage of development or deployment and the ability of the team to complete it or get it to market. They will also want to assess the intellectual property rights in the product or service both because IP, especially a patent, can create competitive advantage and because the business needs the freedom to operate without infringing any other party's intellectual property.

- *Market*   Founders need to show that they understand who will buy their product, why and at what price. They need to have a clear understanding of the size of the market and the cost of addressing it (such as developing or exploiting partnerships) as well as the cost of acquiring individual customers. Although challenging, they need to have a clear view of how the market might develop in the future and how this affects their current product or service offering and what innovation they need to invest in.

- *Competition*   Investors will expect the team to have a clear understanding of their competitors, both direct (those who have the same or similar product or service offerings) and indirect (those offering services that, although different to the business's, meet the same customer needs).

- *Cash*   Investors will pay close attention to the cash needs of the business. Even if it is revenue-generating, or even profitable, they will want to satisfy themselves that the business is fundamentally cash-generating or has the financing facilities to support its growth. If it's an early-stage business, they will want to satisfy themselves that it can either get to cash break-even or successfully raise more investment before the cash invested runs out. They will want to see that management has a good grasp of how cash flow works in the business and the ability to forecast it intelligently.

- *Growth and profitability*   Investors will want to understand how quickly the business can become profitable and whether there is any trade-off between growth and getting to profitability. Some investors are likely to be more risk-averse than others, so founders need to ensure that investors' growth and profit expectations are aligned with their own. This is especially important where a business is likely to need successive rounds of funding before it gets to break-even, which is typical of many life science or innovative technology start-ups.

LEVERAGE

Investors may look to adjust the risk/reward ratio in an investment by trying to get providers of other types of finance to take risk on themselves. This process, commonly called leveraging, was the basis of the large buy-outs of the 1980s. Equity investors and their advisers put together deals in which lending, which was not fully secured against assets, was a critical part of the deal structures. The lending banks were prepared to take the implicit risk on the basis that the businesses had strong historic cash flow, the post buy-out plan showed strong growth in net assets and they were offered a large margin on the borrowing (3 to 5 per cent above prevailing base rates). This type of lending is not equity, on the one hand, nor secured (or senior) debt, on the other. Falling between the two, it is often described as mezzanine debt.

Approaching investors

The landscape for both venture investment (investment in high-growth businesses) and private equity (investment in established businesses) has become much more diverse than before the internet boom of the late 1990s. Most major economies (e.g. members of the G20 group of developed economies) now have developed venture industries and one or more networks of angel investor.

What kind of investor do I want?

Assuming that a business has already exploited its opportunities for borrowing and operational finance – which may be none for a start-up or early-stage business – it will need to approach equity investors. Broadly, these divide down into:

- *Business angels*   investing their own money under their own control.
- *Venture investors*   managing and investing money for other people under a formal mandate.

The boundaries between these may be blurred. A syndicate of angels operating together with one taking a lead role is likely to operate in a way similar to a venture fund manager. Equally, an EIS fund – investing under the rules of a UK tax concession designed to encourage investment in early-stage businesses – will be managed like any other venture fund but will need to structure its investments in the same way as individual angels, also taking advantage of the EIS concession.

That said, there are some clear distinctions between angels and venture investors:

Table 4. Approaching investors: angels vs. funds

	Angels	Venture investors
Approach	Less formal, more personal – personal chemistry can help or hinder	Systematic, process-driven, less personal
Objective	Capital gain, retain tax concessions where applicable, less time-sensitive	Capital gain within the harvest period of the fund (i.e. between 3 and 7 years)
Involvement	Variable – domain-specific or general management experience can be valuable in non-executive director role Risk of excessive and unpredictable interference Complexity of larger number	Variable – likely have right to board seat (or observer rights); may nominate third-party with domain or general management experience Most likely to be involved immediately post-investment, when new investment is being raised or exit imminent
Due diligence	More informal, most likely to focus on product and market	Comprehensive/formal – more financial emphasis
Deal structure	Often tax-driven, less likely to have liquidation preference. May invest at a higher capitalisation than venture investors. Fewer control rights	Structured, extensive control rights and liquidation preference. May include redeemable shares or a mandatory dividend mechanism

Who does seed and early-stage investment?

In reality, there is a tendency towards doing larger deals as a venture investor becomes more established and develops a successful track-record. All deals take similar amounts of time and effort to complete, so economies of scale make it more attractive to do larger deals.

This phenomenon, combined with a rapid growth in numbers of business angels in most developed economies, has led to seed investment becoming increasingly the preserve of angels. Both private sector and publicly subsidised networks and brokerages have developed to make access to angel investment easier and faster.

Approaching investors

PERSONAL NETWORKING
The most important activity for any entrepreneur is building a network of relevant contacts, such as:
- Key players in the industry in which the business operates (larger companies in the sector, potential customers, suppliers, etc.)
- Other successful entrepreneurs with whom there is a connection (e.g. school friends and acquaintances, university or graduate school alumni, members of professional networks, etc.)
- Bloggers and journalists interested in the industry sector or in growth business/investment stories
- Venture investors who invest in the industry sector at the right stage of investment (less value connecting with a late-stage VC than an early-stage investor if the business is a start-up)
- Angel investors who have invested in the sector

LinkedIn, Meetup and other digital networking platforms are a good way to start networking with relevant people. Make the effort to meet new people at meet-ups, conferences and seminars, and be prepared to make/take meetings where there may not be an obvious immediate agenda but the person falls into one of the target networking categories.

DATABASES
There are several online databases where it makes sense to put up a profile of the business and the investment requirements. Obvious examples are:

- *Crunchbase* the database of start-up and growth companies created by TechCrunch and a starting point for anyone looking at new businesses in the space. The profiles include details of funding rounds, although they are not specifically designed for fundraising.
- *Gust* the global database founded by David Rose for matching early-stage businesses to early-stage investors and used by groups such as New York Angels (US) and Cambridge Angels (UK).

Databases also work the other way and investors can be identified though online databases of:
- Venture capital firms (such as the BVCA (UK) and NVCA (US) websites).
- Angel networks (such as EBAN (pan-European), Angel Capital Association (US) and NBAA (Russia)).

Direct approach

Don't be afraid to approach investors directly but do try to make your approach stand out:
- Make sure you know the investment criteria and previous investments made by the investor and demonstrate why you think they should take the time to look more closely at your proposal.
- If you can, get a personal introduction to the investor (this is one of the principal benefits of having an extensive personal network: you're much more likely to be able to find an introducer – LinkedIn even has a widget to enable you to do this).
- Try to make it interesting. Tell a story, even briefly, which gets attention and that is based on some demonstrable success that the business has had ('we're the first business to have licensed X's technology where they've taken equity in lieu of cash up front' is the sort thing, where X is a credible player in its industry and especially if it's well known for driving hard deals).

Advisers

SELF-EDUCATION

Always start with self-education. Find out as much as possible about the investment landscape that's relevant to you through desk research. Good places to start are:

- *News sites and blogs* that report on early-stage investment (e.g. TechCrunch, Mashable or Strategy Eye)
- *Public sector information resources*: central and local government and development agencies and organisations
- *Universities and other education organisations*, which often make excellent educational resources about entrepreneurship publicly available. Two examples are:
  - Stanford University Entrepreneurship Corner[64]
  - Management Technology prodcasts at the IfM of the University of Cambridge[65]

SELECTING ADVISERS

There is a plethora of potential advisers working in the fundraising space, ranging from asset finance brokers to corporate finance boutiques. Assessing the likely effectiveness of a potential adviser can be hard, but there are a few things that can help sort the less likely from the more likely:

- *Specialism.* Do they specialise in the type of finance that the business is looking for and in the industry sector in which it operates? There's an enormous difference between a science-based biotech spin-out from a university and a food service or retail start-up. Treat generalist advisers, such as accountants, with some caution and make sure they really do have a track-record of success in fundraising.
- *Track-record.* Can you check their track-record out easily, that is, find and speak to businesses that have previously been advised by them?

---

64 http://ecorner.stanford.edu/.
65 http://www.ifm.eng.cam.ac.uk/resources/podcast/.

- *Bona fides*. Are they members of the trade associations relevant to the finance they offer or the industries they're active in (such as associate members of the BVCA)? This is no guarantee of quality but it can be a useful first indication of specialism.
- *Social media*. Especially if your business is digital or technology-based, check out their activity and profile on Twitter, Facebook, LinkedIn and the web as whole. Any problems are likely to have surfaced in social media.

TERMS AND FEES

Fees are usually based on a combination of time-based and success-based payment, usually related to the amount of capital raised (the latter can vary between 1 per cent for simple asset finance broking and 5 per cent for a corporate finance adviser). If the fee sought is much more than 5 per cent, it's worth challenging the adviser to demonstrate an outstanding track-record of success.

There's also a balance to be struck between getting the attention of the adviser and ensuring that they are motivated to succeed in the fundraising. Too little time-based fees and they will find it hard to give the consistent attention needed for success – since fee-paying clients are likely to get first call on their time and resources. Too high a level of time-based fee and there's a temptation to string out the task and keep on submitting the invoices. Again, use the experience of previous clients that the adviser has helped to gauge the right level and mix of fees.

The case study included here is very much from the heart of the person it describes. It's the true story of the relatively short life of one company he founded. One of the authors of this book was an investor in this company, served on its board and was its chairperson; he associates strongly with the entrepreneur and his feelings. The case study is included as an authoritative account of how things can go 'not according to vision and plan'. This book is not written to promote venture capital or any particular form of finance, and the authors include information on pitfalls and real-life failures in order to give the entrepreneur a balanced view of funding young companies.

CASE STUDY
An innovator founder's tale in four parts

*Pilgrim Beart, Silicon Valley and Cambridge-based entrepreneur,
currently CEO of AlertMe, in conversation with Alan Barrell*

I'd like to tell you the story of an innovator's start-up. It's not intended to be an historically accurate re-enactment of any one person or company in particular (in fact, specifically not!) but rather an amalgam of lessons learned by various friends and myself in the start-up world, time after time.

I used to think that some of the less positive outcomes were just a result of doing something wrong, but after nearly 30 years in start-ups in Silicon Valley, Oxford and Cambridge, and 15 years in companies I have started in Cambridge, I've come to the conclusion that there are some inexorable consequences of certain actions, even if things generally go well with your start-up, and even if all the actors involved in the story are generally competent, well-motivated and people with great integrity. So if you don't like the consequences, then you should seriously consider taking different actions at key stages in the process – particularly when it comes to funding. See page 106 for the key to the abbreviations used in the diagrams below.

1. The blank sheet of paper

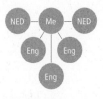

To begin with, there's just you. You're an innovator – like many in Cambridge. Maybe you're working in a company or in an academic lab. Why do you decide to start a company? Perhaps you have a great idea, or at least a fuzzy vision of how the future might be, and how your knowledge could shape it, make it happen better and faster. Perhaps you're frustrated at the slow pace of change in your current situation and want to strike out to do something bolder, something that's yours.

Perhaps you want to do more than work 9–5 on other people's ideas. Perhaps you want to make lots of money (although in my experience this isn't a strong motivator for most innovators).

You start with a blank sheet of paper. Can you give birth to something that will live beyond you?

Perhaps you raise some angel funding, or find some other useful people to join you as advisers. To use fancy terms, we can call them non-executive directors sitting with you on the board, but at this stage everything is informal. You start to build your team, probably of engineers, since it's a technical innovation that needs to be engineered into reality.

Everyone knows everyone else and communication happens as if by magic. You are wearing many hats (product definition, marketing, sales, technology, finance…). You feel incredibly motivated, like you're really making use of every minute of your (long) days.

It's challenging, too – can you make the technology work, can you find a customer, will you run out of money? But it's incredibly fulfilling.

2. Under way

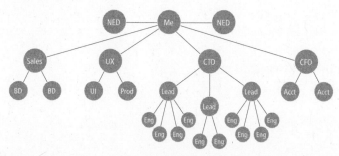

The company starts to grow, and therefore to become more defined. This is good, because the team has a clear unifying goal, and the company a clear marketing message and therefore market traction.

But equally, you gradually realise that this clearer definition also means that several dice have now been cast – 'pivoting' if necessary to change the direction of the company (as it often is!) becomes increasingly more painful, as it's likely to require writing-off some of your investment in technology and people.

You're still spending some time focused on what you love – innovation

– but you have hired the beginnings of a management team, and handed some hats over to them. An increasing amount of your time is spent finding and inspiring great people, organising them, making decisions about how money gets allocated and so on.

You may be living on a shoestring, but these are the 'good old days' when miracles are performed by a small team, and everyone can see that the whole shebang is absolutely dependent on their personal contribution.

You start to need to introduce some lightweight processes, just to keep things running smoothly, although it's amazing how the company is still able to self-organise very well, without any need for lots of meetings, policies, IT or an HR department.

The company remains incredibly agile – probably its greatest strength.

3. Venture capital

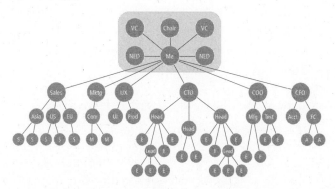

You probably started the company a bit 'ahead' of the market, i.e. before your product or service was mainstream – by definition, since you're an innovator. But now the market is starting to catch up – your vision is becoming reality. Great news! But it means that competitors are springing up too, and it becomes apparent that it's going to be a race to grab market share. You may also be running into some of the classic challenges of a growing company, such as cash flow.

You find that banks won't lend to start-ups. Your angels are tapped-out. And so you take a few million quid in venture capital, perhaps because you need the cash, perhaps just to ensure you're a winner. There's no going back now.

There are many kinds of VC firm, and many kinds of VC people in them. The good ones are generally entrepreneurs-turned-VCs who not only have the right kind of experience but also some degree of empathy with the founder because they've been there. The bad ones are City boys who know nothing about technology or start-ups. Ignorance leads to fear, and fear leads to all sorts of bad behaviour. So we'll assume here that you manage to pick a competent VC.

The thing to understand about VC – in contrast to every other relationship or contract you will have signed to this point – is that the terms of every VC deal I've ever seen means that they have pretty much absolute power over your company.

So it's not your company any more; it's theirs.

Some VCs even refer to themselves as 'owners' – even if they only hold a 15 per cent stake. I used to think that was rather cheeky, but now I just see it as honest. When you started the company, you were definitely the owner, right? And now somehow they are the owner, yet without them having given you any money (they've given the company money, but not you).

Welcome to VC!

Your board structure is now largely window-dressing, because the VC can always cast the winning vote, even if they represent a minority on the board. And even the original meaning of a 'share' (as in everyone owning a share of the company in return for investing in it) has been distorted beyond recognition – the VC's shares are of a different class, and all the previous shares will be worthless unless they get an excellent return first (more on this later). You and your employees are now utterly reliant on the VC's competence and goodwill.

Which should give you pause for thought.

In fairness, though, your idea has now got millions behind it, without you having to put your house on the line. So just for a moment let's take off the innovator's hat and put on the VC hat. As a VC we have taken a few hundred million from fund managers prepared to take higher risks in return for higher rewards, so we need to take that risk to get that potential reward. So our strategy will be to invest in, say, ten companies and then do everything we can to make at least one of them have a 'home run' –

become a Google or a Facebook – giving us a 20x overall return; then it doesn't really matter what happens to the rest of our portfolio.

Of course, we spend time trying to predict what will be successful in the market, and pick the right companies to invest in, but once we've invested we have to gamble everything on that home-run outcome. Our main tool is money, but money on its own is rather useless – we have to also have the <u>power</u> to use that money in whatever way we see fit to achieve our goal, which is why we insist on such draconian terms.

We'll also use our much-vaunted 'Rolodex' to find a chairperson who is well-networked, and we may also decide it's time for a new CEO – someone with commercial experience of the company's sector, who will be absolutely focused on driving operational excellence and returns. We may even have a policy (stated or not!) of always replacing the CEO when we invest, to crank the company into its new 'growth' phase. We like the idea of stock options, because they lock everyone in until the company succeeds.

4. Exit (stage left)

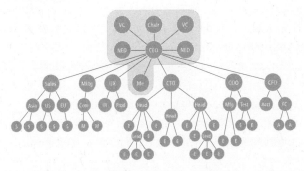

Let's put the founder innovator hat back on. The company continues to grow, develop increasing layers of management and processes, and become slower and slower at innovation.

Suddenly one day you wake up and realise:
- You've lost control (not that you wanted it for its own sake anyway).
- You're now 'just' an employee of the company you founded.
- Innovation is starting to take second place to operational growth, and you're just not getting the 'thrill of the new' any more.

Somehow you've lost the very thing that drove you to start the company in the first place: control over your own destiny, and the freedom to follow your dream. It was great while it lasted.

And so far, we've only just taken our first round of VC. You probably said to yourself and your investors that one round of VC was all that was needed, but the company may well take longer to reach success, or may hit some bumps in the road that require more funding – most ultimately-successful companies do. Serious dilution may beckon, with the VC on both sides of the table (if the VC believes the company is going well they'll want to put in as much cash as possible at the lowest possible price).

You'll also find that pivoting has become almost impossible – VC is like a rocket-booster, and doing a mid-course correction once the blue touch paper is lit can be 'challenging'.

Taking VC can feel like playing a game against an opponent who holds an unbeatable piece. Arguably, many VCs use far too much leverage over founders: leverage works both ways so this can work against the VC's interests if it demotivates and marginalises the founder.

Until the late 1990s, VC was about helping a company that was already successful get into orbit a bit quicker. But with the dotcom boom it became possible to start a company with VC, which is a very different proposition, and it is as yet unclear whether this really makes any sense or is a good idea for most founders. Good companies always used to take 5, 10, or 15 years to reach success, and maybe this is still true.

Finally, let's try to reduce a VC deal to its barest bones. Figure 14 shows possible ways in which the value of a start-up can change over time.

The darkest area shows failure – the company fails to build sufficient value over time and ultimately goes bust or is acquired for a nominal sum. Maybe it was just a dumb idea, or too early, or the tech didn't work. VC is unlikely to change this.

The lightest area shows stratospheric success. In certain circumstances, VC can help make this scenario happen.

The mid-grey area is the interesting bit. This shows a range of growth options that the company can follow leading to moderate or great success. This might mean that it ultimately makes its founders multimillionaires after, say, ten years. It may be what VCs disparagingly call a 'lifestyle' business, and what most people in the street would call a 'normal' business. It can adapt its growth to changing circumstances, for example pulling in its horns in tough times or in good times even choosing to take VC to drive towards an initial public offering (IPO). Because the company doesn't have to take this route, it can probably negotiate terms that retain control for the founders.

But the real point of this picture is to explain that, for a VC-funded company, the mid-grey area represents *failure*. Failure for the VC (only interested in home runs) and failure for the founder who either won't see any return, or at least one commensurate with their effort and risk, because they've been diluted to hell.

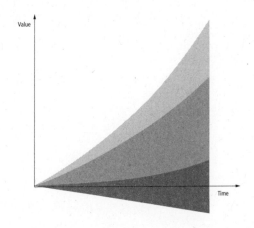

Figure 14. Possible ways in which a start-up can change value over time

The most coherent reason I remember for starting my first company was simply 'to see if I could'. One of the most surprising findings for me was that, as the company grew to about 30 people strong I discovered I really didn't enjoy being the CEO any more, and wasn't doing a very good job of it. On reflection, I shouldn't have found that surprising – being CEO of a growing company requires specific skills and personality, and it's quite unlikely that a creative founder will have those skills or that personality.

I think the reason that it is a surprise is that the very few company founders we tend to hear about in the popular press tend are those who did go all the way as CEO – those such as Bill Gates and Larry Ellison. But I think these people are very much the exception and for most founders it would be better to plan on bringing in a CEO while somehow capturing the value they have brought to the company; at that point however, such value may increasingly be in the past.

VCs tend to insist that founders are 'first in, last out'. This means that founders not only take all the early-stage risks, but also have to take the later-stage risks which they probably don't have so much influence over. I believe it might make more sense for the start-up ecosystem if innovator founders could exit after a few years, typically as the professional CEO is brought in – allowing them to quickly recycle their experience in the early stage which they thrive in. This would also allow them to build up a serial portfolio, which over time would give them something approaching the parallel portfolio of the VC.

KEY TO ABBREVIATIONS USED IN DIAGRAMS ON PAGES 99–103	
ABBREVIATION	MEANING
A	Accountant
Acct	Accountant
CEO	Chief executive officer
CFO	Chief financial officer
Chair	Chairman of the board of directors
Com	Communications/PR
COO	Chief operating officer
CTO	Chief technology
E	Engineer
Eng	Engineer
FC	Financial controller
Lead	Lead manager
Lead	Lead (engineer or other role)
Me	Pilgrim Beart, company founder
Mfg	Manufacturing
Mktg	Marketing
NED	Non-executive director
Prod	Product (manager)
UI	User interface
UX	User experience
VC	Venture capital investor

CHAPTER 3

PREPARING FOR FUNDRAISING

All the forces in the world are not so powerful as an idea whose time has come.
– Victor Hugo

Overview

So far we have covered how to start up, forming a company, building a team, different sources of funding, what investors are looking for and the current funding climate. It's now time to start putting together your proposal in a coherent way – and in such a way that it fits with the market and investor expectations.

This section deals in some detail with five related ways of conveying your proposal to potential investors:
- The business model (the underlying concept of how you are rewarded for producing something people want).
- The business plan (a more detailed take on implementing the model).
- The executive summary (the first two or three pages of the plan).
- The full live pitch (when you present to investors – for five or fifteen minutes).
- The elevator pitch (the spoken version of the executive summary – the compelling essence of your proposal in just a couple of minutes).

'How do I know what I think until I see what I say?' E. M. Forster once wrote. We must emphasise from the outset that, although presentation matters fundamentally to your chances of success – the essence of marketing is minimising the difference between what you say and what your audience hears – this section is focused both on working out the substance of your proposal and on conveying it in as efficient and impactful as way as possible. This section goes considerably beyond presentation skills or business plan writing.

Because angel markets are active and angel investors are likely to be your first port of call, unless otherwise indicated we assume in this section that you are preparing to raise equity capital from business angels. But most of what we say would apply to preparing to meet venture investors as well. As with the rest of this book, we've sought to convey the spirit as much as the letter – what it feels like to pitch your case, as well as the detailed preparation required.

Bank finance and grant applications are covered in Chapters 4 and 5. Loans and grants are sufficiently different from equity investment to need to be treated separately.

Business models and business plans: what are they and why have them?

Most of us at some stage in our lives have probably had at least one teacher or manager, sports coach or scout leader whose general approach to getting things done was, 'Action this day! Quick march! Map to follow!' After the initial adrenalin rush wears off, you realise that much energy has been expended but little achieved, and demoralisation beckons: luck aside, it is unlikely that such an approach will lead to the *right* actions or to marching in the *right* direction.

This chapter is about making sure that your dynamism and enthusiasm are not dissipated but instead are leveraged through securing the right focus. 'Leverage' since the financial crash of 2007–08 is a tainted word, but here we are not thinking of harnessing the power of debt so much as harnessing the power of your ideas by concentrating on the right pressure points and finding ways of applying the weight of the team most effectively to the things that really matter.

The mathematician Archimedes (third century BCE) is reputed to have said, 'Give me a lever long enough and a fulcrum on which to place it, and I can move the world.' Devising a business model is about deciding where your fulcrum is and which levers to pull. The business plan is the instruction manual for how to do so. Together the model and the plan represent an important stage in your transition from 'just an idea' to plausible business and – crucially – investable proposition.

We have stressed throughout this book that entrepreneurial businesses are qualitatively different from others, such as mature or lifestyle firms. This applies at the level of the model and the plan as well. Groucho Marx is (perhaps erroneously) credited with saying, 'These are my principles. If you don't like them, I have others.' In the context of building a business model, this dictum is not at all cynical and should be your mantra: in our experience, many of the most successful start-ups have used the crucial information they received from negotiations with potential customers and investors to modify their original proposal, often quite radically so that it meets a real not a theoretical market need.

This process is sometimes referred to as *pivoting* or *getting to Plan B*: you thought that people would buy your dog food because their pets loved the taste, but as you talked to retailers and domestic customers you find that what really excites them is your just-in-time delivery system, which you originally thought was a secondary consideration. So you decide to pivot from being a pet food producer to a pet food distributor. You may have to pivot several times over.

Does this mean that there is little point in coming up with a plan in the first place if you are likely to move on to Plan B or even Plan F sooner rather than later? Far from it. Having a model you can test with customers is like having a scientific hypothesis which you then seek to disprove with additional data. If you don't have a hypothesis, you can't try it out, find that customers want something else that you hadn't anticipated and then pivot to provide it for them. Without plan

A you can't move to Plan B;[66] if you don't have a hypothesis, you can't test it before you go live.

Finally, before we move into the substance of models and plans, we need to shoot a particularly vexatious recent *canard*, the belief that since a tiny handful of the most successful corporations of the past 20 years did not originally have a clear plan, including a monetisation model, you don't need one either – you can just stick with your brilliant idea and really cool technology, and attract investors and customers that way. The sobering reality is that, for every Google or LinkedIn or Facebook that *may* have adopted the 'build it and they will come' approach, there are untold legions of unknown failures. Don't let survivor bias skew your judgement.

Business models: cutting to the chase

You may already have discovered that the 'business model' has become the subject of an extensive, prolix literature that generates more heat than light. If so, you will be relieved to hear that however difficult you might find it to discover the right model – the one you finally put into practice successfully – the underlying concept is simple: *How does your business produce something that users want, deliver it – and ensure that as a result you capture value?* [67]

If this definition still seems a little abstract, it's because over time business models have become more sophisticated. A century ago, the definition might have read: *How do you manufacture goods for customers, deliver them and get paid?* The concept stays the same with the rise of services but, particularly with the growth of internet-based businesses, your 'client' (the person using your app or other service) may not be the same as your 'customer' (the entity responsible for paying for your service); for instance, users might download your music identification app without charge, and you receive payment as a commission when users buy the track identified from iTunes or

66 See, for instance, J. Mullins and R. Komisar, *Getting to Plan B* (Boston, MA: Harvard Business School Press, 2009).
67 A. Osterwalder and Y. Pigneur, *Business Model Generation: A handbook for visionaries, game changers, and challengers* (New York: Wiley, 2010).

the Amazon MP3 music store. Further differences between the era of making and selling goods and the internet age can be seen in the rapid expansion of firms successfully satisfying hitherto unprofitable niches – the so-called 'long tail' discussed in more detail below.[68]

Another way of understanding your business model is to work out where you fit in the value chain: what must you do, how and for whom to make money? To exploit your idea successfully, how do you organise resources – yours or someone else's? Remember, after all, that 'entrepreneurship is the pursuit of opportunity without regard to resources currently controlled'.[69]

Let's consider some specific examples. While the permutations are numerous and becoming increasingly so, we have identified four basic organisational models for turning your original idea into reality:

1. You can sell the concept to someone else.
2. You can license the ideas (such as patents) to one or more other organisations.
3. You can set up a joint venture or partnership with other people or firms – usually better resourced and more experienced than you are.
4. You could grow it all yourself.

Let's have a look at the pros and cons of each model in turn (Table 5).

Business model	Advantages	Disadvantages
Sell concept	1 Often the fastest way to obtain a cash return 2 Dispenses with the often long, arduous task of building a successful business from scratch 3 No need to undertake external fundraising	1 Your return is likely to be small – the purchase is taking on the hard work of commercialisation 2 You have to find a purchaser and negotiate the deal 3 You cannot build out new opportunities from the platform of your original idea

68 Chris Anderson, *The Long Tail: Why the future of business is selling less of more* (New York: Hyperion, 2006).
69 Howard Stevenson, cited in Paul D. Reynolds, *Leveraging Resources: Building an Organization on an Entrepreneurial Resource Base* (Babson College, MA: 1997).

Business model	Advantages	Disadvantages
License idea	1 Cash is generated fast but is likely to be pinned to levels of sales achieved by the licensee 2 You have limited involvement in building the business, though you may be tied in to assist with future product development 3 Limited fundraising required	1 You will likely receive a small proportion of the value generated 2 You need to identify licensees and then manage and monitor the relationship, including accounting for royalties 3 As with selling your idea, you have limited scope for building on success – you have not built a business so much as generated a rental stream
Joint venture/ partnership	1 Ability to leverage the skill and resources of (usually) an established firm 2 Accelerated route to market 3 Opportunity to share in building a successful business 4 Risk mitigation/sharing across the partnership 5 Major capital injection likely to be provided or sourced by established partner	1 No 'free lunch'. Because you share the risks and resource requirements, you also split the upside or value created with your collaborators 2 Working successfully with one or more much larger companies is tough – you have different cultures and long-term goals 3 What happens if you want to unwind the partnership?
Do it yourself	1 If you succeed, you capture all the value generated (at least in proportion to your equity ownership) 2 You are not dealing with numerous different interests competing to run the venture – for good or ill, you are your own boss	1 You are on your own in raising investment 2 At least at the outset, you are likely to have much more limited resources than in a joint venture 3 You are responsible if the new venture does not work out – with potential long-term reputational risks

Table 5. Main types of business model: advantages and disadvantages

It will be obvious that only if you decide on the fourth option – do it yourself – do you experience both the major challenges and rewards of fundraising and running a business. So for now we will assume that you have chosen option four and we'll go back to the initial question we asked about business models: *How does your business produce something that users want, deliver it – and ensure that as a result you capture value?*

In essence, there are six main ways you can now proceed:

1. *Sell a product.* This is self-evidently the simplest business model, perhaps acting as a reseller of goods with little or no adaptation. But the limitations are also obvious: with limited differentiation, it's unlikely you have a defensible niche. And with limited value added by you, your margins are likely to remain thin. To create a sustainable business by selling goods will likely require the ability to come up with a series of evolving products, perhaps based on a platform technology, and developing mastery of one or more key stages of the supply chain: manufacturing, distribution, recycling, etc.

2. *Sell a service.* Here, at least, you must be acting as more than a reseller, and stand a reasonable chance of securing the full fruits of your industry by hand or by brain, to misquote the old Clause IV of the Labour Party constitution. As most developed economies have come to rely more on services than extraction or production, people with rare specialist skills have come to command considerable rewards – think of surgeons, Queen's Counsel or strategy consultants. But the limitations of this model should also be immediately apparent: the key component of your success is skilled people, whose contribution it is hard to leverage. They can only work so many hours a week, and even the ablest command a finite hourly rate of pay. And as any hospital manager will tell you, managing talented people itself requires rare skills.

3. *Sell a product plus services.* Now we're getting somewhere. Classic examples of this model include manufacturers of aero engines, such as Rolls-Royce, who in effect provide plane

operators with an engine but make their return from the associated long-term maintenance, monitoring in detail the performance of the engine, deciding when servicing and repairs are required and even replacing a specific engine with a new one at the end of its efficient life. The manufacturer has unique product knowledge, leading to a defensible niche, and uses the product and associated service to leverage each other.

4. *Sell a product plus consumables.* Sometimes a little disparagingly referred to as 'bait and hook', this model's classic examples include selling a razor for a low price and then selling the razor blades to users at a higher margin over many years to an established customer base, or selling printers at little more than cost and then selling print cartridge replacements at full price to customers who remain 'sticky' because of the difficulty of switching (or inertia).

5. *Sell a product plus accessories.* From the customer's perspective, this business model may feel less cynical than baiting and hooking, but is probably just as attractive to you: consider how often, as the customer rather than the supplier, you have focused your attention on finding the best price you can for a new computer and then happily spent a great deal on peripherals such as cables, adapters, cases and extended warranties.

6. *Offer a 'free' product and then sell a premium version.* A modern permutation of both bait-and-hook and product-plus-accessories, the 'freemium' model is made possible through internet distribution, which offers low production costs and the opportunity to reach a large audience with limited advertising or other promotion. In essence, you hook users into using a basic computer game or software service (the 'free' part) but charge them for the feature-rich enhanced version (the 'premium'). Well-known examples include LinkedIn and paywall-protected newspaper sites such as *The Times* or *The Economist*.[70] 'Free' can also mean a time-limited offer ('six-month free trial') followed by a subscription or a limited

---

70 Also see, Chris Anderson, *Free: The future of a radical idea* (New York: Hyperion, 2009).

number of 'seats' (or simultaneous legitimate users): as the customer firms grow, they are obliged to start paying for new users – which is highly effective if your customers have come to rely on your service.

Once you have an outline of which model you are likely to pursue, numerous resources are available to help you build the detail. For instance, available free under a creative commons share alike licence is the business model canvas (see Figure 15),[71] which sets out nine critical components in a format that encourages you to work out the relationships between them and the impact they have on costs and funding requirements:

1. Key partners
2. Key activities
3. Key resources
4. Value propositions (your customers' belief that you will deliver value that they will experience)
5. Customer relationships
6. Channels
7. Customer segments
8. Cost structure
9. Revenue streams

The leading modern authorities on business models, Alexander Osterwalder and Yves Pigneur, developed the 'canvas' which you can use for working out your own model. It is widely used by growth firms and their advisers.

Writing up a canvas is likely to be the start of an iterative process: it enables you to begin the process of knowing where to start and what needs to be done first, identify what critical information is missing and recognise who (potential customers or recruits or advisers) you need to speak to. You are unlikely, however, to hit upon the full, ideal model at the first iteration.

---

71 www.businessmodelgeneration.com/downloads/business_model_canvas_poster.pdf.

Figure 15. The business model canvas by Osterwalder and Pigneur (2010)

Source: www.businessmodelgeneration.com/downloads/business_model_canvas_poster.pdf

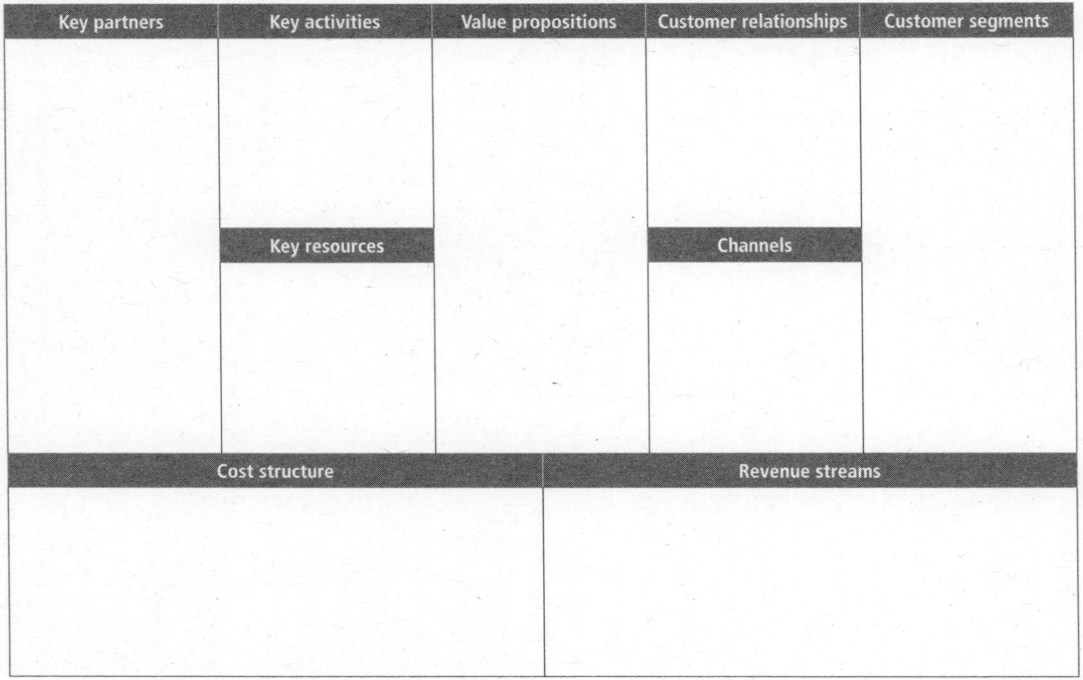

Key partners	Key activities	Value propositions	Customer relationships	Customer segments
	Key resources		Channels	
Cost structure			Revenue streams	

More about business plans

We said earlier that the business model tells you where you need to go and what you need to do, and the business plan is the more developed implementation scheme. It's now time to look in more detail at what a business plan is and what needs to go into it.

Some business plan basics

First, why write one at all? At one level, the plan is a detailed substantiation of your elevator pitch (see the 'Elevator pitch and short slide decks' section later in this chapter) – it is a selling document to be used with potential investors who have already bought the basic vision you presented but now need to drill down deeper as part of the long and winding road they travel before making you a conditional offer of finance – raising equity typically takes six to twelve months. But a good plan is also a summary of responsibilities for the managers of the business: not only the specific tasks you need to perform to succeed and the order in which you need to perform them but also your overall vision and the milestones you've set yourself to reach the end of the rainbow.

A question that comes up frequently among novice teams preparing to raise external funding is, 'Do we have to write the plan ourselves?' The basic answer is, yes: your plan must convey the character of your team and you must be prepared to answer detailed questions about it. By all means use professional advisers to help you with detailed sections, but don't blow your chances of success by having to confess that you don't know how the projected return on capital for investors in year 5 was calculated at 38 per cent 'because our accountants wrote that section'.

If your plan is an extension of your elevator pitch, it also calls for skills similar to those of a public speaker, for whom the best advice is often 'be sincere, be brief, be seated'. Though you need your plan to cover all the essentials of your business, you also have to be aware of the attention span of your audience: many investors receive a thicket of proposals to review each day, and those that do not get to the point and grab interest will be discarded without compunction. There is no hard rule, but if your text before annexes such as financial projections is more than 15 pages long (of which no more than three are the executive summary), seriously consider a further précis.

Tyro (novice) entrepreneurs, especially those from a technology background, are often more focused on the science or the product than the customer and the revenue model. This is a major mistake: you are not making a research application but seeking to seduce investors among whose primary motivations is seeking a significant return on their capital within perhaps five or seven years.

Finally, before we drill down further into the detail of business planning, we need to insert a few caveats. Everything we say here is illustrative: there is no one 'perfect' model, business plan or elevator pitch, or way of dealing with investor questions when you are in front of a panel. You will need to understand your audience (more on this in the 'Planning your pitch' section later in this chapter) and remember that you are selling yourself as much as selling shares in your company.

And sometimes you may be invited to present at business plan competitions (such as those run by government grant or export agencies), for which the criteria are often specific and restrictive. To succeed here, of course, you need to play by those rules. But don't confuse the criteria relevant for such competitions with the criteria used by commercial investors: investors are not especially interested in exports or regional development or encouraging diversity; they are interested in financial return.

Illustrative business plan contents

Because there is no one ideal or 'platonic' template for your business plan to follow, its contents cannot be determined in advance: you have to work out what you need to say and then find a concise and convincing way of presenting the content that is relevant to the individual circumstances of your case. However, as an aide-memoire of likely sections to be covered and a guide to the sequence in which they might helpfully appear, we suggest a table of contents along the following lines:

1. Executive summary
   a. What problem do you solve, for whom, why are you credible?

   b. How much do you need, what for, how long, what's in it for investors?

2. Products and services
3. The market/customers
4. Competition
5. Sales and marketing
6. Operations
7. Roll-out plan
8. Future growth prospects
9. Other risks/responses: for instance, regulatory changes
10. Management
11. Outline financials
12. Appendices
   a. Detailed financial projections
   b. Product literature
   c. Details of patents

THE EXECUTIVE SUMMARY

Je n'ai fait celle-ci plus longue parce que je n'ai pas eu le loisir de la faire plus courte (I have only made this [letter] longer because I have not had the time to make it shorter)
– Blaise Pascal (*Lettres Provinciales*, letter 16, 1657)

The summary is one of the most important pages you will write in seeking to raise funds. If you started with that section to help you map out the rest of the plan, you will undoubtedly have to revisit it once the plan is complete to ensure you have captured as briefly and persuasively as possible everything that needs to be included in, say, the first 1,000 words. The time needed to achieve the desired result is out of all proportion to its length.

The summary matters not least because it is your one chance to make a good first impression. As we've already noted, good sources of funds receive scores of proposals every month and it's your responsibility to show them immediately why your business will be a winner, not their job to hunt for compelling reasons buried among pages of introverted verbiage. As a model you could think of a journalist's introductory paragraph: who, what, when, where, how and why?

In addition to the immediate 'grasp and gasp' of understanding what problem you solve for whom, investors are likely to want an insight up front into you, the team; after all, with early-stage businesses success depends much more on the ability of the founders to deliver against the odds than it does on tangible assets or proven products.

Before you close the executive summary, you *must* have told investors what you are seeking from them and what they receive in return. If you have not made explicit your 'ask', the likelihood is that your plan will simply be rejected, so make sure you say how much you are looking for, what the likely form of investment is (ordinary share, convertible loan note, preference shares, as the case may be), what form of exit is envisaged (trade sale to known and established trading partner, flotation on a stock exchange) and the probable timescale (unlikely to be longer than about seven years for either a venture fund or an angel syndicate).

Strategies differ on whether you should say at the outset how much of the company you would sell to raise the funds you need. Some entrepreneurs omit this figure on the basis that there is no point offering 30 per cent if the investor would have been satisfied with 20 per cent, but even if you do not write down your own implicit valuation be prepared for investors to press you hard for this figure. You can be fairly certain that their proposed valuation and yours will not coincide, but what matters is the cogency of your rationale once you start to negotiate. You can find more on valuation in Chapter 6.

One last point about the summary – and indeed your plan in general. Don't be shy about including your contact details liberally in the plan, not just on the front cover or on a compliment slip or covering email. If investors are interested, they won't waste time looking for your co-ordinates.

DESCRIBING THE OPPORTUNITY

Now you need to drill down in more detail, not just into the presentation of your proposal but into its fundamental contents.

First, to succeed you must be able to articulate what the opportunity is: *what* problem are you solving? For *whom*? How do you get *paid*? Remember that technological breakthroughs of themselves are of no *commercial* value, so for customers to buy from you, your offering must either:

- Relieve the user of a 'pain' (especially in the business to business (B2B) sector); or
- Delight the user (in the business to consumer (B2C) sector).

Sooner or later, investors will expect you to identify *how you make money*. While a tiny handful of exceptional start-ups built a compelling proposition first and then worked out how to monetise the customer base generated, it is important to realise that these successes really are the exception and investors will ask for the systematic *monetisation* of your service or application: simply building a better mousetrap does *not* mean purchasers will come or pay. *Exactly* what will *you* do to generate revenues? This takes us back to the business model: it is a *narrative*, painting a compelling picture, but it must also stand up to detailed scrutiny.

WHAT IS THE PRODUCT OR SERVICE?

In describing your current or proposed product or service, be sure to control jargon and trim unnecessary detail, but do provide analogies and applications to give colour. State clearly what stage you are at: design, prototype, production or even with customers already in the pipeline.

How will you develop your offering further? Will you stop at one product or (better) use your platform to develop a family of related solutions? What is the defensible long-term unique selling proposition, or USP? Thinking back to the more sophisticated examples of business models we discussed above, will your initial products lead to an embedded suite of services? (Think razor blades, printer cartridges, operating systems or aero engines.)

Above all, convey why what you are offering really is different, enough to make sales to people who might right now consider themselves satisfied with an existing solution. And what really makes *you* different from other pretenders?

MARKET ISSUES

In looking at business models, we said that one key consideration is understanding where you fit in the value chain: who do you buy from, who do you sell to, how much, how often, how to get paid, by whom and when? When applying such considerations to the full business plan, an obvious place to start is how large your likely market is.

Here, we suggest that you will save yourself considerable cynical pushback from sceptical investors if you strive as hard as possible to avoid describing your market in abstract, top-down terms and concentrate on bottom-up specifics: investors are generally weary of reading macro figures from generic industry reports to the effect that, by 2018, the US market for aqualungs will be $18 billion, or in 2012 the world market for skipping ropes was €47 trillion 'and therefore if we succeed in capturing 3% global share, our turnover by year 5 will be £128 million'.

Far more convincing is to identify not generic 'markets' but your relevant niche – and specific *customers*. The closer you are to making actual sales, the more compelling your case will be. It is more likely that investors will warm more to a dozen actual sales of £5,000 than to a notional percentage of aggregate market. Traction with real customers is one of the most persuasive arguments you can deploy in showing that, in the hallowed phrase, 'the dogs really will eat the dog food'. So do you already have reference customers? How soon might you recruit them? Will they help you develop the product as engaged early adopters?

That said, you cannot cover market issues without outlining who the existing players are and the technologies or services they provide, together with an indication of emerging trends and investment levels in the industry. Who are the sitting tenants in the sector? Where are they placing their bets? Will they play hard ball in trying to put you out of business?

On a related theme, never claim you have no competition. Perhaps no one else can provide the exact same combination of features that you can, but for every product or service there is at least an indirect form of competition: consumers could read a book rather than play with your provocative new smart phone app. Or they could simply do nothing. Don't underestimate the power of customer inertia.

PRODUCTION AND DISTRIBUTION

You may not at the outset be able to answer all the obvious questions about how you take your product to market, but you do need to convince investors that you are on the case and understand the pros and cons of undertaking manufacturing yourself against subcontracting, how you will win key customers, secure intellectual property and build up channels to market.

Building in-house capacity is expensive. But if you subcontract, how secure is your intellectual property? How does your subcontractor demand to be paid? What strain does this place on your cash flow? Winning a European health service provider as a customer may be your goal, but do you really understand how to break into its procurement cycle, which may be opaque, protracted and time-consuming? How long do government agencies take to pay you? Some EU organisations might take a year to honour your invoice, so how does that affect your funding cycle?

Related questions include:

- What PR, marketing or advertising do you need? How will you cost them?
- If you employ agents as distributors, how will you reward them? Will this prevent you from setting up your own distribution channels? Who has the power?
- Will incumbents seek to put hidden barriers in your way, such as loyalty incentives for retail outlets? Even if this is legally doubtful, do you have the resources to retaliate or seek redress?

Both market/competition and production/distribution issues can be analysed using the structure of five forces first suggested by Harvard

Business School professor, Michael Porter, more than 30 years ago.[72] Numerous variations have since been suggested but the original framework has the virtues of clarity and simplicity. Our interpretation of Porter's five forces model is illustrated in Figure 16.

Figure 16. The five forces model

IT'S THE PEOPLE

If prospective investors liked your executive summary, we suspect that many of them will then turn to the section of your plan about you yourselves – the team – not least because with a business with limited sales and few tangible assets the team is the crucial ingredient for turning vision into reality. And wise investors are looking for a team – or at least the bones of one – rather than just one or two potential stars. The *balance* of skills and experience in the team matters, as does the extent to which you have worked together before: if you have, an important experience curve has already been established.

---

72 Michael E. Porter, *Competitive Strategy: Creating and sustaining superior performance* (New York: Free Press, 1980). Later analysts have suggested that government (regulation) or public opinion should be seen as a sixth force, and that complementary products matter as much as competing offerings. See, for example, John Roberts, *The Modern Firm: Organisational design for performance and growth* (Oxford: Oxford University Press, 2004).

Of course, it is highly unlikely that a near start-up team will have been able to fill all the posts the business will need as you grow (you have not had enough time or money for that), but what does matter for investors is that you have identified the gaps in your line-up and are on the case regarding how to fill them. For instance, common lacunae at an early stage include both finance and marketing. If you have an experienced marketing person lined up once funding or other objective milestones are met, you can indicate (subject to confidentiality!) that 'Jane Smith, the marketing director of MNO, Inc., has agreed in principle to join us on completion of our Series A funding round'. Do you have job descriptions for any gaps in the team? Have you investigated how much they will be paid? Does Jane Smith realise that working for a start-up means foregoing a sizable chunk of salary and benefits in exchange for (1) the thrill of building a potential game-changer and (2) reward ultimately in the form of vested stock options?

It is quite common for small, early-stage teams to cherish a 'flat structure' culture: the three of you who founded the business want to continue to be as democratic and non-hierarchical as you were when you first started out in a garage together. Investors are unlikely to be impressed. They know that clarity and speed depend on someone being in charge; they also know that as businesses grow they become more complex, so you need someone responsible for finance, another for operations, a third for marketing – and so on. Work out who will be chief executive officer, who will be chief technical officer and whichever other roles are key for your business. And expect awkward probing on your decisions.

A question we are often asked by first-time entrepreneurs is: 'What matters most for investors: team, product or market?' Almost always the answer is 'the team'. Investors know that an A-team with drive will likely adapt its perhaps initially B-grade proposal into an A-grade one (remember what we said above about Plan B: you'll likely pivot and then pivot again until you find the winning model to pursue relentlessly). In any event, the A-team will execute with skill and competence on a so-so proposal if it turns out the market is not quite as good as originally envisaged.

One way that ambitious but initially thin teams can seek to punch above their weight is to recruit experienced advisers, perhaps as members of an advisory board or even as non-executive directors. We have found this works only when your advisers do evidence engagement with your business, and experienced investors are skilled at spotting names added merely for ornament not use. But if you really are working with a respected industry specialist or influential adviser, that is certainly an advantage worth bringing out.

When it comes to describing your own experience, we have two words of advice: first, don't be shy; and second, be specific. Don't be shy because you can't assume investors know that you already have a string of achievements to your name – whether previous start-ups or in other careers: your leadership skills may have been forged as a platoon commander or your domain expertise evidenced by a research fellowship. Be specific because the fact that you worked for Megabank, Inc. is likely irrelevant – 100,000 other people did, too (and in the words of one of the oldest management jokes about large organisations 'Q: How many people work here? A: About half of them'). But if you successfully ran a squad of 50 people implementing mission-critical software across three continents against a tight timetable, that says much about your team and task skills.

And you won't be surprised to find that, while investors know you have to live and don't want you distracted because you can't pay your mortgage, during the growth phase until the business is funding itself mainly from sales – not new capital – you won't be able to pay yourself nearly as much as you received at Megabank, nor can Jane Smith expect the same salary she earned at Johnson & Johnson. Overheads are to be kept to a minimum.

An anecdote dating back to the dotcom era highlights the point: a partner from one of the then 'big five' (now 'big four' – Arthur Andersen expired following the Enron scandal) accountancy firms joined a start-up based in St John's Innovation Centre. After a week, he asked the office manager for the team of eight when the announcement of his joining the firm would appear in the press. She replied, 'When you write it.' Entrepreneurial firms turn the necessity of travelling light into virtues, one of which is dispensing with the trouble and expense of managing a fleet of hot and cold running support staff.

FINANCIALS: CASH FLOW FORECAST, BALANCE SHEET, PROFIT AND LOSS ACCOUNT – AND EXITS

The depth of information you should provide on your financials will obviously be heavily influenced by how long – if at all – you have been trading and thus how much historic, empirical data you have. Track-record matters to investors, who tend rightly to believe that the best evidence you can deliver on targets is that you have done so already in this or comparable businesses. Few things are more convincing than customers paying you for your product.

That said, many of the entrepreneurs we meet are still one stage behind regular sales. The best plan here is usually to produce outline projections – and to make sure that you have not only thought through carefully the assumptions on which the projections are based, but also that you have clearly spelled out in your plan what those assumptions are. The quality of your assumptions matters greatly in the absence of solid evidence such as actual bill of materials, historic transport costs, achieved payment cycles and return rates.

Including in your appendices something you have called a cash flow projection but with no supporting rationale (*just why* did you say you'd ship 70 units a month, or that your net margin would be 29% or your headcount would be 19 on average salaries of £11,000 a year?) will kill your credibility just as fatally as not saying in your executive summary what you want from investors. If you present your case live, expect considerable pushback on your assumptions; investors are hard-bitten and readily spot flights of fancy. And don't forget that your assumptions must tie in with the narrative in the rest of your plan: if your detailed projections show that you only break even if you sell 10,000 apps a day for a whole year through the iTunes store but your market analysis suggests that most apps have a shelf life of three months, expect at best an awkward cross-examination.

Conventional accounts (the sort you'll eventually have to file at Companies House) emphasise the importance of the balance sheet (assets = liabilities – owners' equity: a snapshot of the historic value of the business *at a moment in time*, usually recorded every 12 months, which is also a means of showing how the assets were financed) and the profit and loss (P&L) account (its US name – income statement – summarises its function well: top line sales minus expenses, producing net income *over a period of time*, typically one year since accounts were last filed). As part of building a 'big company' DNA into your start-up, you will be wise to start producing accounts in this format from an early stage, possibly even monthly.

But be aware that investors probably pay more attention to your cash flow forecast than to your balance sheet or P&L. Why? Because not only is cash king but it cannot be faked, whereas as anyone who has read the financial pages of a newspaper in the past decade will be aware that conventional financial statements flatter to deceive with regrettable frequency, not least because of the complexity of accounting conventions such as accruals: when did you record the income – when you did the deal or when payment was received the following year? Did you incur expenses up front but match them over time to goods as you sold them over the next 24 months?

Either you have cash (in the bank or on hand) or you don't. But what about that net income figure? You reported sales in good faith and cost of goods sold, but did you include a realistic figure for bad and doubtful debts?

Variances between cash and accruals accounting generally reflect timing differences, the realism and honesty of management and its financial advisers, and cash has the merit of simplicity. Since cash is also fundamental to solvency in a small firm (that is less able to raise new loans or make a call on investors than an established competitor), you and your backers will need to monitor cash carefully both to ensure that you can always comply with the legal requirement of being able to meet your obligations when they fall due and to ensure that cash burn is carefully controlled.

Note that trading while insolvent (or 'wrongful trading') is a civil offence under Section 214 of the UK Insolvency Act 1986, and can lead to your personal liability and even disqualification as a director.

Unlike (deliberate) fraudulent trading, wrongful trading occurs when you as directors knew or ought to have concluded that there was no reasonable prospect of avoiding an insolvent liquidation and you did not take every step to minimise the potential loss to creditors – such as suppliers or the bank. Showing that you were monitoring cash carefully through a robust cash flow projection will be strong evidence that you were taking reasonable steps to stay solvent.

Over the years, we have worked with numerous companies in tight financial circumstances that have turned the corner partly by preparing a revised cash flow forecast weekly or even daily. And within that report, the key columns are those that compare actual performance to both budget and previous period: are you up or down compared with projected out-turn? Compared with last month? And above all, why?

Coming back to what you might include in a plan for investors, it is quite likely that unless you are already an established trading company your projections will be somewhat speculative. We suggest that for your first year of projections you seek to break down your figures month by month; though for the next two years quarterly projections may be the most realistic result you can shoot for. Projections – especially if backed up by clear and realistic assumptions – give investors an order of magnitude and a timeframe to chew on. For instance, if even according to your most bullish view your profitability never reaches £1 million, and profitability is the basis on which your exit valuation (what the company is worth when it is sold) is calculated, it will likely be hard to justify the £10 million valuation in year 5 on which you sought to convince a panel of angels that their £100,000 for a 10 per cent stake today will be worth £1 million on exit – a '10x return' to use the jargon. You will need to reduce your company valuation today (on what basis do you really think you are worth £1 million now?), increase the exit value or achieve an exit sooner – or some combination of all of these. Time for investors *is* money, especially for professional fund managers. (Chapter 6 has more on valuation.)

Finally on projections, if you are hanging your hat on a trade sale in year 5 for £10 million, don't just try to show why the numbers work (why on conventional valuation methods you might be worth £10 million) but try also to put a *compelling* case for who'd likely buy your product or service and why. A bland conclusion along the lines of 'a major pharmaceutical company might buy us because we'll have a pipeline of cool products' – variants of which we see with tooth-grinding regularity – will mean your calls won't be returned. Perhaps one of the most revealing differences between the Californian and the European entrepreneurial mindset is the greater propensity of start-ups in Silicon Valley to work out from the outset which established player (Cisco, Intel, HP, Apple, Facebook, Google…) is most likely to buy them once the product is proven. The start-up can even look like a solution to a problem LinkedIn or Twitter doesn't yet know it has.

APPENDICES

What to include among the appendices of the business plan of an early-stage firm seeking funding is a matter of judgement. We suggest you reserve larger items – such as financial projections, patent specifications or graphics of products – for the appendices but, as with the body of the plan, always be mindful that investors need brevity and focus on your part.

Appendices are not the storeroom for the odds and ends of your business plan, and everything you submit to investors should assist in providing them with insight rather than burdening them with undigested additional information. Often more is less: if it doesn't need to be in, it need not be in.

AND FINALLY…

I keep six honest serving-men:
(They taught me all I knew)
Their names are **What** *and* **Where** *and* **When**
And **How** *and* **Why** *and* **Who.**
I send them over land and sea,

I send them east and west;
But after they have worked for me,
I give them all a rest.
Rudyard Kipling, *The Elephant's Child* (*Just So Stories*, 1902)

You will have spent many hours working out your business model, planning how to implement it and presenting it in a form that enlightens and convinces investors (and new hires, suppliers, advisers and so on). Once you have mastered your brief, you need to be able to put your plan and your presentation behind you, to internalise your vision and the details of its unfurling to such an extent that you live it and breathe it. If you met your ideal investor unexpectedly socially and only had three minutes to persuade her that she really needed to see your full plan and quiz you about it, what would you do?

That's what the next section is about.

Presentations and elevator pitches

If you experience great difficulty in raising money, it's
not because VCs are idiots and cannot comprehend your
curve-jumping, paradigm shifting, revolutionary product.
It's because you either have a piece of crap or you are not
effectively communicating what you have. Both of these are
your fault.
– Guy Kawasaki, Garage Technology Ventures

We've spent most of this chapter talking about the substance of your model and your plan but as a wise if wordy Frenchman (the eighteenth-century comte de Buffon) once put it, 'le style c'est l'homme même', and we now need to focus as much on how you say it as on what you say. This section covers both how to pitch to a full panel of investors for five or fifteen minutes and how to put your case in a minute or two to your ideal investor if you meet her by chance and have the luck to travel with her to the executive suite in the penthouse – the elevator pitch.

'I DON'T HAVE TIME TO PREPARE'

First off, let's shoot yet more *canards* and dispense with some of the most frequent mistakes we see entrepreneurs make. Common excuses for not preparing well include the following brief but effective suicide notes:

- *'It's all about the idea.'* If you really think that experienced, hard-boiled investors with a plethora of tempting opportunities (this will *always* be a buyers' market – get over it) will start writing cheques just because you have a stunning idea with no supporting proposal for commercialisation, we have failed in everything we have said so far. By all means write a narky review of this book on Amazon, but for your own survival don't give up the day job.

- *'I have no time to prepare.'* This is your opportunity to start a journey that will change your life – and if you're right about shifting paradigms, that of many others as well. So you do have time to prepare after all.

- *You only see your side: is this a win–win?* The essence of negotiation, diplomacy and advocacy is being able to use effectively your understanding of what's going on in your opposite number's head. If you can understand life on the other side of the table, you're halfway to success already. Why not let them think that your valuation of the business was the one they came up with in the first place?

- *You don't consider the investors.* One of the most stunningly egregious comments from a wannabe entrepreneur we have ever heard was made during a presentation we gave to first-timers. In response to our case that start-ups should consider carefully the position of first-round angels when raising later-round equity from venture funds, she asked, 'Why should I care about the angels?' If you don't care about those who back you during the most challenging, uncertain time of your business, don't be surprised if they tell you where to go … after they've torn your proposal to shreds in front of all the other presenting companies, 'pour encourager les autres'.

• *Financial errors/projections with basic mistakes.* By all means expect angels and others to challenge your assumptions relentlessly, but if you've made basic errors of arithmetic or category (confusing cash and accruals, for instance), the reaction is likely to be, 'don't call us, we'll call you'. Have your most numerate and pernickety friend – the one you frequently want to strangle – review your presentation before you submit or deliver it.

Common pitching pitfalls

Let's assume that your case was compelling enough for you to be invited to present to an angel club. What are the pitching pitfalls you really must avoid?

1. *Assuming that your listeners intuitively understand the magic.* You have lived with what you think of as a life-changing idea probably for months before you broke cover to approach investors. But for angels or venture funds, your summary or your elevator pitch is likely the first time they've heard the story, so make sure it's obvious to newcomers why your proposal is transformative.

2. *Your content has the wrong balance.* Usually this means spending too much time or space on product or technology and not enough on customers or markets. Why will people *buy* as opposed to simply *blog* about your cool gizmo?

3. *Your delivery has the wrong balance.* Whether you have one, three, five or fifteen minutes, the ultimate sin for any presenter is to fail to plan. No doubt you have a wealth of material to cover. Ensure that you bring out all the relevant points, from today's 'magic', right through to the exit five years hence.

4. *Beginning slowly, with no 'gasp and grasp', no 'ask'.* Cheesy as we admit it sounds, we'll keep repeating that you only have one chance to make a powerful first impression. From the first minute you begin, you simply must make a probably polite but jaundiced audience respond to your wow factor, intuitively understanding why it is compelling, and subliminally

acknowledging that you are the only team with the nous, chutzpah, skill and knowledge to make it happen. This is, after all, the balloon debate of your life. The comedian George Burns said of sincerity, 'if you can fake that, you've got it made'. We believe that if you can kick off convincingly with a curve-jumping proposition *and* make it seem perfectly credible, you're halfway to making it.

5. *Presenting information via an illogical flow.* Readers of a certain age may recall another comedian, Eric Morecambe, countering criticism of his (execrable) piano playing from the professional conductor André Previn with the words, 'I'm playing all the right notes – but not necessarily in the right order.' Similar derelictions on your part will not win awards. Presentations, like business plans, require coherent narrative as well as factual accuracy.

6. *Critical sections are missing.* This pitfall is similar to assuming listeners immediately grasp the magic of your proposal. You may be so inwardly focused on your proposal that you cannot see yourself as others see you. You forgot to say that you've already recruited a serial entrepreneur with several home runs to her name as your CEO, that BP and Exxon are vying to buy your fuel additive. Or you simply didn't come up with a convincing monetisation model, so you left that section out completely. And by the way, who *does* own those patents?

7. *Your presentation is overloaded.* You have too many slides, too much information on each slide, different fonts, illegible spreadsheets and pictures that add no information or impact.

8. *Getting the timing wrong.* '*Vae victis*' (woe to the losers), as the Romans used to say. Every pitch panel or application procedure or live presentation has its own rules. They may frustrate you, but if the word count is 1,000, do not be surprised if you are ejected in the first round for submitting 2,000. Always prepare to play by the rules: five minutes does not mean seven, so if you were saving your best argument until last, you'll never

reach it, alas. You will be told when to finish – so practise, practise, practise.

Planning your pitch

Winston Churchill allegedly asked a parliamentary colleague to leave him alone before a major intervention in the House of Commons, saying: 'I'm just preparing my impromptu remarks.' This brings us back to the value of faking sincerity. Thorough and strategic planning of your case is how to ensure you do not leave any material item out of your pitch, even if you are only allotted two minutes. It will also ensure that the flow of information is logical and that you sound confident – even spontaneous – against an unforgiving clock, knowing how high the stakes are.

These are our key questions to help you 'prepare your impromptu remarks'. You may recognise some of them from the business planning section:

1. *Why?* Be sure you understand the main objective of your presentation. You must be able to limit and define what you have to accomplish. Are you here to ensure you make it through to one-to-one meetings? To recruit advisers? To close the deal? Know your audience and be able to say at the end of the presentation *exactly what* you are seeking from them, how much money and for how long.

2. *Who?* From knowing why you are pitching it follows that you need to find out as much as you can about individual panel, club or committee members. Why will they be there, what is their track-record or sector expertise, which other recent deals have they done, what level of funding is their sweet spot?

3. *How?* Always try to speak in plain English, in the first person, with confidence and enthusiasm. Make sure you know what methods of delivery are open to you: slides and visual aids, or simply standing up and talking? Remember that speaking is not the same as reading a report out loud: use short sentences, short words, memorable facts and clear aural cues. If you say you will talk about three things – number them and make

sure you do that many. Visual aids if allowed provide useful 'punctuation'.

4. *What?* Since time will be short, your key decision is what to include and what to leave out. Master your brief and stay concrete – focus on specifics. Think of a well-wrought executive summary, with a logical order and content pared back to the essentials:

   - What need have you identified?
   - What is your solution, and why is it compelling?
   - Do you identify customers and the growth potential of the market?
   - Do you describe your revenue model?
   - Can you identify existing and emerging competition?
   - Do you identify and describe the people in your team?
   - Do you show your ambition?
   - Do you cover timing, or key milestones to market, revenues and exit?
   - Is the Enterprise Investment Scheme applicable (see Chapter 5 for more on this)?
   - Can you show that you are deal ready, not just investment ready?

5. *Where?* Hygiene factors do matter. Do you know how to reach the venue? Room size can affect the presentation you prepare: small and intimate or large and dramatic? Is the layout theatre style or less formal? Do you have a back-up plan if the projector doesn't work?

6. *When?* How much time is allowed for your presentation, at what time of day, where do you fit in the running order, will you be able to speak to interested angels on the day?

7. *Who else?* First, do you know which other companies are pitching? Are any of them potential competitors – or collaborators? Second, do you have a colleague who can come with you, someone who knows the facts and can take notes on which investor asks which question, and can then work the room with you?

8. *What next?* Remember to close as strongly as you started. Know what you want from the audience, and land within time so that how you end is up to you – you don't want your conclusion drowned out by a gong or whistle.

Elevator pitches and short slide decks

As you have probably guessed by now, our final variation on the planning and pitching theme is the elevator pitch. Remember that the scenario – probably imagined – is that you are riding a lift to the top floor with your dream investor, so you only have a minute or two to convince her she really needs to meet you to hear the full pitch and read your executive summary.

If you have crafted the executive summary into a concise, compelling and polished format you're happy with, it's likely you can use that as your starting point. But an elevator pitch must be even more pithy and punchy – and don't forget that the spoken word offers you the chance to convey personality and enthusiasm through tone and presence.

Our ideal elevator pitch covers the following:

- *What* problem are you solving? For whom?
- *Why* will customers buy from *you*?
- What makes *you* compelling in that space?
- How *big* is the opportunity?
- *How* do you make money?
- And depending on circumstances: *What do you want from...?* – and what's in it for the investor?

That's perhaps 20 seconds per bullet point – no time for a sermon on your technology, telling the angel that you have no competition or ruminating on the subcontracting deal you're trying to sign in Shanghai.

As with the full pitch, in organising your material you have to:

- Be (even more) memorable and efficient
- Provide *immediate* gasp and grasp
- Be easy to follow

- Be knowledgeable, realistic and ambitious
- Know how to end on your own terms, as strongly as you started

Elevator pitches are the haikus of the investment world. Below are some compelling examples of successful elevator pitches together with short commentaries (in bold) on why we think each works. (Note that some of the names have been changed to protect confidentiality.)

Boot Camp
Boot Camp, Inc. has developed patent-protected solutions – known as 'Bootware' – for the major billing problem faced by mobile phone operators. **Is it my market?**

$1,000,000 is required to adapt the technology for a trial contract with Verizon. **What do you want? Is it within my criteria?**

Exit by means of IPO or trade sale is expected in year 3. **Is it my timeframe? Do I believe in IPOs?**

No supplier currently addresses emerging market requirements directly. **Creating the market ... but will still have competitors**

Boot Camp's experienced team of entrepreneurs, led by Dick Dastardly. **Track-record**

Will grow Bootware to be the market leader. **Ambition**

Demand for billing software is estimated to grow to $3 billion by 2015. **Indicative risk/reward ratio**

Golf Chipper
The Walker Chipper – a revolutionary approach to chipping that can improve play and eliminate the yips. This new chipping design uses different gripping and swinging techniques that are

more natural, improve accuracy and avoid motion patterns associated with the yips, the loss of motor co-ordination skills without apparent explanation. **Clearly sets out the pain and its solution**

There are over 17,000 golf courses and 25,000,000 golfers in the United States. Of the golf players, over 48% of those purchasing putters have the yips. In addition to facilitating anyone's chipping, the Walker Chipper offers particular hope for those players with the yips. **Size of market and likely price elasticity for purchasers**

We are offering very attractive returns on what we believe to be a low-risk opportunity. We are also offering investors, especially golf enthusiasts, the opportunity to be part of a fundamental change in the great game of golf. The Walker Chipper could be to golf in 2015 what mid- and oversized rackets were to tennis in the 1980s. **Persuasive use of analogy, enthusiasm, ambition**

Back where you started – but different

Earlier we quoted Kipling: 'But after they have worked for me,/ I give them all a rest.' You may hate us for saying this, but once – and only once – you have mastered your plan and your pitch, you can give serious thought to putting the full, written versions away – giving them a rest – and boiling your core presentation down to just a handful of slides and a two-page summary. Several variants exist.[73]

Although you may feel as though you've gone round the houses, almost all start-ups need to experience the full, iterative process of modelling, planning, writing and pitching before they can strip the core of what they are trying to achieve back to just a two-page précis or a dozen slides. If your short-form pitch succeeds, you'll probably still need the full plan for due diligence purposes.

---

73 The following websites provide short templates showing how to put your case forcefully in a handful of slides: http://www.slideshare.net/huer1278ft/the-art-of-the-start-37633; http://venturehacks.com/articles/deck.

Selecting and targeting investors

This book is written primarily with early-stage companies and those starting up in mind. The world of investors is broad and complex. As well as family and friends (and fools), the investment horizon embraces business angels and venture funds large and small; thus some overall knowledge of the equity investment industry is helpful. Early-stage investing, especially in start-ups, obviously carries higher risks. But investors in early-stage companies can enjoy high rewards as a result of getting in early at a favourable share price.

The first stage in targeting investors, then, is to decide on (having taken appropriate advice) the category or type of investor to consider for further study and focus. Having decided on the category of investor, you need to match interests and agendas. Investors at all levels have investment criteria, and a typical set of these is included a little later in this chapter. Investors may have general interests or very specific and narrow criteria. Therefore the targeting process needs to be based on good knowledge of not only who the investors are and where they are located, but also what they want to invest in. This means carrying out careful research (with help, if needed). It is very helpful at this stage for the entrepreneur to be supported by an adviser or mentor with knowledge of the investment community – especially those investors who may be interested in the company seeking finance. Among the key issues to consider will be:

- The nature of your company – the type of business/sector. Will it become international? Some investors will only invest in companies with global potential.
- Clear understanding of investors' targets and interests.
- The stage you have reached – are you a start-up or have you some results and a track-record to demonstrate?
- Your location – private investors such as business angels will often only invest in companies they can easily visit because they want to take an interest in the business and its team.
- The amount of money you are seeking. Investors and investor groups usually have 'bite sizes' they will invest. Also important will be the equity share they seek.

- The investor's integrity, knowledge, expertise and interest in engaging with your business.
- Special connections you or your valued network partners may have with the investors. Personal introductions can be very important.
- Possibilities of further investment should you need it.
- Willingness to syndicate with other investors to provide the company with sufficient capital if the investor does not wish to or cannot provide the entire amount required.

Research can be conducted with the help of advisers or directly. Business angels may operate individually and independently, but generally belong to organised groups, for example London Business Angels, Cambridge Angels and Yorkshire Business Angels. Many of these organisations are members of the UK Business Angels Association – UKBAA, and also EBAN – the European Business Angels Association. Individual business angel groups have their own websites, as do UKBAA and EBAN. These sites are excellent sources of information and can guide the entrepreneur during the process of enquiry and application for funding.

The value of networking and building connections cannot be over-emphasised since informal meetings and introductions are a key part of the lives of private investors and venture capital investment partners. If starting from scratch, constructing a database of potential investors and specific information about them is essential. Entrepreneurs may need experienced help with this.

In the venture capital sector there are many funds and all will have clear investment criteria. All these funds have websites which typically give details of the partners and their individual expertise as well as their investment criteria. If venture capital funding is sought, the processes involved in selecting and targeting investors are especially important. Much time is often wasted trying to speak to or arrange meetings with investors who will never invest because of divergence of interests. Time can be saved by carrying out thorough research. The British Venture Capital Association (BVCA) and the European

Venture Capital Association (EVCA) are substantial organisations and have websites and handbooks which provide a wealth of the information required.

Having established a target list, a database of the selected targets can be prepared which will form the basis of the forward action plan and the means to record responses, progress and frequently asked questions (FAQs). It may take weeks or even months to attract investors from your target list. Getting attention and setting up meetings is time-consuming and there is significant competition for funding.

In the next section we cover planning for fundraising using your target list and approaching investors through a structured plan.

Setting up a structured plan for approaching investors

Your first approach to an investor or investor group can be critical. You may only get 'one shot'. Careful thought and preparation will pay dividends. Make sure that you have all the preliminaries in place, such as a business plan or at least a clearly defined business model, an executive summary and a presentation before you set up meetings with investors. The presentation needs to be in a flexible and changeable format to meet specific investor needs, interests and preferences. A two-minute elevator pitch should by now be well-rehearsed and ready to go whenever opportunities present.

Before making any approaches to investors collate all your research about them on a spreadsheet. This spreadsheet will be your core document as approaches are made and meetings take place. Keeping track of all contacts with each investor will ensure attention to detail in follow-up and tracking. In addition to this spreadsheet, priorities should be set for the sequence of contacts to be made. Those 'most likely' to be interested and invest will naturally come at the top. Timing is an important consideration so that you can deal with a manageable number of approaches at any one time, be confident of having time for follow-up and arrange subsequent meetings at times convenient to investors as well as yourself.

Investors can be approached by telephone directly or through network connections who know them well. Wherever a key adviser or other network colleague is well known to a prospective investor a personal approach is most likely to get a response. An approach in written form by email (rarely these days by regular mail) will be your first step. This can take the form of a friendly but clear and professional message accompanied initially by an executive summary of no more than one and a half or two pages. This document must be very clear and engaging. See Chapter 3 for more on writing effective business plans. Follow-up will usually be needed to activate the next steps in the process. In summary, events should be planned as follows:

1. Send emails inviting declarations of interest. Attach your executive summary. It is important to request responses by a specified date to add a note of urgency/importance. Offer to set up a meeting or offer more information. No detailed financial information should be sent at this time. The executive summary can include a few financial projections and requirements.

2. Either receive responses requiring more information and continue dialogue or follow up by email and telephone if you get no response. There are likely to be requests for your business plan. While you can provide your business plan at this point, it is best to press for a meeting at which it can be made available, usually after a presentation.

3. Record responses on your investor spreadsheet and in narrative form if needed. All business plans should be numbered and records kept of each recipient.

4. Review progress, responses, next steps and so on on a weekly basis with all those involved in fundraising. Documents may need revising as a result of ongoing progress.

Meetings with investors

First meetings are most likely to take place at investors' premises rather than yours. Before the meeting, take the following steps:

- Make sure that everyone who will attend the meeting reviews all the data available on the investor(s).

- Plan your approach with a view to exerting appropriate control over the meeting. Plan to take the initiative following introductions to direct the meeting in the way 'most comfortable to you'.
- Check out all materials to be taken and decide who is to be the main presenter. Experience shows that it is helpful to have two people representing the investee at these meetings – but rarely more than three unless the investor has asked at this early stage to meet the whole team and there are more than three. It is not necessary for all who attend from the company to participate in the main presentation. Better for one to take the lead and best if this is the lead entrepreneur.
- Ask the investor in advance what kind of presentation they prefer. Some investors have strong preferences regarding the type and nature of the information they see. Some do not like PowerPoint, so sailing in with a big slide show without checking out first can result in disappointment for all. Sometimes investors indicate that they want the first meeting to be informal, just to get to know you and your plans. Others will require hard copy information which can be talked through and left behind.
- If you are going to the investor's premises, check out who will provide the necessary equipment for a PowerPoint presentation – you or them. This may sound basic but it certainly avoids embarrassment all round.

DOING THE DEAL – NEGOTIATION

The value of your business will ultimately depend on what someone is prepared to pay for it and what you are prepared to sell it for. You will come to the final price through negotiation. The key to successful negotiation is preparation.

Before attempting a negotiation you must know your business plan inside out – what your product is, what your business is about and who your target customers are and the kind of value you will be providing to them through your products and services.

Work through a number of deal options and work out the range of prices you would be prepared to accept, or the 'zone of best agreement' (see Figure 17). This range will be bounded by the ideal price (the greatest value that you could possibly expect from the deal) at the top end and the walk-away point (the lowest price that you could possibly accept, below which you are no longer interested in the deal). You will also need to think about why you would be prepared to drop the price over this range.

Figure 17. Zone of best agreement

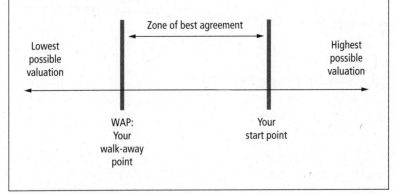

At the meeting

- Determine at the outset how long the investor(s) have allowed for the meeting. It will usually be one to one and a half hours for the first meeting. Indicate at the beginning that you would like the investor(s) to explain their investment process and the sequence of events if they decide to explore an investment further.
- Propose a sequence and format so as to maintain a degree of control over the discussion.
- Present in the way the investors indicate they prefer. For example, you may be given 15 minutes to set out your stall and then 45 minutes for questions and discussion. Alternatively, the investors may prefer an interactive discussion – intervening as points arise.

- Always have at least one other person present on the investee side. This person should make careful notes on responses and identify questions that need to be addressed. If there are questions which cannot be answered on the spot – say so – and promise to provide an answer in an agreed period of time. Do not waffle!
- When the main discussion seems to be coming to an end, ask the investor(s) whether they are interested in your proposal and, if they are, clarify the next steps to be taken.
- After every encounter with prospective investors, and without delay, write a thank you note and include any appropriate follow-up information.
- Record the outcome of the meeting on your spreadsheet.

Presenting effectively takes practice. You need to respond to investor feedback and update and modify your presentations accordingly. Genuine confidence, inspiration and passion impress investors as much as technological proficiency.

In Chapters 1 and 4 we discuss the importance of experienced board members and advisers. Investors will be very interested in knowing about and meeting the 'grey-haired supporters' you may have attracted to your board or advisory panel.

CASE STUDY
Cambridge Healthcare Ltd: finding the right investors

This is a study in persistence, learning things the hard way and of success generated by finding investors with genuine interest in and understanding of the field of operations. It is also a lesson in the importance of clarity in company positioning and realisation of future potential.

Cambridge Healthcare Ltd is a highly innovative company that started life as a partnership with the UK National Health Service (NHS). It is a company that has developed a series of international award-winning telehealth and bioinformatics solutions – principally an electronic health record and platform called 'How are you?' (www.howareyou. com). It enables patients to get involved with health professionals to take a much greater role in the planning and implementing of their own health care. This company has been described as 'the social network of healthcare' and is one of many companies competing for attention in the digital market place and in health information generally.

When he founded the company in 2010, Dawson King was 27 years old, an entrepreneur who had already successfully started and exited three companies. His knowledge of bioinformatics and information technology is as extensive as his understanding of the NHS and the challenges involved in implementing health and social care policy. These are important points – knowing your market, customers and those who can influence the success of a new business with new technology – all critical to attracting finance and succeeding over the long term.

Cambridge Healthcare operated for the first 18 months with only the founder as its full-time employee. It raised its outside investment from business angels – but not the 'usual suspects'. Dawson King had worked with a large software company and established a reputation for excellence that resulted in the firm providing the initial private investment. Unusually, King did not go to organised business angel groups and thus avoided the time-consuming processes that are generally involved. The initial investors were uninterested in engaging in day-to-day company operations but were strategically important in the longer term. The company was able to operate for more than a year with the founder drawing minimal living expenses and working long hours to develop the first product. The company structure and organisation was well considered and assembled with the professional help of a quality law firm. It complied with all appropriate aspects of company law from day one.

In Chapter 1 we emphasised the importance of 'getting the basics right from the start'. Dawson King had done just that.

The time for fundraising came again in 2012 as the company sought new capital to support product development and international market entry. The business plan reflected these needs and a number of prospective investors were targeted and approached.

Presentations were made to early-stage venture capitalists with no immediate outcomes. The company was eventually introduced to an American group of health care specialist investors who showed great enthusiasm, and after a number of meetings, it appeared were committed subject to due diligence. However, discussions were protracted and at the eleventh hour it was discovered that the investor had no immediate capital – and was in the process of fundraising itself.

A lesson learned! Always try to find out early whether your prospective investors have the money to avoid time wasted on meetings, presentations, visits and correspondence. Fortunately, Cambridge Healthcare had been in discussions with other interested parties; a fund based in Asia and a well-established technology investor with a European headquarters and a strong presence in the US.

These investors not only had funds, but also leaders who understood Cambridge Healthcare's business and saw the abilities and resourcefulness of the founder as reasons to expect success. Post-due diligence there was a clear matching of agendas and an investment was secured at a favourable valuation, which left the founder with a majority shareholding and fair shareholder agreement.

Cambridge Healthcare is now flourishing. Preparation for entering world markets from a strong position in the UK is going ahead, contracts have been signed with major industry leaders such as Microsoft and overseas agreements are in place in Asia and EMEA. The company has shown itself to be distinctly 'investable' and its investors are ready, when and if necessary, to provide additional growth capital.

It is worth noting that considerable efforts were made by the company to win major international awards as it positioned itself on the world stage and sought industry and peer recognition. In 2011 Cambridge Healthcare was awarded the IT Innovator of the Year award by the Institute of Engineering and Technology and, in 2012, the IT Innovation of the Year award within the Health Investor Awards. Undoubtedly, these accomplishments – highly prestigious and stringently-judged awards – influenced investors as well as prospective business partners.

Since securing new funding, Cambridge Healthcare has sealed a major deal with the largest company in China operating an online social network, which has 500 million users, and is now anticipating major growth in the world's most rapidly expanding health care market.

Many lessons can be learned from the experiences outlined in this case study:

- It is necessary to have efficient company and financial management structures in place.
- Credibility of the leader(s) is a key factor.
- Clarity of identity and planned positioning of the company in very significant growth markets is more important than a 50-page business plan.
- Early funding without too many strings can be secured by entrepreneurs 'in the know and with track-records'.
- Investors do not always reveal truthfully or openly whether or not they actually have the money to invest. Sometimes seeing a really good deal may cause investors to drag out discussions whilst they try to find the money. Simple due diligence by the company can find this out. Beware the effusive and enthusiastic investor with empty pockets!
- Matching agendas and key people in the company and investor organisations is key and takes time, energy and patience.

CHAPTER 4

COMPETITIVENESS: INTELLECTUAL PROPERTY, NEGOTIATING AND DEAL-MAKING

A fair bargain leaves both sides unhappy.
– George R. R. Martin

Overview

Understanding what's 'under the hood' in a venture deal – especially legal issues, including intellectual property – is key to completing a transaction that is well structured and allows all parties to maximise the chance of achieving their aims. Equally critical is negotiating terms that are acceptable to all sides and make for a stable relationship between investors and founders as the business develops.

This section covers:
• Choosing professional advisers
• The importance of identifying, valuing and protecting intellectual property
• The process of due diligence and disclosure
• The key documents used to implement a venture investment
• Guidance on negotiating with lenders and investors

A venture investment is a transaction that creates a relationship – as opposed to the sale and purchase of an asset where the parties may never be in contact again. This relationship needs to be founded on trust and confidence. The best way to build confidence between investors and founders is to have a rigorous deal-making process that allows investors to investigate and understand the business, building their confidence that what they have been told about the business is true and fair.

Maintaining the relationship between investors and founders is made much easier if the investment is based on well-structured agreements that address all the key commercial aspects of the deal. This is especially true of those issues that could become sources of tension between investors and the company or founders as the business develops.

Choosing legal and professional advisers

The voice of the team must be heard

We have deliberately not introduced the topic of external advisers until this stage of the book – raising money must be done principally by the founders or managers of a business, not by anyone else. The reason is obvious: investors want to do the deal with the people that they are actually backing. The contact they get through the investigation, negotiation and completion of the investment is how they gauge the ability of the founders to sell, negotiate and simply get stuff done and, even more important, assess whether they like and can work with the founders going forward. The latter is especially true where the investor is an angel. To paraphrase Bob Marley, it has to be 'you I'm talking to now'!

Choose the right adviser for the right task

This means that the role of professional advisers needs to be tightly defined and controlled to avoid becoming 'noise on the line' between investors and founders. That said, the right advice at the right time is invaluable is getting the optimal possible deal for both founders and investors. Circumstances where professional or external advice could be valuable include those listed in Table 6.

Table 6. Which adviser to use when

Issue	Adviser	Fee basis
Investment readiness – preparing a business plan and presentation	Accountant, corporate finance adviser, management consultant	Hourly or fixed
Finding and introducing investors (a regulated activity in many countries)	Accountant, corporate finance adviser, angel network, placing agent	Hourly or fixed with a success fee related to investment
Protecting innovations in product or service	Patent agent (for patenting), intellectual property lawyer (for other matters – e.g. assigning IP)	Hourly
Preparing for investment (company records, disclosure bundle, accounts, contracts, employment records, etc.)	Accountant, company secretary, lawyer, employment lawyer	Hourly
Reviewing term sheet or offer from investor	Corporate finance adviser, lawyer (possibly)	Hourly
Negotiating with potential investors over detailed deal terms.	Lawyer for legal issues, corporate finance adviser for commercial deal terms, *but* founders should lead	Hourly

Ensure that advisers have a clearly defined mandate targeted on the specific outcomes that the founders want to achieve. This has several benefits:

- Limits unnecessary use of advisers' time (and therefore costs)
- Keeps founders in control of the process
- Avoids delays while advisers seek instructions

Select advisers with care

Advisers should always be selected using a process that is professional and rigorous. Canvass business contacts, mentors and existing advisers for names of new advisers who can fill a specific role. Whittle the names down to a shortlist of at least three and meet each of them. When meeting prospective advisers, investigate:

- Their experience in the type of work you want done (never use a generalist adviser for investment work – it's complex and requires an experienced specialist).
- Their estimate of the time needed to do the work and likely costs.
- Whether they've acted in a transaction with the investors you're considering.
- Whether they've worked with your existing advisers before.
- References from clients whom they have acted for in similar transactions.

Appointing and managing advisers

Once the best adviser for the job has been selected, make sure they enter into a clear agreement that specifies what needs to be done, by when and how much the work should cost. If the job takes significantly more time than expected, require them to come back and get agreement to a revised estimate. If the adviser doesn't do what is required, or is tardy or otherwise performs unsatisfactorily, the adviser must be told early and clearly – so that they can remedy the position or, if they fail to do so, there is a clear pretext for replacing them without having to pay twice.

Managing intellectual property

The value of patents

A business is more valuable the more that its market position has monopoly characteristics – where demand for the product is great and/or growing significantly but is inelastic (i.e. price doesn't deter customers from buying). This gives the business the ability to achieve very high profit margins and, if the market is large or is becoming large, high levels of absolute profit that translate into significant value for the enterprise as a whole.

Governments generally dislike monopolies and have enacted anti-trust laws to control them or, in extremis, break them up (e.g. Standard Oil and AT&T/Bell System in the US). In the case of innovations, however, nearly all jurisdictions worldwide grant legal monopolies (i.e. patents) for a fixed time period. This is based on a *quid pro quo* which requires the applicant for a patent to disclose its workings (and thereby increase knowledge in the application area) in return for the granting of a monopoly on its commercial exploitation.

Investors value strong intellectual property (i.e. where it protects products or services that are key to the business's commercial offering) for two reasons:
- It offers protection from competitors while the business is growing to scale and profitability.
- It enhances the long-term value of the business.

Investors will take considerable trouble (see the 'Due diligence' section later in this chapter) to ensure that the company owns or has unfettered rights to the intellectual property it is exploiting in its products or services. Founders need to make sure that any other claims to the IP, such as by employees or technology partners, are pinned down by means of an assignment of IP to the company or a licence for it to exploit the IP. The former is likely to be more satisfactory than the latter and weak IP position may cause an investor to reconsider the valuation at which the investment is being made or whether to continue with the investment at all.

Other intellectual property

Other types of intellectual property include the following:
- *Trade marks*   A trade mark is a sign, in the form of an image or words or a combination of both, that can distinguish a business's goods and services from those of its competitors. In common law countries[74] there are general protections from 'passing off' provided for any trade mark that is validly used but greater protection in these countries, as well as the rest of the world, accrues from registering the trade mark.
- *Registered designs*   All designs in the UK automatically have protection for their three-dimensional form through the

---

74 Principally the UK, US, Australia, Canada, Hong Kong, India, Ireland, New Zealand and Singapore.

unregistered Design Right (and equivalents exist in some other countries). In contrast, a registered design gives specific protection to both three-dimensional and two-dimensional designs as well as surface patterns and prevents anyone from copying the design.

• *Know-how*   If disclosure of the workings of an invention could lead to its circumvention or in circumstances where it may be hard to demonstrate the inventive step in an innovation, it may be best to protect a business's intellectual property, generally described as 'know-how', through secrecy and binding those people who have access to the know-how.

Advisers

The principal categories of intellectual property adviser are:

• *Patent agents*   These (or patent attorneys) are professional advisers who specialise in the preparation and submission of patent applications and their management after the grant of a patent on behalf of clients. They can also act for clients in registered design applications.

• *Trade mark attorneys*   These specialise in the registration of trade marks and issues surrounding their protection in home and overseas markets. This is a distinct profession in the UK and Commonwealth countries; in the US any qualified attorney or patent agent can represent clients in trade mark matters.

• *Intellectual property lawyers*   These act in legal matters relating to intellectual property, which can include preparing documents that protect trade secrets, bind employees in connection with innovations and confidential information or mortgage, sell or otherwise dispose of intellectual property.

Due diligence, disclosure, term sheets and legal agreements

Due diligence

Investors need to satisfy themselves that they understand the business in which they are proposing to invest and that the case put forward by founders in the business plan is a fair reflection of reality. This potentially could impact on valuation (see Chapter 6), especially if the investor's investigation (termed 'undertaking or doing due diligence') reveals that the business's market, product or financial position is significantly weaker than it was held out to be.

Due diligence can take several forms but usually comprises *commercial due diligence* (most often undertaken by the investor themselves) and *legal due diligence* (undertaken by lawyers acting for the investor). In larger or more complex transactions, the investor may require an *investigating accountant's report* on the company's financial position, the accuracy of its management accounts and the future financial projections provided to investors.

COMMERCIAL DUE DILIGENCE

This is usually conducted as a site visit including interviews with key team members as well as detailed investigation of:
- product and marketing strategy
- competitors
- costs, margins and growth
- detailed plans and forecasts
- innovation and market development
- operations
- cash generation and use
- management accounts and other management information and their accuracy

LEGAL DUE DILIGENCE

The investor's lawyers will require sight of a full range of legal documents prior to completion of the deal. These will almost certainly include:
- current articles of association (or equivalent company governance documents)
- any preceding shareholder agreements
- contracts with suppliers, partners and customers
- employment contracts and service agreements

- bank facility letters
- operational finance agreements
- intellectual property documents (including patents, patent applications filed, IP assignments)
- leases or other documents relating to the company's right to occupy its premises

Disclosure

WARRANTIES

Nearly all investment agreements will include warranties (see the 'Term sheets' and 'Legal agreements' sections below). In essence, a warranty is an assurance by one party to another that specific facts or conditions are true. The other party is entitled to rely on that assurance and seek some type of remedy if it transpires to be untrue.

There are two aspects to disclosure in a venture investment context:

- It is an important general principle to bear in mind when dealing with investors. Clear disclosure of any material fact about the business, including weaknesses, problems and challenges, is an essential part of engaging effectively with an investor and building confidence between the investor and the founders.
- It is the management team's primary defence against liability under the warranties. Anything formally disclosed cannot be used to make a warranty claim.

★ KEY CONCEPT

DISCLOSE FULLY AND EARLY
- Investors should never discover key weaknesses in the business for themselves
- Disclosing fully and early maintains confidence and keeps the deal on track

---

Term sheets

A term sheet (or 'heads of terms' or just 'heads') is a summary of the terms of a proposed investment. Term sheets are widely used by venture investors and some angel investors. The principal terms of the deal can be negotiated and agreed without delving into the detailed terms, saving wasted time and effort if the principal terms cannot be agreed.

Legal agreements

BINDING TERM SHEETS

There has been a tendency to use simplified legal agreements, which have some of the characteristics of a term sheet, to make the venture investment process faster than using a term sheet followed by a full shareholders' agreement. Clearly, these work better in a simpler transaction, such as a straightforward angel investment or one where many of the investor rights and provisions can be incorporated into the articles of association.

STANDARD AGREEMENTS

The conventional way to structure a venture investment is to use a combination of amending the company's primary governance document (articles of association in the UK and most Commonwealth countries; articles of incorporation in the US) and executing a shareholders' agreement (or 'investment agreement' or 'subscription agreement').

- *Articles of association (articles of incorporation)*   A company's articles regulate the relationship between the company and its shareholders, including the division of its share capital into different classes of shares and the rights of those classes to participate in distributions of capital or income or vote in general meetings. They also regulate other matters of governance, such as the appointment of directors and the process for liquidation or sale.
- In venture investment transactions the principal amendments likely to be sought by investors could include:

- Creating one or more **new classes** for investors' shares which may have priority over ordinary shares in the distribution of capital or income.
- Defining other rights (normally referred to as **control or consent rights**) that will accrue to the new class of shares (such as the right to nominate one or more directors to the board or a requirement that holders of the class consent to significant changes to the business such as issuing new shares, mortgaging its assets or selling or licensing its trade or assets).
- Fixing '**drag and tag**' provisions: drag (or 'drag-along') is the ability of the holders of a given proportion of the shares in issue to require the remainder to join them in a sale of the whole of the issued share capital; tag is the requirement on the holders of a given proportion of the shares in issue, having negotiated a sale of their shares, to ensure that all other shareholders are offered the same sale terms.
- Defining **pre-emption rights**: the degree to which existing shareholders are given first refusal to subscribe for new shares or buy existing shares for sale in proportion to their shareholding prior to the transaction.
- Defining compulsory share transfer provisions in the event that a founder leaves the business – called **good leaver/ bad leaver provisions**. Good leaver provisions occur when a founder leaves because of ill health or as the result of a mutually agreed departure (likely to be more attractive from the founder's perspective), and bad leaver provisions occur when the investor loses confidence in the founder or the founder leaves the business other than by mutual agreement.

• *Shareholders' agreement (investment agreement or subscription agreement)*   Every investment will have some form of legally binding agreement between the company and the investors, which may also bind all existing shareholders (in addition to the founders). The terms set out in the shareholders' agreement are likely to include:

- *Reporting*   The requirement for the company to report

progress and other matters to the investor on a periodic basis or as otherwise required (i.e. when something exceptional but significant occurs).

– *Control and consultation rights* Provisions for the investor to be consulted on major decisions affecting the company (duplicating or adding to similar rights set out in the amended articles), including setting budgets and agreeing the business plan; issuing new shares; founders' remuneration; borrowing, sale or mortgage of assets including intellectual property; acquisition of other businesses and agreeing joint ventures; entering into large or exceptional contracts.

– *Board representation/attendance* The right to nominate one or more directors to the board of the company (which may duplicate similar provisions in the amended articles in respect of appointing directors), but also to attend board meetings if a director has not been appointed by the investor or where an appointed director is a third party.

– *Ratchets and Reverse ratchets* It can be hard to agree the valuation of a business at the time of investment, especially if it is pre-revenue or loss-making. One way to get round an impasse between investors and founders on valuation is to implement a ratchet – a mechanism for adjusting the relative shareholdings of investors and founders dependent on the achievement of mutually agreed goals. A recent phenomenon, especially in seed investments in the US, is the reverse ratchet, where a proportion of founders' shares have their rights to voting and/or return of capital taken away. The rights are restored progressively as the business achieves agreed milestones over time. Ratchets and reverse ratchets may be implemented through the articles as well as the shareholders' agreement.

Negotiating with investors and lenders

Founders will want the best possible terms for an equity investment or other financing. This is natural: they have confidence in their own abilities, believe in the potential of the opportunity and will want to concede as little value as possible to the potential investor or lender. That said, they will often be unfamiliar with the investment process and when and how to negotiate with investors.

Founders also need to know where to turn for advice and to know what alternatives exist to the investment terms proposed by the investor.

When to negotiate

NEVER NEGOTIATE TOO EARLY

The obvious first opportunity for negotiation is when the investor makes an offer, whether in outline or in a formal term sheet. The investor is showing a willingness to try to do a deal and will expect some response from the founders.

However, if the investor is a venture fund, the executive will already have crystallised a deal outline and may well have tested it with the investment committee or other sanctioning authority needed to sign off the final deal. Clearly, it's harder to change the terms of a deal once crystallised than beforehand.

This means it is essential that founders express their aspirations and expectations as effectively as possible before any valuation or structure is crystallised by the investor. The investor is also likely to want to understand the founders' position on valuation and terms to avoid having an offer rejected outright, so will listen to a well-made case on valuation and terms.

UNDERSTANDING THE PSYCHOLOGY OF THE INVESTMENT PROCESS

It is possible to identify four phases in the process of making an investment, and the psychology of an investor is likely to be substantially different during each of these phases:

- Investors start out in **selling mode**: demonstrating experience, track-record and commitment in supporting excellent management teams.
- Once a pitch has been made, the investor becomes a **sceptic and inquisitor** seeking out weakness and inconsistency in the

business product or plan and in the experience and capacity of the founders.

- When an investor decides to invest, a Rubicon is crossed. There may be several weaknesses or threats that need investigating and understanding, but the investor is working to make the deal happen. Although likely to still be negotiating with the founders, the investor's main challenge is getting the deal agreed by colleagues or an investment committee – acting as an **internal product champion** for the deal (this can even apply to angels who need to justify a new investment to a partner, spouse or trustee).

- Once the deal is done, the investor should settle into the long-term role of **supportive shareholder** and, potentially, non-executive director.

Making the most of management's negotiating opportunities

SUCCESSFUL TRADING BUSINESSES

In a management buy-out or any transaction involving a successful and profitable business with reasonably predictable future performance, it won't be difficult to attract investors. The business may even end up in the enviable position of asking potential investors to take part in a 'beauty parade' where they present their bona fides and track-record to convince the management team and existing shareholders to select them. Inevitably, the price and terms on which they might do the deal will be among the most important issues in selecting investors. Under these circumstances, the negotiating pressure is thrown onto the investors and managers will have real choices from the outset.

SEED AND EARLY-STAGE BUSINESSES

More usually, the deal will be less straightforward. Seed and early-stage businesses carry a degree of risk and uncertainty that is difficult to assess. Under such circumstances, it is easy for the initiative to pass to the investor, especially if there is a dearth of investors who want to take the proposal beyond the initial pitch. This is when the founders must work, with some subtlety, at maintaining or regaining the initiative:

- *Name the valuation or not?* Nearly all investors, especially venture investors, like to feel that they are good deal makers, not only in the way they conduct negotiations, but also in the way they 'tailor' a deal to the circumstances of the company (and, of course, their needs or those of their fund). This means that they will react badly to a proposal where the manager, or his advisers, has devised a deal structure and is saying, 'here's the deal: take it or leave it'. There are circumstances, however, where this approach may be appropriate, such as pitching to an angel network or where the founders have already raised the majority, or a significant proportion, of the funds required, on terms already agreed

- *Nuancing valuation expectations.* The founders' opening gambit needs to be more subtle. They need to convey confidence in their projections and the value of the opportunity, combined with a clear understanding of the way a rational investor would tackle valuation and therefore have a sensible range of values for the business in mind. Founders should flag the deal terms they feel are appropriate but do this at the right stage of the investors' appraisal process (i.e. when interest is clear but before a firm deal outline has emerged; see the 'Understanding the psychology of the investment process' section on pages 162-63).

REALISM

If management can make this negotiating process work, their opening position will have had an impact on the investors' initial offer. So long as management, with the help of their professional advisers, have been realistic in their opening position, the investor will have to take that position into account in designing any deal. The better the investors understand the founders' position, the more likely it is that any offer will meet the expectations of both parties.

EXPLOITING AN INVESTOR'S COMMITMENT

In the later stages of the investment process management can still have considerable influence on some of the terms of the deal. The investor will be increasingly committed to the deal as the process continues and won't want to imperil it over an issue of detail. Therefore this can be a good stage to exert pressure to change some of the details of the deal, especially where a venture investor doesn't have to seek approval for any changes. These details might include the process for appointing any nominee directors, fixed or participating dividend rights or, in the case of loans, the repayment timetable.

What to negotiate

Negotiation has two central objectives for founders: first, raise investment or other finance on the best possible terms and, second, ensure that the investor's desire to invest is strengthened in the negotiating process. This means that careful thought needs to be given to ensuring that any negotiating position is realistic and that it is consistent with the view of the business and team presented to the investor.

Successful negotiation is a two-way street. The investor, as well as management, will want to reach an agreement on the best terms available, although be sensitive to the need not to demotivate the management team or run the risk of rejection of the terms by a majority of existing shareholders. More important still, the investor will want to ensure that weaknesses in the plan are addressed and that the deal provides enough influence over the business to keep it on track.

Tables 7 and 8 are designed to give founders a feel for the issues that can be negotiated with an investor, the stage at which to raise them and the possible trade-offs.

Table 7. Equity investment

Issue	Investor sensitivity	Trade-off
Equity % (pre-offer)	Very sensitive	Increase management subscription or improve profitability offer ratchet
Total facility (pre-offer)	Sensitive (it may need regional or board approval)	Seek deferred consideration or more bank borrowing. Consider offering equity ratchet tied to drawdown of cash
Exit (pre-offer)	Very sensitive for limited life funds; less sensitive for bank subsidiaries	Find investor who agrees with management aims for realisation
Management subscription (pre-offer)	Very sensitive (rule of thumb: each manager should put up one year's salary)	Show previous salary and personal financial circumstances; don't be greedy in first year
Loan/equity mix (pre-/post-offer)	Dependent on fund constitution and need for running yield	Demonstrate strong profit potential but less predictable cash need. Suggest preferential shares or participating dividend on ordinary shares instead of loan
Ratchet (pre-/post-offer)	Disliked by some investors, but widely used	Useful in impasse over equity % (driven by profit) or over total facility (driven by drawdown of cash)
Drawdown of funds in stages (pre-/post-offer)	Reassuring for most investors when the stages are performance- rather than time-driven	Useful for closing a gap where management and investors disagree on total facility needed or on realistic projected performance
Special share rights (post-offer)	Inevitable with most investors	Use as a reason for not conceding a debenture on lending
Security/ debenture rights (post-offer)	Important to investors with significant loans; can be important where the investor wants the right to change management	Look for investor with all equity philosophy; ensure balanced, well-qualified management team with track-record; don't concede security easily – it will limit future bank borrowing

Issue	Investor sensitivity	Trade-off
Dividend rights (post-offer)	Important to investors who need running yield; desirable to others, if no realisation plan	Useful for closing a gap where management and investors disagree on total facility needed or on realistic projected performance
Repayment or redemption schedule (post-offer)	Sensitive but not vital to investors who use loans or preferential shares in deal structures	Concede early redemption schedule (i.e. shares) but fight tight repayment schedule (i.e. loans)
Nominee director (post-offer)	Very difficult to avoid (Note: some funds always nominate one of their own staff, others look for the suitable outsider)	Try to insist on named individual (if fund nominates one of its staff); otherwise seek right to nominate director subject to Investor's approval
Support/training	Dependent on fund's philosophy	Useful concession if management think it is worthwhile

Table 8. Lending

Issue	Lender sensitivity	Trade-off
Total facility (pre-offer)	Sensitive (it may need regional or head office approval)	Consider alternatives (factoring, leasing or venture capital) to fill any shortfall; demonstrate strong cash flow and asset growth to give added security
Margin on loans (pre-/post-offer)	Sensitive	'Beauty parades' of potential lenders are possible, but not worth prejudicing long-term relationships
Security (pre-offer)	Most sensitive	Haggle to demonstrate quality of assets (i.e. debtors, stock and property); resist 'shrinkage' factors (i.e. 50% of debtors); suggest Government Loan Guarantee Scheme
Personal guarantees (pre-offer)	Not essential if adequate business assets, but often required	Negotiate proper security cover based on business assets sought; consider venture capital
Repayment schedule (post-offer)	Not sensitive within bank's standard loan criteria	Provide well-argued cash flow forecasts and insist on repayments matching business need

Figure 18 below shows in simplified form how some trigger events become inflexion points affecting how investors view an early-stage company.

Figure 18. Events impacting business valuation at early stages

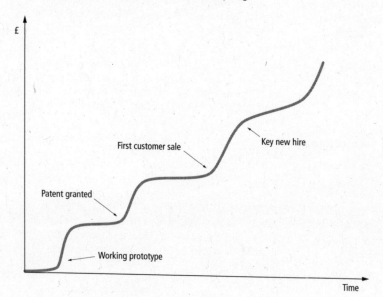

CHAPTER 5

BANKS, GRANTS AND NEW SOURCES OF FUNDING

I went to my bank first and met a very nice chap, very friendly. It turned out he was normally doing things like lending money to people to set up newspaper shops. He did not really feel qualified to comment on my adaptive non-linear pattern recognition technology. But he did give me a good piece of advice, which I carry with me even now, which is that people will always buy confectionery.
– Dr Mike Lynch, founder of Autonomy Corporation plc, quoted in *The Observer*, 5 December 1999

Overview

In your earliest phases, before your venture has a regular income from customers, it is highly unlikely that bank funding will be suitable for your needs. But don't ignore banks completely, for two reasons. First, you will require somewhere to deposit the funds you do raise elsewhere (if only from family and friends or grants); second, you will need to have access to a means of money transmission to pay staff and suppliers – a core banking service, even if overlooked in the years before 2008. You may also find other non-lending services useful (such as insurance), as is building up a 'behavioural' track-record with a potential future lender. Also, once you hit the growth phase it's quite likely you will be suitable for carefully considered bank debt to supplement equity investment and cash from customers.

Then there is the third component of the funding trinity to grapple with – grants. Grants are usually provided by public bodies (charities and other foundations are other possible sources) and have the advantage that – if you do as you're asked – you don't have to pay them back or part with ownership in your business. But to receive a grant, you will normally have to commit to delivering work packages that are not all directly relevant to your core commercial mission. And meticulous record-keeping is also generally a requirement. The grant scene is often opaque at best, but we've sought to bring out some general principles as well as outline those sources of grants most likely to be of use to entrepreneurs currently.

Finally in this chapter, we look at some minority but intriguing additional forms of funding: crowd-sourcing and corporate venturing.

Banks: the basics

Remember the analogy that borrowing from a bank is akin to renting a car: you must return both the car and the money on time and undamaged, and you'll likely pay up-front fees and a daily rate in each case. Though as an ambitious entrepreneur you'll likely find dealing with banks a frustrating experience initially (you never realised there'd be so many ways of being told 'no'), real bankers are doing their job well when they adopt a conservative approach.

It's in your interests – as well as theirs and society's – that only those ventures that have convincing prospects of repaying loans should receive them in the first place. Since a bank is only renting you money (much of it the savings of depositors like yourself) it has no stake in the event that your business is a remarkable success – unlike angels, the bank has no share of the equity. Its reward comes in the form of the interest charged on the loan and fees such as an arrangement fee for reviewing your application in the first place. Even though interest margins have risen since the crash, banks have little room for error: it takes the return on scores of good loans to make up for the loss on one bad one.

Consider the following simplified example. Megabank lends your friend's business (boom.com) £100,000, with a 1 per cent arrangement fee and an annual 5 per cent interest margin over the base lending rate set by the Bank of England, with no repayments until the first anniversary of the loan and with an interest 'holiday' for six months (so no interest is payable until halfway through the first year). Your friend convinced Megabank to make this loan because she is naturally persuasive but, it goes without saying, she is nowhere near as competent a manager as you are. Boom. com went bust in month 6 so comprehensively that, even though the bank had a charge over the assets, it received back none of its original £100,000.

The only return Megabank has is the original £1,000 arrangement fee. To make up for the lost principal of £100,000, you may think that it will need 20 other similar loans – each generating £5,000 in interest income a year – to perform impeccably. In fact, it is much worse than that because banks have relatively high fixed costs, paying for staff, premises or compliance as well as cost of funds. So boom.com's demise may well mean that not 20 but 40 other similar loans have to perform impeccably to restore the *status quo ante*.

Post-crash banks again rely heavily on depositors for the funds they then lend on to borrowers. Depositors include start-ups like yours, looking for a safe haven for your angel round. So whether it's a relief to know that old-fashioned credit standards are back may depend on whether you're a depositor or a frustrated lender.

Fundamental credit principles

Which brings us on to how well-drilled lenders will review your proposal. Gallows humour at the darkest moments of the 2008 financial crash produced one very revealing joke. Among the banks galloping to the brink of oblivion in Britain were Royal Bank of Scotland and HBOS, which were led by Fred Goodwin and Andy Hornby, respectively. The former was a chartered accountant and the latter held an MBA from Harvard Business School. Neither had a banking qualification, let alone hands-on lending experience. Hence the question: 'Who's the odd one out – Fred Goodwin, Andy Hornby or Terry Wogan?'

The answer was Sir Terry Wogan, the popular entertainer, as the only one of the trio to have been a branch banker. As recent history has shown, no amount of clever software can replace the experience of sitting across the table from a potential client, deciding whether or not to offer a loan.[75]

In addition to judgement and personal experience, lending bankers do also use structured frameworks when appraising lending applications. These differ from institution to institution but the fundamental issues remain constant and can be illustrated by the mnemonic 'CAMPARI & ICE'. In other words, lenders will be seeking to answer these seven sets of questions when looking at your proposal:

- *Character*. Are you 'respectable and trustworthy'? While the proposal must have commercial merit on a stand-alone basis, experience suggests that strong plans need dependable people to deliver them.
- *Ability*. What is your track-record, how strong is the team, what's your potential? This question matters much more to an investor, but a lender needs to consider it, too. If everything you've ever touched turned to lead, don't be surprised if lenders shy away even if you can supply security for your loan.
- *Margin/means*. What percentage above base rate would be a suitable margin if the loan were made? Too low and the bank is not being rewarded for the risk; too high and it might damage your cash flow. Also – and this is critical – don't expect the bank to supply all or even most of the funds you need for your proposal. If your analysis shows that you require £100,000 to proceed, don't assume that a meagre £5,000 from you as shareholders and directors will be enough. Since you'll take the reward if the plan succeeds, expect also to take much of the pain if it fails. (As a rule of thumb, start with a 50:50 ratio and then compare your proposals to others to determine relative risk.)
- *Purpose*. Specifically, what is the bank lending for? Are you undertaking a well-thought-through expansion, seeking to rescue

---

75 See, for instance, Ray Perman, *Hubris: How HBOS wrecked the best bank in Britain* (Edinburgh: Birlinn, 2012).

a business buffeted by events, or are you really just buying toys such as new cars?

- *Amount.* Is the amount requested realistic? You may have asked for too much or too little – often a certain amount of headroom, even though it increases the principal, provides both you and the lender with the comfort of knowing that you can deal with unexpected events, such a customer paying you a month late.
- *Repayment.* Do your projections show that you can both pay the interest *and* repay the principal? A common mistake for first-time applicants is to show interest being repaid month on month but for no plan to be put in place to repay the principal. For small firms in particular, repayment will often be expected to come from profits on additional sales enabled by the loan. But always remember the car rental analogy: banks want their money back on time and undamaged.
- *Insurance.* Does 'insurance' really mean tangible security, or an alternative means of repayment if required should trading not go to plan? If a loan is approved in principle, expect the bank to seek to take a charge over either or both business and personal assets. Again, the rationale is based on relative risk and reward: if your proposal is successful, you stand to make considerable gains; and since no one will know your business as well as you do, a bank will be loathe to fund the proposal if you won't. The responsible balance seasoned lenders strive for is that you should have enough 'skin in the game' to focus your mind on success; but you should not have so much to lose that you are distracted by anxiety or your behaviour becomes reckless.

If that is Campari, what of the ice? This second aide-memoire is for the banks to assess what's in it for them if they do decide to advance the loan:

- *I* is for interest, or the margin over a benchmark lending rate (such as that set by the Bank of England or other central bank) that the lender would need to charge you to make a commercial return having assessed the risk using the CAMPARI exercise.

Calculating the margin is increasingly complicated and technical because of standards being imposed by international bank regulators (the so-called 'Basel III' rules). At their simplest, these rules require banks to 'weight' loans according to risk guidelines such as whether or not tangible security is available. The riskier the loan, the more of its own capital the lending bank has to set aside; since most banks lend the money they borrow many times over ('fractional lending', in the jargon), the more capital they have to set aside or leave untouched, the less they can lend and the less income they generate.

- *C* is for commissions or charges. In addition to the regular interest payments you will make in exchange for 'renting' the bank's money, you will likely be expected to pay other fees, such as an arrangement fee to cover the investigation costs of approving the loan in the first place or a renewal fee for an overdraft, perhaps also an early repayment fee or a monitoring fee for a larger, more complex loan. Be sure to look at all the terms before signing and ask yourself if the business can afford the full cost of the loan, especially if adverse changes – such as an increase in base rate for a variable rate loan – happen.

- *E* is for extras. Post-crash, banks will be much more prudent in making sure that each lending transaction stacks up in its own right – that all the issues set out in CAMPARI have been addressed. But most lenders will also be looking to see if the loan itself can be a platform from which to offer you other products with better margins for the bank, such as insurance, trade finance or credit cards, and now that the basic fact-finding exercise has been completed the bank in theory 'knows its customer' and will have greater knowledge and experience the next time you make an application.

Varieties of debt

For the sake of simplicity, so far we have talked about debt mainly in the form of a term loan – as if the bank proposed to offer to lend you a set amount of money for a fixed period of time, with repayment of principal taking place in tandem with the payment of interest. These general principles apply, with the necessary changes, to other forms of lending also, some of which will become increasingly relevant as your business grows over time. Several of these later forms are based on assets you seek to acquire or use; others are more heterogeneous. The basic schema for all these products is as follows:

1. Asset finance:
   a. Leasing
   b. Debtor finance
   c. Mortgage finance
2. Bank lending:
   a. Term loan
   b. Overdraft
3. Government schemes:
   a. Enterprise Finance Guarantee
4. Regional loans:
   a. Local variations

Asset finance

LEASING

Leasing comes into its own when you don't need to own a productive or 'fixed' asset – such as vehicles or machinery used in the business – outright. 'Fixed asset' in this case means one which has more than just a short life of a few months; it refers to assets that you'll likely keep to help you produce goods and services for sale to your customers (a lathe, a van, a server). The opposite is a 'current asset', one which can readily be converted into cash.

Advantages of leasing an asset include the fact that if numbers stack up (and similar procedures to CAMPARI will be used by the lessor), facilities can usually be arranged quickly (think of vehicle finance arrangements when you buy a car as an example). The assets continue to be owned by the lessor and the initial down payment is usually lower than it would be if you were buying an asset in instalments. That said, a **finance lease** may give you the opportunity to purchase the asset at the end of the leasing period. And provided that you are leasing under an agreement in writing for a period exceeding one year, the payments you make are tax deductible.

DEBTOR FINANCE

One of the biggest drags on the growth of ambitious smaller firms is often the length of time it takes their customers to pay for goods and services delivered. Imagine the simple example of making office furniture for Bigco Ltd. You were delighted to win the account; it is prestigious, and Bigco is likely to have a high 'lifetime customer value' to you, because now that you are one of their accredited suppliers their premises manager will be coming back to you on a regular basis over the years to supply more chairs and desks.

However, Bigco has turned into a lousy payer. Your terms of trade clearly said that you expected to be paid within 30 days of delivery of any goods, but Bigco regularly takes at least 90 days to pay. This ties up a great deal of your working capital. To make the furniture in the first place, you had to buy raw materials, pay your workforce, pay for rent, rates and utilities on your factory and then lease a van to deliver the finished goods.[76]

And since none of your workforce, your landlord or the local authority will extend the same 90 days to you that Bigco has extracted from you, you need to find some way of bridging the finance gap before you run out of cash. What's more, you've noticed that, although it's encouraging that over the past two years you've managed to attract more and more household names as customers (in addition to Bigco, Megabank, Monolith Holdings, Goliath Inc and Nondom LLP), they are all remarkably late payers, with Nondom in particular taking 150 days to settle. Given your respective, highly asymmetrical bargaining strengths you've run out of ideas for persuading them to pay you on time.

---

76 The number of days allowed for an invoice to be settled is part of the 'terms of trade' agreed between you and your customer. 'Agreed' here is a legal issue: if you write to Bigco stating 'our terms of trade are 30 days for payment' and Bigco replies enclosing its terms of trade stating it will pay within 90 days, as the 'last person to speak' Bigco will see its terms prevail as a matter of law. So keep reminding your customers how long you extend credit for!

Instead, what about raising cash based on the strength of your customers' debts to you? There are two distinct ways of doing this:

1. *Factoring.* A factoring company takes over your sales ledger and the debtors. This is *not* a loan. In substance, you have sold your invoices to a professional debt-collecting company to raise cash immediately. You could typically expect to receive between 85 and 70 per cent of the face value immediately, with the balance – minus the factor's commission, bad debts and other charges – once the account has been collected from your customers.

2. *Invoice discounting.* Here, a discounter lends against the security of your debtors, so this is a loan. You are using the unpaid sales invoices as security or collateral to borrow a percentage of the value of your total sales ledger – perhaps around 80 per cent of eligible invoices. As your initial customers pay their invoices, you will be able to draw further advances and still stay within the agreed percentage of eligible invoiced and/or total facility limit.

The outcome appears the same with invoice discounting as with factoring (you receive most of the invoices' value upfront), but with invoice discounting you remain in the driving seat; the debts are still yours to collect and you owe money to the bank or other provider of the service. Each solution has its pros and cons: a generation ago, factoring looked like an admission that your business was in bad shape, but such a preconception is less prevalent today. With factoring the hassle of reminding debtors is now in the hands of a third party, who specialises in chasing late payers and has the systems, people and processes to do so. You can return to doing what you do best, making furniture and winning new orders. Either way, you are now working with financial professionals with extensive knowledge of your clients derived both from public sources and from their own dealings over the year.

Both are good facilities to support growing businesses as the facility 'grows' with your turnover. With both factoring and invoice discounting, the quality of the debtors is key. We cheated a little in this example by assuming that all the furniture manufacturer's clients were blue chip firms. Debtor finance would be less forthcoming if the book had been not so obviously 'clean and collectable' – for instance, if you were contracted to supply not just the original goods but also an ongoing maintenance contract (as is often the case with software suppliers), or if there was a dispute between you and your client about merchantable quality.

However, in the early days of your business – even once you have started shipping product on a regular basis – you should be aware of the following likely limitations on how applicable debtor finance is until you have a good mix of reasonable-quality clients:

- Insurance of debtors has been volatile since financial markets started to wobble in mid-2007.
- Costs depend on the quality of debtors and type of facility, and may include both a charge calculated on the basis of monthly outstanding amounts and a service charge related to how complex analysing your total sales ledger is.
- Both tend to be more expensive than bank loans, partly because more work is involved and partly because debtor finance is typically 'stand alone' rather than secured on the total assets of the company.
- The quality of your management systems will be key: can you show a clear trail back to when the customer placed the order, delivery of goods and aged debtors after delivery? (An 'aged debtors report' is essential for working out how old/overdue your debts are. It normally sets out debts by months; those over, say, 120 days late you are unlikely to recover.)
- Debtor finance is often seen as less relationship-driven and so more price-dependent than your main bank relationship, for good or ill.
- International trade can be a problem, especially if you are dealing with locations off the beaten track, with unreliable legal systems or political volatility.

COMMERCIAL MORTGAGES
After several years of successful trading, you may decide that your

business is now large and settled enough to seek a long-term home in premises you own yourself rather than paying rent and moving on every few years. The most common form of facility for this type of acquisition is a commercial mortgage, which may be supplied by a bank, building society or other long-term institutional funder against the security of the real estate you are purchasing.

Though the market for commercial mortgages has eased since the major contraction of 2009–10, one key number to look out for is the **loan to value ratio**. Say that your bank has indicated a willingness to lend 70 per cent of the value of the office block you have your eye on, which the agents are marketing at £1 million. One of numerous precautions that the bank will insist on before proceeding is that you obtain a professional valuation (PV) from a reputable firm of surveyors. You will pay for the survey, but it will be addressed to the bank, who will use it both for an independent take on how much the property is worth and – if things go seriously wrong later – to have a fall-back in the form of someone it can sue (the valuer), someone with the benefit of a professional indemnity insurance policy – 'deep pockets', to use the common phrase.

So concerned were valuers about their potential liability in the depths of 2009–10 that we sometimes saw PVs as low as 70 per cent of the asking price for commercial premises, with vendors nevertheless holding out for the full asking price so as not to fall into 'negative equity' – that is, receive proceeds of sale lower than the debt secured on the premises. Probably its own bank was only exercising 'forbearance' – that is, not going for repossession for breach of valuation covenants – in the hope of a sale at the full asking price soon. So if banks would only advance 70 per cent of the PV and the PV was 70 per cent of the asking price, the value of the commercial mortgage might only be ±49% of the price.

Commercial mortgages can be offered on flexible terms. For instance, the rate of interest may be fixed for at least part of the length of the mortgage or it may be floating in line with a benchmark rate such as the lender's base rate; the length of the loan may be as much as 25 years, and in the first 6–12 months or so you may be able to negotiate a capital repayment 'holiday' so that you are paying interest only in the early days.

With participating banks, commercial mortgages are likely to be covered by the government's **funding for lending scheme**; see below.

Bank lending: term loans versus overdrafts

Despite the financial tempest of recent years, banks are still the first port of call for most smaller firms. A recent government survey summarised the position as follows:

> Whilst around half of businesses use external finance, a smaller proportion (around 20%) is actually seeking finance at any one time. Of those who have used external finance in the last year, bank finance is still the primary source of finance. In the last year, 28% of all SMEs have used an overdraft and 11% have used a bank loan.[77]

While overdrafts were more than twice as popular as term loans, they are something of an oddity. Overdrafts, unlike other loans, are *repayable on demand*. To understand what this means in practice, consider the following example:

- You manufacture large volumes of low-cost pens, sold mainly to commercial stationery outlets.
- You have an agreed overdraft limit with Megabank of £100,000, which you use to help with your seasonal cash flow cycle, with peak requirements hitting you in July and December.
- You have never exceeded your limit and you normally swing from relatively low indebtedness (£5,000) to about £80,000 utilisation.
- At Christmas in each of the past three years utilisation has gone up to about £90,000 and to keep this flexibility you are prepared to pay slightly higher fees to the bank.
- Out of the blue, Megabank finds that it has lost heavily on trades

77 SME Access to External Finance, Department for Business, Innovation and Skills, January 2012, p. vi. Available at: http://www.bis.gov.uk/assets/BISCore/enterprise/docs/S/12-539-sme-access-external-finance.pdf.

in paperclip derivatives in New York and so decides that it is overexposed to the stationery sector.
- Consequently, Megabank informs you that it is withdrawing your overdraft forthwith (adding helpfully in the covering letter that it is doing so to 'enhance its service to you as a customer').
- Despite your impeccable track-record, since your facility was repayable on demand there is little you can do.

Fortunately, this does not happen often but it is still a risk you run if you are heavily reliant on overdraft funding. By their nature, overdrafts are short-term (maximum 364-day) facilities and in addition to interest payments you may expect to pay an annual renewal fee and even non-utilisation fees (commitment fees on undrawn balances, typically 1.5 per cent).

A term loan, by contrast, may be more effort to set up in the first instance but once established will likely provide both greater security and lower costs. Loans can be flexible as to duration and, as with commercial mortgages, you can seek to negotiate an initial capital repayment holiday and choose whether to fix the interest rate for a while. The conditions (or 'covenants') applied to a term loan often act as a discipline for the borrower, too: typically you can expect to be required to provide a minimum level of net interest cover and a maximum level of loan to value, for instance:
- Earnings before interest and tax (EBIT) to be not less than twice net interest payment; and
- Value of the loan to be no more than 75 per cent of the value of the asset purchased with and providing security for the advance.

Security is likely to include either or both a debenture over company assets and personal support from directors.

Government help

ENTERPRISE FINANCE GUARANTEE
Because lending from conventional institutions slowed considerably

with the financial crash, early in 2009 the government introduced a new scheme to make borrowing by SMEs from banks easier. The Enterprise Finance Guarantee (EFG) scheme replaced the Small Firms Loan Guarantee Scheme (SFLGS) that had evolved since the late 1980s and in a number of ways is more 'generous' than the SFLGS: the SFLGS upper lending limit of £250,000 is raised to £1 million under the EFG, and turnover limits were previously only £5.6 million. But a key change for you to ponder is that, under the new scheme, participating banks can insist on a personal guarantee from you.

To be eligible for the EFG, firms must have turnover below £41 million and not operate in a prohibited sector (restrictions are few but agriculture, coal and transport may be caught by state aid rules).[78] Loans between £1,000 and £1 million are available, for terms between three months and ten years. Businesses without a track-record are eligible but may struggle to demonstrate viability.

The government does not lend directly to you as an SME but provides a guarantee to your bank for up to 75 per cent of the value of the loan in circumstances where the bank considers that your business is viable but you have no or insufficient security to provide (the I in CAMPARI). The cost of the guarantee is around 2 per cent a year, payable quarterly. Your bank, not the Department for Business (BIS – the sponsoring government department), makes the decision on your loan, which can be new borrowing or a means of converting an overdraft into a loan. As a boost to working capital, EFG funding can suit businesses where contractual obligations put invoice-discounting houses off (for instance, ongoing maintenance clauses mean the debt is not 'clean and collectable').

We have found that SMEs' experience of dealing with banks in applying for EFG funds has been mixed. This is largely the result of the overall *portfolio* limitations placed on banks by BIS in using the guarantee. Although 75% of any one loan is guaranteed, banks using the scheme can only claim up to 13% of the total amount they have advanced under the EFG. Since the guarantee covers 75% of 13%,

---

78 http://www.bis.gov.uk/efg.

9.75% of the eligible portfolio is the most a bank could claim to cover losses. While bad debts at that level would be exceptional, lending banks cannot be certain how close they are at any given time to the ceiling and so tend to err on the side of caution.

FUNDING FOR LENDING SCHEME

Aware that net lending by banks continued to drop (see Figure 1 in Chapter 1, page 8) despite programmes such as the EFG, in July 2012 the government introduced the Funding for Lending Scheme (FLS) to improve the supply of money available from the Bank of England to banks and building societies for lending on to both businesses and householders.

Under the FLS, banks can borrow from the Bank of England at around 0.75 per cent including fees (market rates at the time of announcement were around 1.25 to 2.5 per cent) over a four-year period, provided that they increase the availability of loans to their customers. For every additional £1 lent, a participating bank can access £1 of cheaper funding from the scheme, up to 5 per cent of its current lending stock, a percentage that will increase if net lending expands by the end of 2013. If lending decreases, higher fees will be payable.[79] Some 35 institutions (including most major banks except for HSBC) are taking part and the aim is to increase net lending by £60 billion by January 2014.

Unlike the EFG, the FLS affects small firms only indirectly: the Bank of England lends to commercial banks on favourable terms, and SMEs do not receive a special lending 'product'. How successful has this been? The Bank of England undertook to publish a quarterly breakdown of figures, and as at the end of 2012 early signs were that the FLS was making only limited progress. At the end of September, participating banks had drawn down £4.36 billion under the FLS and increased net lending by £496 million, mostly increasing the supply of mortgages.[80]

What this means for entrepreneurs is that policy measures are slowly improving the supply and cost of bank finance. But borrowing

---

79 See http://www.bankofengland.co.uk/publications/Documents/inflationreport/ir12nov1.pdf, p. 14.
80 http://www.bankofengland.co.uk/publications/Pages/news/2012/153.aspx.

from a bank only makes sense once you have regular sales to support repayments. Time to look at ways to supplement what your angels are prepared to provide.

Grant funding: the basics

Occasionally you can find a middle way between the rock of giving up some ownership when you sell equity and the hard place of having to find security to make regular repayments when you take out a loan. This financial 'third way' is a grant. Many early-stage entrepreneurs – especially those from academia, which is largely funded by research grants – look to this middle way with keen anticipation, but may soon find themselves bemused when analysing grants in the commercialisation arena.

Why? Well, the good news first: if you win a grant, it does provide cash, which will almost certainly be in short supply for an ambitious start-up. And unlike the money you rented from the bank, you don't have to give the grant back – provided that you have observed its terms and conditions meticulously. Above all, you are not parting with equity.

Now the bad news: there are thickets of grants out there (national, local, sectoral, European…) but the great majority will not be relevant to you. You may have to wade through oceans of websites to find the one that is, and then spend considerable time, effort and even money preparing and submitting an application. Success rates for applications are variable across schemes and across time.

And grants are usually created in the first instance to satisfy an aim of the grant-making body – not specifically to help your business. These aims are often related to government policy, such as developing new sectors (nanotechnology or DNA, say). Do not apply for a grant simply because it looks like 'free money'; you will have fiduciary reporting responsibilities and other onerous obligations, so make sure that the grant fits with work you had intended to carry out anyway. This is another good reason for having a business plan: if you don't know where you intend to go, you will find it hard to tell whether or not the grant will help you get there.

If you're already a long way down the road to delivering your prototype or undertaking your market research, remember that grants almost invariably only cover future activity and won't reimburse you for work you've already undertaken. And with a few exceptions, the most you could expect to recover of future expenditure is 50 per cent, so you will still have to locate other monies as matched funding.

With those caveats, we set out below some of the 'hardy annual' grants that are most likely to be relevant to early-stage entrepreneurs. Details of existing grants change regularly, new ones come along as single spies (rarely as battalions) and others fade away. Keep looking, keep checking and seek advice.

But a quick word of advice about advice. While we do consider that the complexity of the grants world may well justify using a professional adviser, take soundings from your own network to ensure you only work with advisers who will give you realistic, independent advice. We have come across advisers claiming to be able to prepare 'unrejectable applications', which strains credulity at best as even well-targeted proposals will be up against a competitive field.

Finally, always remember that grant applications tend to be heavily prescriptive. If the EU website says the deadline is the 31 March, all your hard work will be wasted if you submit on 2 April. If the SMART application form says that you must explain your innovation in no more than 500 words, don't submit multiple pages. And above all make sure that you have understood the purpose for which the grants are being made so that you can show how effectively your proposal will meet that aim.

The SMART scheme

One of the most successful of UK government schemes to help high-potential firms, Small Firm Merit Awards for Technology (SMART) date back to 1988, when they were administered by central government. After the formation of the Regional Development Agencies (RDAs) in 1998, the scheme was devolved and different names were applied to separate components of it (proof of market, proof of prototype), which lost the SMART label in 2005.

By 2010, the RDAs started to be wound down and responsibility passed to the Technology Strategy Board (TSB), which in December 2011 reinstituted the SMART label, and the current position is as follows:[81]

A total of £75 million over three years has been allocated for innovative small firms, with three different categories of award:

1. Grant for *Proof of Market*, covering market research and intellectual property issues
   a. Awards are available for a maximum of £25,000, covering up to 60 per cent of total project costs
   b. Project can have a maximum duration of nine months
2. Grant for *Proof of Concept*, for feasibility studies, prototyping and testing
   a. Awards are available for a maximum of £100,000 to cover a maximum of 60 per cent of total project cost
   b. Projects may last up to 18 months
3. Grants for *Development of Prototype*, such as demonstration models, and protection of intellectual property
   a. Awards are available for a maximum of £250,000 to cover up to 35 per cent of the total project cost for mid-size firms
   b. Limits for small firms are higher: up to 45 per cent of costs
   c. Projects must have a maximum duration of two years

Knowledge Transfer Partnerships

Knowledge Transfer Partnerships (KTPs)[82] are a graduate placement scheme, part-financed by a government grant, enabling firms to take an employee (usually a recent graduate) with specific technical expertise and work with a university, college or other knowledge-base partner. The rationale for using public funds in this way is that knowledge developed in the research base often needs intensive adaptation to a particular business application, which is best delivered

---

81 www.innovateuk.org/competitions.ashx.
82 www.ktponline.org.uk.

in the form of know-how gained by a trained individual working in the business. Innovation of this sort in turn generates sustainable commercial success. So, in seeking a KTP relationship, you should be focused on a strategic need where working with a research partner will deliver measurable benefits.

Several KTP variations are available:

1. The basic permutation is for a 'graduate associate' (at NVQ level 3 or above) *to be employed* by the knowledge-base partner but *to work* in your company.

2. Typically, two-thirds of the necessary funding is provided by the KTP grant for an SME and half for a large company. The average annual contribution by an SME is £20,000 – meaning that if your graduate associate is the right person for the job, the value to you of the partnership is considerable.

3. KTPs can last between six months and three years.

Our experience is that KTPs work well, embed innovation and help increase profitability. The programme claims that about 75 per cent of associates are offered permanent employment by the business they were placed in on completion of the project, often at senior level. That said, it will be obvious to you that unless you are both engaged in innovation where working with academia is an obvious benefit and you can afford the contribution of £20,000 or so towards employment costs, then the KTP grant is not for you.

EU Seventh Framework Programme

Reading the official literature, you might think that the EU's Seventh Framework Programme (FP7) was devised specifically for the ambitious, innovative but impecunious SME:

Small and medium-sized enterprises (SMEs) have a special place in the current round of calls with a package worth around EUR 1.2 billion. This includes financing for SMEs of around EUR 970 million under the 'Co-operation' Theme, where ring-fenced budgets for SMEs will account for up to 75% of available funding in specific calls. There will also be EUR 250 million for the dedicated SMEs programme 'Research for the benefit of SMEs', including demonstration actions for FP7 research results.[83]

But the reality is tougher. Applying for EU funding can be daunting for first-timers and you may be best advised to be a partner in a consortium with other players who have undertaken such work before. The type of grant applicable to an innovative younger firm as part of a consortium would likely be made under FP7, covering trans-European collaborative research and development projects in specified areas of technology and the application of technology.

The important facts you need to know are as follows:

1. The FP7 is open to a wide range of organisations and individuals. The minimum requirement is for at least three partners from two countries – but typically a wider range is needed to enhance your chances of success.
2. The FP7 was launched in 2007, with a budget of €55 billion.
3. Typical projects have a duration of two to five years, and typical budgets run to hundreds of thousands or millions of euros.
4. The standard reimbursement rate for R&D projects is up to 50 per cent but SMEs can sometimes get up to 75 per cent.
5. Calls for proposals appear regularly – check websites for details.[84]

FP7 is expected to be replaced in the near future by Horizon 2020,[85] the name for the EU Framework programme for research and innovation 2014–2020. The Commission's proposed budget for Horizon 2020 is €80 billion, against the current FP7 budget of around €54 billion. The principal aims of Horizon 2020 are:

- responding to the economic crisis to invest in future jobs and growth

---

83 http://cordis.europa.eu/fetch?CALLER=FP7_NEWS&ACTION=D&RCN=34831.
84 http://cordis.europa.eu/fp7/home_en.html; https://connect.innovateuk.org/web/fp7uk.
85 The authors are grateful to Dr Huw Edwards for considerable assistance in the preparation of this section as *Show Me The Money* went to press.

- addressing people's concerns about their livelihoods, safety and environment
- strengthening the EU's global position in research, innovation and technology

The new features for the new programme include drawing three separate initiatives under FP7 into a single programme, coupling research to innovation, reinforcing the focus on the challenges of society (such as health, energy and transport) and simplifying programme access significantly.

A budget of about €2.4 billion is proposed for the four measures supporting scientific excellence, with the biggest part proposed for the European Research Council. To promote industrial leadership the Commission proposes a budget of €13.8 million for enabling industrial technologies (ICT, nanotechnologies, materials, biotechnology, manufacturing, space), €3.6 million supporting Access to Finance and about €7.4 million fostering innovation in SMEs.

New approaches and new instruments have been developed to support R&D partnering in the European Union. Public–Private Partnerships and Public–Public Partnerships will be supported through new funding instruments such as the Pre Commercial Procurement mechanism. European Innovation Partnerships are not funding instruments but will co-ordinate broader policies and programmes.

Participation in Framework programmes will be facilitated by a single set of simpler participation rules and an improved contracting approach for projects. The current complex funding rate arrangements for different project partners and activities will be reduced to two cases; similarly the four methods of overhead calculation will be replaced with a single flat rate. The Commission anticipates major simplification of its financial regulation, making project liaison with Commission financial services easier. Finally, the Commission has set a goal of reducing the time from bid to grant to 100 days against the FP7 average of 350 days, to allow applicants to get working much more quickly.

Strong participation of SMEs in the programme is a key objective.

Of the total programme budget for societal challenges, 15% will go to SMEs. SMEs are to benefit from a single entry point to the programme. A new SME instrument, built on the Small Business Innovation Research model, will be used across all societal challenges. A dedicated activity for research-intensive SMEs is planned and 'Access to risk finance' will have a strong SME focus, and a strong agenda in 'international co-operation' has been established.

Help where you least expected it: the tax system

In recent years, the UK government has recognised the need to encourage research and development in the private sector. If you are an innovative small firm, these policies may turn out to provide a surprising source of funding for you in the form of tax breaks. Two schemes in particular are relevant here, the R&D tax credit and the Patent Box regime.

R&D tax credits

R&D tax credits are not a grant scheme but a form of corporation tax relief, which in some circumstances can actually provide you with cash. The basic rules since April 2012 have been as follows:[86]

- The relief is applicable to companies of all sizes with qualifying R&D revenue expenditure (there is no minimum).
- It allows for 225 per cent (in the case of SMEs) or 130 per cent (for large companies) of R&D expenditure to be deducted for tax purposes. Some SMEs not in profit can surrender R&D tax losses for cash.
- State aid or subsidies can reduce the amount of eligible R&D expenditure or deduction percentage, sometimes to zero.
- For capital R&D expenditure, 100 per cent capital allowances may be forthcoming.

Patent Box

A new scheme for 2013, the Patent Box allows for a favourable

---

86 www.bis.gov.uk/policies/innovation/business-support/rd-tax-credits/about;
www.hmrc.gov.uk/ct/forms-rates/claims/randd.htm.

tax regime for profits generated from intellectual property (IP).[87] Key features of the Patent Box are as follows:

- From commencement of the new regime in April 2013, the tax rate applicable to relevant IP-related profits will be 10 per cent.
- The Patent Box regime will be phased in over five years, with 60 per cent of the full allowance from 2013–14, rising to 100 per cent in 2017–18.
- Companies need to own or have exclusive rights to IP, and be *actively* involved in the management and development of that IP.
- Patents issued by the European Patent Office, the UK Intellectual Property Office and certain other EU country patent offices will qualify.
- The calculations required to arrive at profits attracting lower rates of tax are multi-stage (see below).
- The Patent Box regime applies to both new and existing patents.
- Profits accruing up to six years before patent is granted can be clawed back and taxed at the lower rate.
- Companies need robust accounting systems and policies to ensure compliance.

How is the tax calculation made to identify those profits to which the 10 per cent rate applies? The 10 per cent tax rate does not apply across the board to R&D firms, but those profits attributable to the IP are taxed at 10 per cent. HMRC applies the following formula once you have established that you own, manage and are developing the IP:

1. Determine how much of your company's revenue relates to the exploitation of IP rights, then express that as a percentage of the company's total revenues.
2. Apply this percentage to the company's profits to determine the *qualifying profit*.
3. Deduct from this the profit the business would have earned

---

87 http://www.hmrc.gov.uk/ct/forms-rates/claims/patent-box.htm.

from routine trading in the absence of the patent; HMRC have decided this represents 10 per cent of trading expenses excluding R&D costs.

4. Deduct from this how much of the profit is derived from the marketing strengths of the business (branding, advertising) – the 'notional marketing royalty', though there is currently no agreed mechanism for calculating this.

5. Apply 10 per cent to the resulting profit – known as the Relevant IP Profit.

6. Apply usual tax rates (20–27.5 per cent) to the residual profits.

Note that steps 5 and 6 are arrived at by deduction of an appropriate amount from the profits taxed at the full rate.

The absence of any agreed mechanism for calculating the notional royalty (step 4) could lead to lengthy disagreement with HMRC. But there is fortunately a simplification for companies with claims below £1 million, who can elect to deduct a notional 25 per cent.

Confused? Then study the two worked examples on the following pages (Tables 9 and 10) to see how Patent Box might work in practice. Each case assumes that the Patent Box regime has been fully phased in. Note that the figures in the shaded section will be subject to substantiation and negotiation with the tax authorities.

Example 1. Company A – small company tax band

Company A has profits of £300,000 and so falls right at the top limit of the small corporation tax band. It judges that 90% of its revenues are attributable to its IP and chooses to adopt the 25% marketing royalty. Its effective tax rate drops from 20% to 15%, saving nearly £14,000.

Table 9. Patent Box calculations: small company tax band

Firm in lower corporation tax band		Profits without Patent Box £	Qualifying profit ratio	Qualifying profits for Patent Box £
Stage 1: Calculating profit before tax				
A	**Sales**	1,400,000	90%	1,260,000
B	**Expenses**			
C	R&D	150,000	90%	135,000
D	Marketing	50,000	90%	45,000
E	Other	900,000	90%	810,000
F	**Subtotal**	**1,100,000**		**990,000**
G	**Profit before tax**	**300,000**		**270,000**
Stage 2: Net Patent Box profit				
H	Proposed mark-up rate		10%	
I	Mark-up on trading expenses (D+E)			85,000
J	Profit on qualifying income (G–I)			184,500
K	Standard rate for marketing asset return		25%	
L	Relevant multiplier (100%–K)			75%
M	**Net Patent Box profit**			**138,375**
Stage 3: Corporation tax calculation				
N	Small business rate		20%	
O	Tax without Patent Box (G*N)	60,000		
P	Patent Box tax rate		10%	
Q	Tax on PB profit (M*P)			13,838
R	Residual profit = profit without PB less NET PB profit (G–M)			161,625
S	Tax on residual profit (R*N)			**32,325**
T	**Final corporation tax charge (O or Q+S)**	**60,000**		**46,163**
U	As % of PBT without PB	20%		15%

Example 2. Company B – higher corporation tax band

Company B has £3 million taxable profits before taking account
of Patent Box but after the benefit of R&D tax credits. Its internal
working papers show that 80% of income and expenditure qualify
for Patent Box. From 2013, mainstream corporation tax will be
23%. Company B's effective tax rate drops from 23% to circa 16%,
assuming a notional marketing royalty in the region of 9%.

Table 10. Patent Box calculations: higher rate tax band

Firm in higher corporation tax band		Profits without Patent Box £	Qualifying profit ratio	Qualifying profits for Patent Box £
Stage 1: Calculating profit before tax				
A	**Sales**	12,000,000	80%	9,600,000
B	**Expenses**			
C1	R&D	1,500,000	80%	1,200,000
C2	R&D tax credit enhancement	−450,000		−
C3	Consumables (for R&D)	3,500,000	80%	2,800,000
D	Marketing	1,700,000	80%	1,360,000
E	Other	2,750,000	80%	2,200,000
F	**Subtotal**	**9,000,000**		**7,560,000**
G	**Profit before tax**	**3,000,000**		**2,040,000**
Stage 2: Net Patent Box profit				
H	Proposed mark-up rate		10%	
I	Mark-up on trading expenses (D+E)			356,000
J	Profit on qualifying income (G–I)			1,684,000
K	Standard rate for marketing asset return		9%	
L	Relevant multiplier (100%–K)		91%	
M	**Net Patent Box profit**			**1,532,440**

Stage 3: Corporation tax calculation			
N	Main rate of corporation tax from 2013	23%	
O	Tax without Patent Box (G*N)	690,000	
P	Patent Box tax rate	10%	
Q	Tax on PB profit (M*P)		153,244
R	Residual profit = profit without PB less NET PB profit (G–M)		1,467,560
S	Tax on residual profit (R*N)		337,539
T	**Final corporation tax charge (O or Q+S)**	**690,000**	**490,783**
U	As % of PBT without PB	23%	16%

New sources of funding

If necessity is the mother of invention, the past five years have been remarkably maternal. Many conventional sources of funding went into hiding and others – such as private individuals with savings – sought unsuccessfully to obtain a meaningful return from bank deposits or government bonds when base rates fell below 1 per cent. In the gap between savers looking for a return and entrepreneurs looking for new sources of funds emerged a number of mechanisms whose time appeared finally to have arrived.

We discuss two here: the increasingly complex and fast-moving world of crowd-funding and the sporadic re-emergence of corporate venturing.

Crowd-funding

Crowd-funding is a (mainly) commercial subset of crowd-sourcing, or the outsourcing of individual tasks to a group of people (often self-selecting) as part of a wider project. Crowd-sourcing exploits in a positive way the 'wisdom of crowds' and the piecemeal spare capacity of volunteers, enthusiasts or subcontractors to provide feedback, ideas or solutions.[88] Crowd-funding harnesses the techniques and motivations of crowd-sourcing to raise funds from a wide audience (hence 'crowd') through donations, loans and equity investment:

> Crowdfunding involves an open call, essentially through the internet, for the provision of financial resources either in the form of donations (without rewards) or in exchange for some form of reward and/or voting rights in order to support initiatives for specific purposes.[89]

Typically some emotional identification with the project being funded and a greater level of engagement with its founders supplement financial return as motivations to invest. An online crowd-funding platform (CFP) provides the mechanism for both information exchange and money transmission. CFPs have started to complement traditional seed-funding sources, especially at early stages.

CASE STUDY
The Small Business Research Initiative (SBRI)

Encouraging the delivery of innovation in support of public procurement and the development of more new technology-based businesses

For a significant number of years now, in the US, the Small Business Innovation and Research (SBIR) program has run so successfully that it has been labelled by some as 'The Largest Seed Fund in the World' (according to Dr David Connell, in *Secrets of the World's Largest Seed Capital Fund*[90]). Since 1982, in most years the SBIR has awarded to some 4,000 small companies, funding totalling $2 billion of public

---

88 See, for instance, Clay Shirky, *Cognitive Surplus: Creativity and generosity in a connected age* (London: Allen Lane, 2010).

89 http://www.isi.fraunhofer.de/isi-media/docs/p/de/arbpap_unternehmen_region/ap_r2_2011.pdf

90 Published by the Cambridge Centre for Business Research.

money – not by way of grants but as contracts to develop defined new products to fill needs in the public procurement area. One hundred per cent of funding is provided against a development plan to cover all costs and there is a small profit margin included too. Literature indicates the scheme has enabled significant numbers of early-stage companies to develop successful new products which have immediate access to a market, and many of these companies have been able, as a result, to thrive and grow, some becoming very large indeed.

In the UK, since 2009, with the government-funded Technology Strategy Board leading the way, a scheme based on the US model and titled similarly – the SBRI – Small Business Research Initiative – has been piloted and, after early successes, extended and expected to receive more funds from the government progressively in an economic, business and political environment demanding the formation and successful growth of more new innovative companies.

For the entrepreneur, the SBRI scheme represents real opportunity to obtain non-equity-based early-stage funding, accompanied by professional guidance and mentoring with procurement of products successfully developed in line with recognised needs finding immediate sales. There has been particular success recorded in the life science sector with the NHS as the procurement body driving the processes; these have been designed to be every bit as demanding in terms of rigorous examination of proposals as with venture capital, which are made on a competitive basis. In the first region to pilot the scheme in the UK NHS there were 177 applications, resulting in 21 being shortlisted and 11 contracts being awarded for stage-one funding (usually £100,000 per company). Similar numbers of applications and awards have now been recorded in other health regions. Numbers of companies receiving phase one contracts have gone on following a year or more of successful development to receive phase two funding of up to £400,000. The Technology Strategy Board now runs SBRI schemes across numerous sectors; details can be found at www.innovate.uk.org.

Benefits of the SBRI to business

The SBRI offers numerous benefits to business, including:

- Intellectual property remains with your company.
- One hundred per cent of funding is by contract – not grant.
- It provides a route to engage the public sector as a customer.
- It provides a clear route to market.
- As lead customer, the public sector body will be the research and development partner, testing and validating the solution as well as providing inputs to the product requirement.
- Successful contracts provide not only seed funding but create credibility, which encourages other forms of funding in (this has been very notable in the pilot studies carried out and is a repeating pattern).

The SBRI benefits government, too

Government departments and agencies benefit as follows:

- Access to new innovative suppliers – mostly small companies.
- Ability to reach out to organisations from a wide range of different sectors.
- A way to find and exploit companies previously unknown.
- The potential to act as the lead customer – managing contracts to:
  - Enable early access to new technologies
  - Shape solutions to meet specific needs
  - Enhance ability to deliver a major improvement in meeting operational or policy objectives
  - Provide simple, accelerating processes to support the public sectors in procuring the development of new technical solutions and faster technology adoption
  - Better manage the risk associated with innovation through a phased development programme running a portfolio of the most promising projects.

In terms of 'show me the money' for entrepreneurs and innovative early-stage companies working in technology sectors, the SBRI scheme is worthy of close study on the Technology Strategy Board website and by reference to expert advice available at innovation centres, science parks and from financial advisers. Experience has shown that companies obtaining SBRI contracts definitely enjoy enhanced ability to attract business angel and venture investments.

The European Commission foresees more widespread adoption of the SBIR scheme – predicting that up to €7 billion may be made available over a seven-year period. Definitely something to be kept under close review by those intent upon exploring ongoing access to early-stage business finance.

NESTA[91] and Crowdsourcing.org[92] both identify four emerging models:

1. *Donation-based.* For non-profits and projects with social or charitable benefits, for which returns are intangible or altruistic.
2. *Reward-based.* This also relies on donations from funders, with return being a combination of altruism and rewards, which can vary from receiving a signed first edition of a sponsored book to being thanked by a personal email from the artist or social entrepreneur to being credited on the release of a new album.
3. *Lending-based (ECFs).* As in the personal P2P space, CFPs provide credit scores to businesses seeking loans and information on proposals to lenders (for instance, FundingCircle[93]). The lender usually expects repayment of the loan with interest, but some socially motivated lending is interest free.
4. *Equity-based.* Mainly for financial investment at pre-start-up, start-up and established business stages. In some cases, non-financial rewards are also offered.

Each ECF operates a different model, but the process in most cases is designed to ensure that to a greater or lesser degree some level of vetting beforehand and monitoring and aftercare post-investment is facilitated:

---

91 Liam Collins and Yannis Pierrakis, *The Venture Crowd – Crowdfunding equity investment into business* (NESTA, 2012). Available at: http://www.nesta.org.uk/library/documents/TheVentureCrowd.pdf.
92 Massolution, *Crowdfunding Industry Report – Market tends, composition and crowdfunding platforms.* Research Report, abridged version, May 2012. Available at: http://www.crowdsourcing.org/.
93 https://www.fundingcircle.com/.

- Following application by the business for funding, the site manager scrutinises the proposal to ensure it meets the site's criteria.
- A proposal developed by the business is uploaded and may be subject to due diligence.
- The proposal will be given a specific amount of time in which to raise a set target level of capital.
- The project is distributed through the ECF's networks.
- The business interacts with potential investors online to address questions for a specified time only.
- If the funding target is met by the end of the fundraising period, the business receives the funds via an escrow arrangement. Most sites operate an 'all or nothing' policy (if your target was £50,000 and only £49,000 was raised, the funds will be returned to investors).
- Policies on fees vary widely, with various combinations of upfront listing fee, share (5–7.5 per cent) of money raised and share of uplift in value over time.

Equity funding is the most controversial form of crowd-funding, not least because it is seen as the riskiest and because the activities it covers fall in a grey regulatory area. As of late 2012, no specific regulation had been proposed by government or the Financial Services Authority. Crowd-funding organisations have started to join the UK Business Angels Association.[94] But other angel-related groups remain sceptical. As the Angel Investment Network put it:

> Crowdfunding platforms are poised to make fools out of a generation of amateur investors, triggering waves of lawsuits.[95]

---

94 http://www.ukbusinessangelsassociation.org.uk/news/seedrs-becomes-first-online-investment-plat-form-to-join-ukbaa.
95 http://www.angelinvestmentnetwork.co.uk/article/crowdfunding-platforms-are-poised-to-make-fools-out-of-a-generation-of-amateur-investors-triggering-waves-of-lawsuits.

The Breedon Review suggested that P2P generally could become an important new source of risk-funding, and hinted that regulation could be a help not a hindrance if intelligently devised:

> These markets have been allowed to grow in the UK, partly as a result of a permissive regulatory environment. However, some operators perceive the lack of regulatory underpinning as inhibiting potential investors and regulatory uncertainty may prove to be a barrier to other entrants joining and growing the market. The Taskforce has considered these arguments and sees some sense in proportionate regulation, to protect investors and provide confidence. However, there is a strong counter-argument that over-zealous regulation would add to costs, destroying this market before it has a chance to gain scale organically.[96]

What does this mean for entrepreneurs? Table 11 sets out a snapshot of some leading crowd-funding offerings as at early 2013 (the scene changes fast; we have used the table provided by NESTA in July 2012 but have updated the details). Most comment on crowd-funding, especially equity crowd-funding, has wobbled uneasily between the hype of its promoters and the jeremiads of its detractors. Of course, both investors and aspiring investees are at risk in a fast-changing sub-sector. But since crowd-funding cannot be ignored – numbers of sites and values raised are growing year by year – if this looks like a good potential source of funds for you, do due diligence on the sites you shortlist in the same way that you would with potential angel investors. How many deals have they done? What is the profile of their supporters and investors? Are the fees reasonable? Who controls the escrow? Opportunity is risk well-managed.

---

96 Report of industry-led working group on alternative debt markets, BIS, March 2012, p. 34.

Table 11. Matrix of equity crowd-funding platforms in Europe

Source: Liam Collins and Yannis Pierrakis, *The Venture Crowd – Crowdfunding equity investment into business* (NESTA, 2012). Available at: http://www.nesta.org.uk/library/documents/_eVentureCrowd.pdf

Platform	Location	Capital raised so far through the platform	Fees	How investment is facilitated	Vetting / Due diligence by platform	Decision on how much equity to offer	Funding window	Post-investment
Crowdcube	UK	£4.9m	For businesses: 5% of amount raised + £1750 legal fees if successful	Both investor and business become members of Crowdcube for the period of the raise	Vetting done before businesses accepted on platform	Entrepreneur decides. Can increase equity during funding window	60 days as standard	Business decides threshold for voting rights
Symbid	Netherlands	€1m	For businesses: €250 upfront for existing businesses (start-up ideas can place in for free) + 5% of amount raised + legal fees - only payable if successful. For investors: 3% of investment amount + transaction costs	Investment is via a co-operative established in the Netherlands	Perform due diligence once target raised	Entrepreneur decides. Can increase equity during funding window	Maximum of 1 year	Indirect voting rights for all investors via co-operative
MyMicro Invest	Belgium	€500,000	For businesses: 12% of amount raised if successful + €6,000	Investment through an investment vehicle	Board of professional investors do their own due diligence before investing	Agreement reached after negotiation	1 month as standard	Voting rights for professional investors only
WiSeed	France	€2.8m	For businesses: 10% of amount raised if successful. For investors: 5% of amount invested if successful	Investment through dedicated investment vehicle for each raise	Perform due diligence before raise	Negotiation between platform and business after due diligence is performed	3 months as standard	Platform manages voting rights

Table 11 (cont.)

Platform	Location	Capital raised so far through the platform	Fees	How investment is facilitated	Vetting / Due diligence by platform	Decision on how much equity to offer	Funding window	Post-investment
Innovestment	Germany	€500,000	For businesses: 10% of amount raised if successful	Investment through dedicated investment vehicle for each raise	Selection process with multiple stages and a board before business allowed on to platform	Uses auction to decide on valuation	30 days as standard	No voting rights for investors
Seedrs	UK	£400,000	For businesses: 7.5% of amount raised if successful. For investors: 7.5% of profit from investment	Seedrs hold shares on your behalf as a nominee manager	Approve disclosures as financial promotions beforehand and perform legal due diligence once target raised	Entrepreneur sets amount which cannot be altered	3 months as standard	Operate nominee model where they represent the interests of post-investment
BankTo TheFuture	UK	£30,000	For businesses: 5% of amount raised + £1750 Company Secretarial fee	Facilitates financial promotion via membership model. Working on next phase with FSA	Vetting performed before business allowed on to platform	Entrepreneur makes decision. BankTo TheFuture provides training to assist them	Maximum of 90 days	Investors are collected into private group for updates. Entrepreneur sets minimum investment amount to qualify for voting rights
Syndicate Room	UK	Launching in April 2013	For businesses: 5% of amount raised if successful	FSA regulated investment. Active Business Angels become direct shareholders. Nominee structure for passive Business Angels	Deals need to have an active Business Angel investing their own capital to be posted on platform	SR members get same terms as active Business Angels	Maximum of 60 days	Shareholders' management tool available for entrepreneurs and investors

Corporate venturing

We have cheated a little here. Corporate venturing (CV) isn't really new; it's simply that as a means of supporting innovative ventures in particular it seems to be rediscovered every dozen years or so, notably when the economy catches a chill.

Apart from use of the term in the tax code (see below), CV is not a precise term and covers some combination of the following:

- A simple financial investment by one (usually large) firm in another (often in the early-growth phase) and with mixed objectives ranging from straightforward financial return to joint product development and strategic research.
- A co-operation arrangement – formal or informal – focused more on the transfer of know-how than an injection of tangible resources, which at the more formal end shades into a strategic alliance.
- An investment via a separate fund in which the corporate is the – or at least a – major investor. From your perspective, this may feel like a conventional venture holding but with the mixed blessings of industrial and technical expertise being available to you from the 'parent' organisation.

CV activity is most likely to be found in science and technology-based sectors, and in the pharmaceutical industry in particular. 'Big pharma' – the handful of worldwide, multi-billion dollar drugs companies – has found it harder and harder to come up with the next blockbuster product and uses venturing as a means of outsourcing its innovation.

In order to stimulate collaboration and equity investment, the government has devised tax breaks for established firms investing in smaller ones in the UK. The Corporate Venturing Scheme provides advantages for these organisations that are essentially the same as those available to individuals under the Enterprise Investment Scheme and Venture Capital Trusts:

investment relief – relief against corporation tax of up to 20 per cent of the amount subscribed for full-risk ordinary shares, provided that the shares are held throughout a qualification period

deferral relief – deferral of tax on chargeable gains arising on the disposal of shares on which investment relief has been obtained and not withdrawn in full, if the gains are reinvested in new shares for which investment relief is obtained

loss relief – relief against income for capital losses arising on most disposals of shares on which investment relief has been obtained and not withdrawn in full, net of the investment relief remaining after the disposal.[97]

The 'usual' conditions apply when assessing if your company meets the criteria:

- It must be an unquoted company.
- It must have gross assets of no more than £7 million immediately before and £8 million immediately after the issue.
- Throughout the qualification period the issuing company must not be a member of a group of companies, unless it is the parent company of the group, nor be under the control of another company.
- At least 20 per cent of the issuing company's ordinary share capital must be held by individuals other than directors or employees (or their relatives) of an investing company, or any company connected with it.

What does CV mean for you as an entrepreneur? Regrettably, in many instances the aspiring smaller firm feels vulnerable. If you are visibly partnered with one giant in your industry – Vodafone, say – the others (O2, Everything Everywhere…) may look on your world-class software with suspicion.

The founder of one of the most successful CV funds once explained to us that his remit from head office was 'to invest in the guys who would otherwise eat our lunch' – which suggests that often the

---

97 http://www.hmrc.gov.uk/guidance/cvs.htm.

larger partner is more defensive than genuinely co-operative. There are exceptions to this, some of them culturally based. When asked why corporate venturing had benefited his business so much, one entrepreneur we know said, 'because our partner was Japanese, with a long-term strategic view, not a short-term financial one like the Anglo-Saxon guys'.

Touché.

We asked Barry James of The Social Foundation to comment on crowd-funding and its pre-sales or reward-based variants, in particular. His response is given in the box below.

STOP PRESS!
The latest on crowd-funding!

Crowd-funding is ideal for start-ups and very early-stage businesses because
- You raise the money you need with few or no strings – you decide on what it is you'll offer and how much you need
- You keep 100 per cent of your equity
- You don't have to repay the money you raise
- You don't have to convince an angel (or dragon) that it will make them richer – just find a market
- You create a customer base and a community of advocates at the same time as raising cash

In doing this you prove to yourself and potential future funders (should you need them at a later stage) that there is a market for your product or service. No small thing. Better still because the process is a two-way street, via social media you'll hear from and gain valuable insights from your market throughout the process. The fact that you can work with the 'crowd' in this way, rather than being locked away in a back office doing research and second-guessing, is revolutionary in itself. Also in the absence of a gatekeeper whose perception of what will work in the market may be as flawed as your own. The removal of any requirement to meet their investment or lending criteria allows you to

---

focus on your market – rather than on needing to provide an early exit with a good multiplier.

It also means that you can 'iterate' to success rather than having to live or die by decisions made in a vacuum before you launched. This both increases your chances of success and means that if you do fail to reach your target in the time available you can learn a lot and apply it next time. Indeed this kind of 'failure' lies behind two of the most often quoted crowd-funding success stories – the Pebble Watch and the Nifty Mini Drive, both on KickStarter in 2012. It's less well known that their massive success (100 times target and 38 times target, respectively) was built on a previous offering that failed to achieve its target. In each case the team learned very quickly from the experience, sharpened their pitch and offering, and moved on to a massive success. Their 'investment ready' training came 'on the job'.

It's widely acknowledged that early-stage seed-funding has been ineffective and that attempts to remedy this by government over the years have failed and so it's now largely absent. Which is why this is a sterile debate given that repeated attempts have failed.

Similarly VCs and angels aren't equipped to play in this market. It's a truism that the amount of work for them to do a £100k deal is not much less than for a £1 million one (and anything much less is generally considered not worth the effort) so unless there's a really compelling case driven by the vision of the angel or VC, who are constantly inundated with pitches, naturally gravitate away from the 'seed' stuff.

Crowd-funding has the potential or relieve this bottleneck in the economy that chokes off access to the market for entrepreneurs and start-ups by allowing direct access.

For the entrepreneur it provides a powerful new way to raise the cash needed to launch at the same time as honing the proposition and garnering sales, customers and advocates. Not to mention proving themselves and the proposition and potentially growing to a size where they are candidates for the next stages of growth.

If past history was all there was to the game, the richest people would be librarians.
– Warren Buffett

CHAPTER 6

VALUATION AND KEY FINANCIAL RATIOS

Overview

This section is about valuing your business – or at least part of it when it comes to selling a portion of equity to raise vital risk capital. But the next few pages may not contain what you are hoping for: there is no magic formula somewhere 'out there' that will enable you to compute an incontrovertible value for your start-up. Ultimately, 'the' price is a win–win point where risks and rewards are perceived by both sides to be even, or at least capable of becoming even over the life of your journey together.

Valuation for early-stage firms is not a science, it is a negotiation. Various technical practices assist with valuation discussions between you and your potential investors, and we set out the major ones below, including some techniques for calculating the possible value today of your profits several years from now.

It is said that Michelangelo believed that inside every block of marble was a statue looking to get out. We do not think the same holds with start-ups: there is no single 'right answer' in valuing pre-revenue firms, no valuation looking to get out of your pages of projections. Despite that, we recognise that the valuation of your business achieved in early funding rounds is critical. And valuations can – surprisingly – be too high as well as too low:

- An excessively high first-round price (from novice angels, say) may limit your ability to attract future investors. More experienced later investors would seek to 'crush down' the first-round funders (that is, invest at a lower valuation, thus compressing the value of the first-round funding), a move resisted by the novice angels and leading to an impasse in which you receive no new funding and become a 'living dead' company.

- Entrepreneurs often say, for instance, 'I don't want to give up more than 50 per cent' or 'I want to give away as little as possible'. The underlying mindset in each case is simply wrong. With equity, you are not *giving* anything away, you are *selling*, and you must negotiate the/a right price.

- We also hear entrepreneurs say, 'If I sell at a low price, I surrender control and value'. But it is more complicated than that. Investors use clauses giving them more control than their nominal percentage reveals. Control is not a simple function of percentage shareholding but of ratchets, rights to nominate members of the board, contractual vetoes on capital spending and other similar checks and balances. And the value to you of the 'right' investor at a lower price may be greater than a passive investor at a very high price.

Finally, never forget that if you are too proud or greedy, you may receive no funding.

Getting started: a value, not 'the' value

In Shakespeare's *Troilus and Cressida*, Troilus and his brother Hector argue about whether to hand Helen, whose kidnap sparked the Trojan War (then in its seventh year), back to the Greeks. Surprising as this may sound, their reasoning reflects fundamental and irreconcilable approaches to business valuation – opportunity cost, inherent value and market sentiment:

> **HECTOR:** Brother, she is not worth what she doth cost
> The holding.

> **TROILUS:** What is aught, but as 'tis valued?

HECTOR: But value dwells not in particular will;
It holds his estimate and dignity
As well wherein 'tis precious of itself
As in the prizer [...][98]

We frequently run seminars and classes in preparing a business for investment or trade sale. Each time – without fail – before we reach the substance of how to negotiate a value, one or more participants will ask, 'so what's my business worth, then?' The true answer is not the one the questioner wants to hear: whether raising equity or selling the whole operation, your business is 'worth' what someone else is ready and able to pay, when and where you are looking to sell. Which is why we say it is *a value* – depending heavily on a combination of luck and your skill as a negotiator – not *the value* in the sense of an objective, mathematical constant. Often you may feel slightly aggrieved ('I should've got more!'), but now and again one of the glamour stocks *du jour* will start making offers to small firms they can't refuse: if yours is a lucky recipient of such an offer, remember that Napoleon asked of his generals that they should have luck.

The less data you have (sales, margins, repeat business, range of customers, product pipeline), the more room for disagreement even on the appropriate *method* of valuation. The longer established your business is, the more data there will be for experienced negotiators to agree a *range of values*, but even then the final strike price will depend on a wide range of circumstances, such as other opportunities available to buyer or seller, supply of credit to fund the purchase, complementarities assessed by the purchaser – as well your skill as a negotiator.

If most people implicitly think like Hector and believe that there is an inherent value in an object (or at least its value should be not less than what it costs you to 'hold it'), to succeed in attracting investors you have to think more like Troilus: 'of course, *today* we have only limited sales and no profits yet, but just look at our potential – how

---

can you afford *not* to invest in us?' The balance you have to strike in your salesmanship is knowing when you've pushed as hard a bargain as you can so that you don't nudge your potential investors over a cliff.

Life on the other side of the table

The starting point for your negotiations will be understanding how investors (and potential acquirers) think. Two key components of investor thinking are:

- Both angels and funds *need an exit.* Your vision may be to run the business into your dotage, growing it from humble start-up to international corporation and handing on the CEO's chair to your granddaughter, but with a vanishingly tiny number of exceptions, external investors have to sell their stake (preferably at a substantial uplift in value) to provide the funds for further investments over time.

- Investors often start to appraise the potential value of the business into which they are buying by *working backwards from what an investment can be expected to be worth when it is sold in three or five or seven years from now.*

INTERNAL RATES OF RETURN SIMPLIFIED

In working out the potential value seven years (say) from now, angels tend to use terms such as '10x return' or '40% IRR'. These phrases are critical in understanding and persuading your investors. They mean essentially the same thing. A financial dictionary will tell you that the *internal rate of return is the discount rate at which net present value of costs (negative cash flows) of an investment equals the net present value of the benefits (positive cash flows) of that investment.* And you will be relieved to know that is a lot simpler than it sounds.

Take the following example. Imagine that you have £250,000 to invest and that your time horizon is seven years – a long time for many investors these days.[99] You could be wearing one of three different hats:

---

99 Dominic Barton, in 'Capitalism for the long term' (*Harvard Business Review*, March 2011), suggests that institutions hold quoted stocks for seven months. John C. Bogle, in 'Restoring faith in financial markets' (*Wall Street Journal*, 19 January 2010), suggests five months.

- In Scenario A, you are a mainstream fund manager investing in quoted equities. After buying £250,000 worth of shares in Amalgamated Holdings Inc (a utilities conglomerate) today net of all expenses, over the next six years you receive dividends worth around 5 per cent of your initial investment, year on year. In year 7 you received a dividend of £11,000 as in the previous year and – since the share price had gone up to value your stake at £324,000 – you decided to stick with your seven-year timetable and sell all the shares, so in that last year you received a net £335,000. The uplift in capital value, assuming no extraneous factors such as inflation or taxes, was nearly 30 per cent. That sounds quite good, but what do you compare it against?

- In Scenario B, you are acting as a classic lead angel. You invest £250,000 today in TxtApp Inc (which makes specialist voice-recognition software enabling parents to understand the grunts made by teenagers), but this time you receive no income (dividends or director's fees) until year 7 when the company is bought by Soonbust Inc, the darling of NASDAQ, for a valuation enabling you to double your original investment. So over seven years, your total capital return is 100 per cent, but in the intervening time you had nothing to show for your trouble. Was it worth it?

- In Scenario C, you decided to buy a new press for your own factory, to make specialist sprockets for asbestos manufacturers. The press had an upfront cost including installation of £250,000. In each of the following six years it enables you to generate additional net cash returns of between £70,000 and £90,000. In year 7, the press becomes completely obsolete because of new environmental legislation, and the cost of disposing of the machine in compliance with the law is exactly the same (£80,000) as the cash generated from sales, so your net cash in the final year is £0. Over its lifetime, the machine generated net cash to you of £240,000. Is that good or just okay?

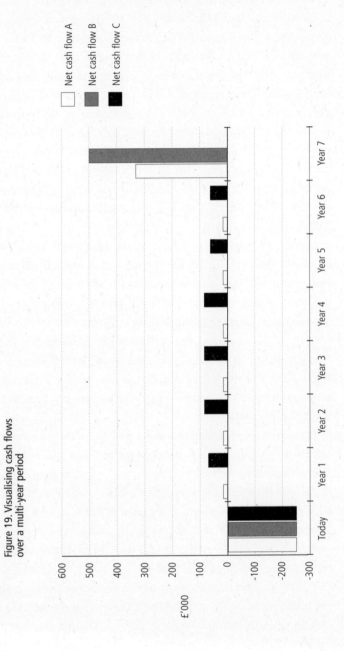

Figure 19. Visualising cash flows over a multi-year period

To help appraise the respective merits of each scenario, we can put them on a spreadsheet[100] and then represent them visually, as shown in Figure 19.

Scenario A gave us a net positive cash return of £191,000 and an internal rate of return of 9.91%. This probably makes reasonable back-of-the-envelope sense as you were receiving dividends of about 5% and you had a capital gain at the end. But look further and something is happening that defies mental arithmetic. First, the difference in IRR between Scenarios A and B is 0.5% (9.91% compared to 10.41%), but the cash difference is nearly £60,000. Second, net cash in Scenarios B and C is the same (£250,000) but the IRR of C is more than twice that of B. What is going on?

The answer lies in when you received the money. Consider the three separate flows of funds in Table 12. Except in a completely risk-free world, £1,000 today is worth more to you than £1,000 ten years from now. If you have cash now, you do not have to worry about inflation or whether your investee will go broke, leaving you with nothing. The key lesson for present purposes is this. Look at the simplified angel return: doubling your money sounds good, but compared with running productive machinery for goods in demand, as an angel you run the risk of receiving a low or even no return at all. What if Soonbust bought your competitor and not you? Or if Soonbust paid you in shares but its share price then tanked when irrational exuberance gave way to panic selling as the market realised Soonbust only had vapourware? At least with the machinery in Scenario B you benefit from interim payments each year.

Investment multiples

We will come back to cash flows later. Meanwhile, let's turn to IRR's much friendlier twin, the investment multiple. If institutional investors tend to talk about internal rate of return (and look for 30 or even 40 per cent), angels often use the easier shorthand of saying they are looking for a multiple of their original investment within a

---

100 All major spreadsheet programs (such as Microsoft Excel, Apple Numbers or Google Docs) contain IRR functions to simplify calculations.

Table 12. Simplified net cash flows and internal rates of return over seven years

Cash flows vs IRR (£'000)	Cash flow timing								Value?	
	Today	Year 1	Year 2	Year 3	Year 4	Year 5	Year 6	Year 7	Total CF	IRR
Net cash flow Scenario A	–250	18	17	18	17	18	18	335	191	9.91%
Net cash flow Scenario B	–250	0	0	0	0	0	0	500	250	10.41%
Net cash flow Scenario C	–250	80	90	90	90	70	80	0	250	24.73%

middling period of time, for instance 'I need 10x in 5 years' means 'I need ten times my original stake back' no more than five years from now.

Looking at Scenario B above, you'll have worked out already that the multiple and the IRR are essentially the same. We could rework Table 12 as shown in Table 13.

The original Scenario B was based on angel investors receiving twice their original investment at the end of seven years. This would be lower than most experienced private investors would target. In recent years we have found angels look for closer to ten times their money back (2x is not enough, for reasons we discussed earlier, in Chapter 1 – this is not naked greed). From the revised Scenario B, you can see that over a longish holding period '10x' is about the same as the IRR a fund manager would be looking for, or near enough 40 per cent.

For a ready reckoner converting multiples to IRRs, have a look at Table 14.

Table 13. Comparing net cash flows, internal rates of return and investment multiples

Cash flows vs IRR vs Multiple (£'000)	Cash flow timing								Value?		
	Today	Year 1	Year 2	Year 3	Year 4	Year 5	Year 6	Year 7	Total CF	IRR	Exit X
Scenario B	–250	0	0	0	0	0	0	500	250	10.41%	2
Scenario B revised	–250	0	0	0	0	0	0	2,500	2,250	38.95%	10

Table 14. IRR/multiple returns quick conversion table

Free smart phone apps are available providing instant IRR calculations, for instance at:
http://www.collercapital.com/Publications/Publications.aspx

Multiple	Year 2	Year 3	Year 4	Year 5	Year 6	Year 7	Year 8	Year 9	Year 10	Year 11	Year 12
0.50	−29	−21	−16	−13	−11	−9	−8	−7	−7	−6	−6
1.25	12	8	6	5	4	3	3	3	2	2	2
1.50	22	14	11	8	7	6	5	5	4	4	3
1.75	32	21	15	12	10	8	7	6	6	5	5
2.0	41	26	19	15	12	10	9	8	7	7	6
3.0	73	44	32	25	20	17	15	13	12	11	10
4.0	100	59	31	32	26	22	19	17	15	13	12
5.0	124	71	50	38	31	26	22	20	17	17	17
6.0	145	82	57	43	35	29	25	22	20	18	16
7.0	165	91	63	48	38	32	28	24	21	21	21
8.0	182	100	68	52	41	35	30	26	23	21	19
9.0	200	108	73	55	44	37	32	28	25	22	20
10.0	216	115	78	58	47	39	23	29	26	23	21

Conventional valuation methods

If you are feeling better informed but none the wiser about IRR and related calculations, bear with us. The short answer as to why they matter is that more 'conventional' forms of asset valuation rely on reasonably consistent historic results (sales, margins, pre-tax profits), but the great majority of early-stage firms cannot provide such data. If you fall into that category, at some point you will need to make well-thought-through projections covering future trading, and then work back from that projected value for the whole business to negotiate a price for some of the equity today.

Before we look at projections in more detail, a short word about some more conventional valuation methods by way of context – even if they are unlikely to apply to you in the start-up phase.

Net assets

Pick up the financial pages of a broadsheet newspaper and somewhere amid the commentary on recent company results you will likely find a discussion of why 'Flip Fund Inc is trading at a discount to net assets' or 'StartaHomes plc is on a premium to net assets'. In the case of large, well-established companies with relatively stable prospects, net assets can be a guide to accumulated value:

- Think of a commercial property company, for instance: assuming it has a fair spread of assets (and hence risks) in its portfolio, it would be reasonable to expect that the whole company will be worth approximately the sum of the individual office blocks in the portfolio, and those offices in turn will be worth a multiple of current year earnings, adjusted in line with industry norms and subject to the skill and judgement of the valuers. If so, the company as a whole can be expected to be valued by the stock market at close to net asset value, or NAV.
- On the other hand, as at the end of 2011 Lloyds Banking Group plc had net assets as per its audited accounts of £46,594 million but by the end of 2012 had a market capitalisation (the total value of its shares in issue traded on the London Stock

Exchange) of only £32,282 million, a discount of 30 per cent, when its share price reached 48p/share (it had been down to 25p in June). Investors were taking the view that Lloyds still had many problems to resolve (further write-downs of poorly-performing loans, new banking regulations, possible management changes, sell-off of branches to comply with EU rulings, further compensation claims for insurance mis-selling, possible fines for LIBOR fixing) before the risks associated with buying the stock ceased to cast a shadow over its reported asset value.

Both property companies and banks are (in theory!) businesses with potentially unlimited lives: well-managed property companies will put aside funds on a regular basis to upgrade or replace their estate; and banks that survive crises can gain stability through reduced competition and seasoned management, as various waves of bank mergers over the past 150 years have shown. People still need somewhere to store cash and a means of transferring payments, even when the savings and investment functions in banks dry up.

But some asset-backed companies may be seen as having a finite life, such as those involved in primary extraction (oil fields, gold mines): unless Consolidated Coal plc has a strategy for replacing its assets, its market valuation will begin to resemble a short-life annuity, declining fast in its final decade.

The take-aways for you as an entrepreneur are that:

- Net assets shown on a balance sheet prepared for statutory accounting purposes may not accurately reflect the true value of the underlying assets and liabilities, even in well-established, publicly-traded companies.
- At best, the balance sheet is a starting point. We saw with Lloyds Banking Group that investors made adjustments to the balance sheet value by reference to numerous complex trading issues. Even if Consolidated Coal does have an asset replacement strategy, investors have to form a view on how well its management is likely to execute the plan relative to

other companies in the sector.

- With public companies, investors will look for 'hidden debt' in off-balance sheet vehicles. With early-stage firms, investors will be looking for 'informal' loans, such as an arrangement you may have had with a family member that needs to be unwound before your venture is investment ready.
- Whichever way you look at it, net assets are unlikely to be much use to your prospective angel investors. Your net assets are likely to be worth roughly the value of cash invested in the business minus expenses and plus anything of value you have acquired or generated with the cash.

Comparative transactions

If audited net asset values offer spurious accuracy, a less specific but sometimes more helpful approach is to identify recent transactions reasonably akin to what you have in mind for your own business. For instance, can you find a company similar to yours that was recently acquired by a bigger competitor? Or one that underwent a management buy-out, as you propose to do?

If so, to start your negotiations with investors you can argue that the basis of the transactions is more important than the specific company details. Perhaps your chosen comparative transaction was based on seven times ('7x') earnings before interest, tax, depreciation and amortisation (EBITDA being an approximation for underlying profitability, stripping out non-cash accounting items and levelling different financing methods)? If you are showing positive EBITDA, that metric may suit your case. Or other details of the deal might help you: perhaps the management was tied into a two-year earn-out (that is, they have to carry on working for the company after the trade sale), or final remuneration was set as a percentage of sales or increase in sales?

Well, as a basis for negotiation comparative transactions are a start. And you can be sure that, if your intended investors have done deals recently that they consider similar to yours, they will invoke those other transactions as benchmarks. But since more often than not details of deals done by actively acquisitive companies are not released (beyond the bare disclosures required of listed entities, or accounts filed at Companies House many months after the event), you are likely to find making meaningful comparisons frustrating. If you only know half the deal, can you be sure it's the relevant half?

Sector comparison

Never fear, we are now getting warmer. The basic concept of sector comparators is to find a company similar to yours by sector and type of business, then to 'work back' from its valuation. If your comparators are quoted companies, then information such as market capitalisation and price/earnings ratios will be in the public domain but will need extensive adjusting to reflect the greatly reduced liquidity you offer as a small, unquoted stock.

Consider among other approaches making adjustments to reflect, for example:

- How early-stage you are.
- Your more limited range of products and geographies.
- Your likely more constrained financing mix: it is probable that your comparator has the benefit of leverage (debt supplementing equity) but if you are at the pre- or early-stage revenue stage, will you be funded by equity alone?

If you are struggling for direct comparators with similar products to yours, you can still look for companies with similar revenue models (such as franchising, R&D, consumables – bait and hook (as described in the 'Business models: cutting to the chase' section in Chapter 3, pages 110-17), and adapt their earnings per employee or other metrics to your own case.

Table 15 contrasts two companies operating in the industrial ink jet sector. They entered the sector at different times and were differently financed.

Using financial projections

Comparators will come into their own when you start building

Table 15. Contrasting case studies: same business sector – similar companies – similar valuations. Equity finance is not the *only* way – but valuation counts anyway

Domino	Willett
• Venture capital	• Organic growth and bank borrowing
• IPO – LSE 43× oversubscribed	• **No** equity investments
• Growth financed by rights issues	• No public offerings
• Significant acquisitions to buy new technology (e.g. laser coders)	• New technology 'developed within' – at controlled costs (e.g. laser coders)
• **Always** profitable	• **Always** profitable
• Half-yearly reporting	• No public reporting other than annual accounts
• 1,500 shareholders	
• Regular dividends	• No dividends for first 10 years
• Shareholder-driven – business ratios and 'bottom line' focus	• Growth- and ambition-driven
• Founder **reputedly** realised £21 million	• Owners' re-investment policy **minimises** reported bottom line and taxes
	• Founder **reputedly** realised £60 million – cash

your own financial projections. And these will be the basis of the relationship between you and your investors. To a large extent, how much you have put into the business so far (in cash or sweat-equity) is irrelevant unless it has brought the company to the point where it has assets and/or broadly quantifiable earning power.

Your investors will not care that you gave up your job as chief executive of the Lilliput District Council on a salary of £250,000 a year to work in your start-up full time two years ago – your input will only be 'worth' £500,000 if you have brought the start-up to the point where its potential is moving away from mere aspiration and into the zone where credible projections based on its current competences can be constructed. Their investment will make your joint future possible, a future based on a serious though always imperfect attempt at valuing the company at some point in the future when the investors can realise their investment and work out if it was a '10x', a big loss or just the opportunity to get their original stake back.

Financial projections of this sort require considerably greater thought than the conventional accountant's extrapolation ('last year plus 5%'). The younger your business is and the closer it is to take-off, the less likely it is that recent performance will be directly relevant to how you see progress in the next three to five years: you may well be transitioning from the development phase to commercial take-off. So your model will need to be built bottom-up, with great care given to the underlying assumptions you make about costs, sales, margins – and problems such as late payment by major debtors or what-ifs such as your overseas suppliers not being able to keep up with your change of pace. The more your risks are unquantifiable, the more investors will apply a discount to your projections.

Investors appreciate that you will have less detail the further into the future you look, so you might start by preparing monthly cash flows for year 1, followed by quarterly numbers for years 2 and 3. Your assumptions should always be clearly stated – their quality, and your ability to defend them with fact and logic, will be key to how persuasive investors find you. Realism matters, as does identifying the critical variables and other mnemonics such as your cash burn rate (how much cash do you use up each month; can you reduce it; if so, what impact does it have on your time to market?) and how long until you are out of cash.

And while you are reliant on external equity, do not assume that you will be drawing a generous salary. Investors know that you will work best when you do not have anxieties about keeping a roof over your head, but staying lean and hungry is part of the start-up DNA: your reward comes when you sell out to a major corporation or list on the stock exchange.

Bringing it all together: valuations, projections and investors

Nowadays people know the price of everything and the value of nothing.
– Oscar Wilde

The projected value of your business a few years from now, made possible through the combination of your skill and the investment of your chosen angels or venture funds, is the foundation of your joint future together. In most cases, future value based on earnings and an exit price matters much more to investors than your current balance sheet value.

The underlying logic is as follows. Remember that investors need a high return on those investments that do succeed to make up for the losses on the (majority) of deals that don't – hence their pursuit of a '10x' or '40% IRR' exit. Investors work back from that point. At its simplest, their reasoning will be as follows:

I know that I am looking for a return of X in year Y. Having undertaken extensive research on the company and its management, identified comparables and applying a material discount to those similar companies to take account of their relative maturity, as an experienced investor I know that to obtain my specified return of X I need to acquire a minimum of Z% of the company today.

To give an implausibly simplified example, let us assume that you are the founder of 'HearCorp', which has patented a new, slim-line and highly effective hearing aid called HearSlim. It has already obtained all necessary regulatory approvals in the US, EU and Japan. You and your investors – Unicorn Fund LLP – have agreed on a detailed analysis of what you need to do today to ramp up production to fully commercial levels, recruit a sales team, market the device and keep working on product improvement. This analysis shows that you need £8 million now. How does Unicorn value HearCorp today and work out what percentage of the equity it needs to own to hit its desired rate of return?

Worked example: venture fund valuation model

Unicorn starts by working backwards from the likely exit timing and valuation (remember we assumed that the financial analysis and projections have been agreed between you as the negotiation on fundamental issues has been concluded). It has used the following key facts in its arithmetic:

- Unicorn knows that £8 million is required today and believes that your projections show that HearCorp can achieve net profits after tax (or earnings) five years from now of £15 million.
- You both believe that selling the company to an established medical devices conglomerate in five years is realistic, and you agree to work together to make HearCorp attractive to the conglomerates, working on your already good relationships with them through trade shows, professional conferences and studying the gaps in their product line-up.
- After extensive research, you and Unicorn both believe that medical device companies comparable to yours in terms of activities are trading on multiples of earnings of 15. You have examined in detail the impact of HearCorp being smaller than these comparables, with a less extensive portfolio and no entrenched market position. As a result, you have concluded that your exit multiple will be nine times ('9x') year 5 earnings, rather than 15 times.
- Unicorn's internal investment guidelines require it to seek a 40 per cent IRR on exit.
- You do not consider that a second funding round will be required and the number of shares reserved for employee options is minimal.
- The management currently owns all the 100,000 shares in issue.
- Unicorn does not expect to receive dividends or other forms of remuneration before the final sale of HearCorp.

This simplified information will allow Unicorn's analysts to work out key numbers such as the value of the company at exit, the value of today's investment at exit (or payoff), the fraction of ownership required and the share price in the current round. The easiest place to start is with the fraction of ownership required today, as follows.

Fraction of ownership required
$V_{t, company} = Earnings_t * Multiple_t$
$V_{t, investment} = V_0 * (1 + r)^t$
$F_{required} = V_{t, investment} / V_{t, company}$
$S_M = (F_{req} * S_{pre}) / (1 - F_{required})$
$P_M = M / S_M$

where:

$V_{t, company}$ = value of company at payoff
$Earnings_t$ = the earnings of the company at payoff
$Multiple_t$ = the P/E multiple expected to reflect the market at payoff
$V_{t, investment}$ = the value of the current round at payoff
$F_{required}$ = the fraction of corporate ownership required
S_M = the number of shares issued in the current round
S_{pre} = the number of shares in existence pre-funding
P_M = the share price at the current round
M = the amount of funds raised in the current round
r = desired internal rate of return

Taking these one by one:

$V_{t, company} = Earnings_t * Multiple_t$

The value of HearCorp after five years will be its earnings of £15 million times the agreed multiple of 9 = £135 million.

$V_{t, investment} = V_0 * (1 + r)^t$

The value of the investment after five years will be its value today times 1 + the desired IRR to the power of the number of years of the life of the investment.

$V_{t, investment} = £8m * (1+.4)^5$
$= £8m * 1.4^5 = £8m * 5.38$
$= £43,025,920$

$$\boxed{F_{required} = V_{t, investment} / V_{t, company}}$$

The fraction of ownership required by Unicorn is derived from the value of its holding at the time of exit or payoff as a proportion of the total value of HearCorp:

$F_{required} = £43,025,920 / £135,000,000$
$= 31.87\%$

$$\boxed{S_M = (F_{req} * S_{pre}) / (1 - F_{required})}$$

How many shares will Unicorn require to be issued to it in this round to achieve its desired ownership fraction?

Number of shares issued in current round
= (Ownership fraction required * Number of shares in existence) / (1 – Fraction required)
= (31.87% * 100,000) / (1 – 0.3187)
= $\dfrac{31,870}{0.6813}$
= 46,778 shares

$$\boxed{P_M = M / S_M}$$

What will be the share price at which Unicorn buys its shares today?

Share price at current round
= Funds raised in current round / Number of shares issued in current round

= £8,000,000 / 46,778

= £171.02 per share

We hope that working through that simple example helps unpack the key stages required when a knowledgeable investor has to work backwards from the exit value to find the value of the company today and hence the proportion of equity it needs to acquire to hit its desired rate of return. The maths is not really as hard as it looks when you break it down line by line. However, because transactions are rarely quite as straightforward as this, at the end of this chapter we have included a somewhat more complex variation on this case study, which also sets out the formulae you would need if you were looking at two separate rounds of investment in the same company.

But first, a short reminder of how you can negotiate with investors when you find it hard to reach agreement on exit values, the timing of your exit and other critical factors.

What if you can't agree on key items?

You will recall that in Chapter 4 we went through the different instruments used by professional venture fund managers to protect the value of their investment. Some instruments can be complex, covering every possible outcome – think of the cumulative, convertible, redeemable, participating preference share. Here we touch on something with a similar philosophy but which is much simpler in design, and often used by earlier-stage investors – such as angels – where there is insufficient empirical data to start arguing with about price on an informed basis: convertible instruments and options.

Suppose that you are the founder of QuickCharga, and you have used grant and family investment wisely to develop a new charging pack for smart phones and tablet computers that has the twin advantages of working with most major brands and taking up half the physical space of existing adaptors. It looks like a winner but because of confidentiality issues you have not been able to test it yet with any of the device manufacturers – in the jargon of the trade, you don't know if the ducks will feed.

You only need £500,000 to set up manufacturing and distribution channels and a group of super-angels is looking seriously at providing that sum. But because you have made no sales yet, you and they cannot agree on some of the key numbers needed to form a valuation of the company now and derive the fraction of ownership they would receive. Furthermore, you both know that if your initial sales to the Danish handset manufacturer, Sonerik, are successful, you will need considerably more funding to build capacity to serve it and its much larger Norwegian competitor, Kianor – probably £3 million, which is way beyond what your super-angels can provide on their own.

Fortunately, your super-angel syndicate contains seasoned investors who recognise the value of ratchets in settling on mutually acceptable terms when you have critical factors that cannot be quantified at the outset. They propose two possible solutions: first, they will invest initially using a convertible loan note; second, they will take warrants to ensure that they obtain an increased ownership percentage later on if you do not hit your agreed targets.

How does this work? The great advantage of a convertible loan note is that it is a form of debt that will convert to equity later on once events make valuing the company easier in the light of subsequent information. So the angels can provide you with the £500,000 you require today (they did accept your budgeted costs) as a loan so you do not have to haggle over company valuation today ahead of market data giving you a fix on price. But when later on you do raise your second round of investment with the benefit of a year's worth of sales to Sonerik behind you, the angels can fix the price at which their debt will convert to equity based on the price that Unicorn Fund LLP pays for shares then. And to reflect the higher risk that they have carried, the angels write in a discount for their conversion price.

As for options, it is quite possible that you and Unicorn were not so far away in terms of valuation, so you did agree a target exit date and valuation and hence ownership fraction today. But because there are numerous assumptions in your calculations that will need to be revisited in the light of experience, to protect their position the angels write in an option allowing them to acquire a greater proportion of

QuickCharga at low cost so that their ultimate exit value is what they need it to be to obtain the 30 per cent IRR they were looking for.

Numerous variations and combinations of these ratcheting techniques can be used to fit your – and investors' – circumstances when unknown factors at the outset make agreeing on values and percentage of ownership impossible. We summarise the key features, including:

- *Convertible loan notes or shares*:
  - Loan or preference share that converts to ordinary shares with the strike price based on later events
  - Can be redeemable with a long-stop date (for instance, five years), to prevent management relapsing into a 'lifestyle' company
  - Often carry a coupon, for instance, 5 per cent cumulative per year, based on face value
  - Equity conversion may take place at a discount (for instance, if a venture investor later pays £1 per share according to an agreed timetable, the initial angels receive 1.15 shares per £1)
- *Options and warrants*:
  - The investor has the right to acquire more shares (usually at par or at a discount to latest valuation) if agreed milestones are not met

- *Advantages*:
  - Resolves conundrum of equity being impossible to price
  - Incentivises management to hit (or beat) milestones as ratchets may also work to the advantage of management
  - Prevents relapse into lifestyle company
- *Disadvantages*:
  - Investors and founders begin their relationship by disagreeing about valuation
  - Disincentivises management if targets are too stretching or only operate in favour of investors
  - Complexity and potential added legal costs documenting ratchets

CASE STUDY
Calculating values over multiple rounds

Introduction

Earlier on this chapter, we took the relatively simple example of HearCorp and its advanced hearing aid, HearSlim, to see how venture investors work back from a projected exit value and their desired rate of return to calculate a value for the company today and the required fraction of ownership. We will now make matters a little more complicated, not least by asking what would happen if not one but two rounds of investment are required to see HearCorp through to sustainable profitability.

The basic facts are the same as before (and – with the necessary changes – reiterated below for convenience), except that this time we will assume you run Unicorn and that HearCorp is managed by its two founders, Lorne and Olivia. What is more, the founders wish to incentivise their long-suffering laboratory technician, Alan, by providing him with a meaningful grant of share options.

Key facts

Lorne and Olivia are the founders of HearCorp, which has patented a new, slim-line and highly effective hearing aid called HearSlim. It has already obtained all necessary regulatory approvals in the EU, US and Japan.

You run a mid-market venture fund – Unicorn Fund LLP – and have agreed with the founders on a detailed analysis of what HearCorp requires now to ramp up production to fully commercial levels, recruit a sales team, market the device and keep working on product improvement. This analysis shows that HearCorp needs £4 million now and a further £4 million in two years from now (note the change).

You accept provisionally the founders' projections showing that HearCorp can achieve net profits after tax (or earnings) five years from now of £15 million. And you and the management all believe that selling the company to an established medical devices conglomerate in five years' time is realistic. So you agree to function together to make HearCorp attractive to the conglomerates, working on your already good relationships with them through trade shows, professional conferences and studying the gaps in their product line-up.

After extensive research, you and the founders believe that medical device companies comparable to HearCorp in terms of activities are trading on multiples of earnings of 15. You have examined in detail the impact of HearCorp being smaller than these comparables, with a less extensive portfolio and no entrenched market position. As a result, you have concluded that your exit multiple will be nine times year 5 earnings, rather than 15 times.

Unicorn's internal investment guidelines require it to seek a 40 per cent IRR on exit.

The second funding round will be required quite soon (end of year 2), and you agree that provided Lorne and Olivia have hit their agreed milestones by then, the round-to-round multiple will be '2x'. You will value the total company then at twice its current agreed value now for the purposes of preparing your financial projections and agreeing a base case with the founders. (This in turn means you will receive half as many shares for your £4 million then as you do for your £4 million now.) Unicorn does not expect to receive dividends or other forms of remuneration before the final sale of HearCorp.

The founders own all the shares in issue and have recently conducted a 10:1 share split such that there are now 1,000,000 shares of 10p each in issue. Each has invested his or her entire life savings of £250,000 in HearSlim, but has no further money to invest. Given the untested nature of the product and the lack of tangible assets, HearSlim cannot leverage equity investment with bank debt.

Lorne and Olivia are benevolent employers and have reserved 1,000 shares for Alan, the laboratory technician, using a tax-effective share scheme allowing him to exercise his options on the earlier of (a) the fifth anniversary of grant or (b) sale of the company or its flotation on a recognised stock exchange.

Key questions

The issue for you as fund manager is the same as when only one round of investment was being reviewed, but it is complicated by having a second investment round, a round which will be at a different price from the first.

How does Unicorn value HearCorp (a) today, (b) at round two, and then (c) work out what percentage of the equity it needs to own to hit its desired rate of return?

As before, you as fund manager will start by working backwards from the likely exit timing and valuation. But this time, to calculate the number of shares to be issued in round two (S_{M2}) you can substitute *the money raised in round two* divided by *the share price in round one* times *the multiple of the first-round price*:

$$S_{M2} = M_2 / (P_{M1} * \text{round-to-round multiple})$$

In this instance:
$$S_{M2} = M_2 / (P_{M1} * 2)$$

Building a spreadsheet

Taking all this information together, we could work through round one as before, then work up round two by substitution, as discussed.[101] However, since as a diligent investor you will almost certainly need to try out numerous iterations of the same scenario (working out the 'what ifs') to see what the impact might be if one or more key facts changed – such as the number of years until you reach your exit or the ultimate price achieved for the whole company – it is preferable to build a spreadsheet to accommodate your key variables, which will provide an instant snapshot of the impact of changes as you make them.

Table 16 provides a template you may find useful in building your model for round-to-round valuation and share price analysis, together with a full summary of the relevant formulae required at each stage.

The spreadsheet allows us easily to calculate the number of shares to be issued in round two, using the formula as demonstrated above:

---

101 Note that, because of the changes to the basic facts (for instance, splitting the £8 million into two equal rounds over two years, undertaking a share split and including share options), the numbers would not be identical to those in our earlier single-round example.

$$S_{M2} = M_2 / (P_{M1} * 2)$$
$$= £4m / (£19.08 * 2)$$
$$= £4m/£38.16$$

= 104,810 shares to be issued in round two (taking account of roundings)

Apart from its flexibility and the time saved, the other advantage of this modelling approach is to provide an agreed frame of reference for the entrepreneurs and investors to negotiate over price. Realistically, you are both seeking to 'solve for x' where x is your terminal value. If you can do that, you can start to work back through what you need to achieve at each stage to be on track to hit x and by extension what proportion of the company the investor needs to own today to reach their desired rate of return.

However, our usual caveats apply: the earlier the company is in its development, the smaller the amount of empirical data it will have to build its case, and the more the entrepreneurs have to negotiate on the basis of a combination of vision and ratchets.

Finally, we can use the spreadsheet to prepare a simplified capitalisation table for HearCorp, showing at each stage the number of shares owned and their value – a value which remains putative until realised. Note from this two fundamental points:

- First, as we said right at the beginning, with investors you are not giving anything away, you are selling, and with the right deal the outcome is a win–win. Lorne and Olivia have parted with 12 per cent of the equity each, for a total investment in the company of £8 million. Their original stake had a (paper-only) value of £9.55 million per founder. After parting with a minority holding, five years later they would be in a position to sell to their chosen competitor for £51.3 million – each.
- Second, never underestimate the value of share options. Key hires could work elsewhere for considerably more than they are paid in many start-ups, which need to manage their cash burn with fierce determination. The upside for them is partly the joy of working in a creative entrepreneurial environment

Component	Figure	Notes
Entrepreneurs requested first-round investment from VC	£4,000,000	M_1
Earnings of company at time t	£15,000,000.00	Post-tax profit, not revenue
Time t in years	5	t
Multiple company will be trading at time t	9	Assumption; rough P/E ratio for comparables at exit
Terminal value of company, given multiple	135,000,000.00	Terminal earnings* multiple ... call this "X"
Compounded return required by VC	40%	IRR – percentage is fixed as a goal
Terminal value of VC investment at time t, given return rate	£21,512,960.00	Investment* $(1+IRR)^t$
Fraction of ownership needed at payoff	15.94%	F= terminal value of investment /terminal value of company
Round-to-round multiple	2	R-r multiple – assumption: only 8 months out
Cash required by entrepreneur for second round	£4,000,000.00	M_2
Current stock in issue to founders, angels, other investors (given)	1,000,000	S_{out} – given in business plan
Shares reserved for founders and employees	1,000	S_{pot} – assumption: arbitrary
Total 'pre-money' shares outstanding	1,001,000	$S_{pre} = S_{out} + S_{pot}$
Shares VC needs to purchase in round 1	209,620.91	$F*S_{pre}/(1-F-(F*M_2/M_1*r\text{-}r\ multiple))$
Price per share, round 1	£19.08	VC investment / number of shares VC buys
Pre-money valuation	£19,101,148.33	Round 1 price* $(S_{out} + S_{pot})$
Price per share, round 2	£38.16	Price of first-round share*r-r multiple
Shares VC needs to purchase in round 2	104,810.45	SM2=M2/(M1/SM1*multiple of first-round price
Maximum number of shares in issue at exit	1,315,431.36	Current stock in issue + options + VC round 1 + VC round 2
Market value per share at exit	£102.63	Market value / total shares in issue
Post-money valuation	£23,101,148.33	$V_{pre}+M_1=V_{post}$

Table 16. Template for building a spreadsheet. For ease of reference, the figures in white are givens from the business plan or otherwise agreed between the founders and the investors. Those in grey are results provided by the spreadsheet. The target IRR is in black and can alter according to the perceived level of risk of the business case

1. Pre-money valuation

$$V_{pre} = P_s * S_{pre} = P_s * (S_{out} + S_{pot})$$

where:

V_{pre} = the pre-money valuation
P_s = the price per share of the current round
S_{pre} = the number of shares 'in existence' pre-funding
S_{out} = the number of actual shares outstanding before funding
S_{pot} = allowance for potential issuance of shares under
employee stock options or warrants

2. Post-money valuation

$$V_{post} = V_{pret} + M$$

where:

V_{pre} = the pre-money valuation
M = the money raised in the current round

3. Internal rate of return

$$r = \left(\frac{V_t}{V_0}\right)^{1/t} - 1$$

where:

r = internal rate of return
V_t = value of company at time of realisation
V_0 = value of company at time of investment
t = time to realisation (years)

4. Fraction of ownership required

$$V_{t, company} = Earnings_t * Multiple_t$$
$$V_{t, investment} = V_0 + {}_t * (1+r)^{\wedge}t$$
$$F_{required} = V_{t, investment} / V_{t, company}$$
$$S_m = (F_{required} * S_{pre}) / (1 - F_{required})$$
$$P_M = M / S_M$$

where:

V_t = value of company at payoff
$Earnings_t$ = the earnings of the company at payoff
$Multiple_t$ = the P/E multiple expected to reflect the market at payoff
$V_{t, investment}$ = the value of the current round at payoff
$F_{required}$ = the fraction of corporate ownership required
S_M = the number of shares required in the current round
P_M = the share price in the current round
M = the amount of funds raised in the current round

5. Multiple-round dilution

To calculate S_{M2} substitute for it using:

$$S_{M2} = M_2 / (P_{M1} * \text{multiple of first round price})$$

Also substitute for P_{M1} in the equation above, using:

$$P_{M1} = M_1 / S_{M1}$$

This gives an equation where S_{M2} is a constant times S_{M1}
Now substitute into the equation covering fraction of ownership
required:

$$F_{required} = S_{M1} / (S_{M1} + S_{out1} + S_{pot1} + S_{M2})$$

and partly the deferred gratification of a capital gain through cashing out share options, especially where these are structured to be tax effective, such as the Enterprise Management Incentive Scheme.[102] Alan, in this example, would have had pay back for several years at a low salary on under 0.08 per cent of the total equity. See Table 17.

To negotiate wisely, you need to understand how selling equity will yield you a smaller slice of a much bigger pie.

TECHNICAL APPENDIX
Some useful financial calculations

Break-even point or BEP

Your BEP tells you what you need to sell given your current cost structure before you start turning a profit, where:

- costs and revenues are equal
- gross margin = overheads

- gross margin = contribution = price of product – direct costs
- overheads = indirect or fixed costs

BEP formula

$$\frac{\text{Overhead}}{\text{Gross profit margin as \%}} \times 100$$

BEP worked example

Gross profit margin =

$$\frac{\text{Sales – direct costs}}{\text{Sales}} \times 100$$

---

102 http://www.hmrc.gov.uk/shareschemes/emi-new-guidance.htm.

Table 17. HearCorp capitalisation table

	Number of shares	£/share	Portfolio value (£)	As %
Before investment				
Lorne	500,000.00	19.10	9,550,574.17	50.00%
Olivia	500,000.00	19.10	9,550,574.17	50.00%
Total	1,000,000.00		**19,101,148.33**	
After Round 1				
Lorne	500,000.00	19.08	9,541,033.13	41.34%
Olivia	500,000.00	19.08	9,541,033.13	41.34%
Unicorn	209,620.91	19.08	4,000,000.00	17.33%
Total	1,209,620.91		**23,082,066.26**	
After Round 2				
Lorne	500,000.00	38.16	19,082,066.26	38.04%
Olivia	500,000.00	38.16	19,082,066.26	38.04%
Unicorn	314,431.36	38.16	12,000,000.00	23.92%
Total	1,314,431.36		**50,164,132.53**	
After Exit				
Lorne	500,000.00	102.63	51,313,966.03	38.01%
Olivia	500,000.00	102.63	51,313,966.03	38.01%
Unicorn	314,431.36	102.63	32,269,440.00	23.90%
Alan	1,000.00	102.63	102,627.93	0.08%
Total	1,315,431.36		**135,000,000.00**	

$$\frac{600,000 - 240,000}{600,000} \times 100 = 60\%$$

Annual overheads = £216,000
Monthly overhead = £18,000

Monthly BEP =

$$\frac{\text{Monthly overhead}}{\text{Gross PM as \%}} \times 100$$

$$\frac{£18,000}{60} \times 100 = £30,000$$

You may find it helpful to think of the break-even point visually. For instance, you can see in Figure 20 that total costs are equal to fixed costs (a horizontal line, until you go through some form of step-change, such as having to move to more expensive premises as you expand) plus variable costs, a line growing in step with sales. Where sales cross these combined costs on your graph, you have hit BEP. And if fixed costs do increase – the BEP moves further up and to the right – you need more of them.

Your investors will likely use BEP as a key metric, along with cash burn rate: it shows when you will cease to be reliant on them to stay afloat. Note that in Figure 21 there are two break-even stages: at the bottom of the curve, you cease to burn more cash than you generate; then, when you 'cross the line' back to having a positive bank balance, you have paid off external debt and can start to generate a return for your equity investors.

Different types of business have different cash profiles – see Figure 22. Those with long-term ability to scale up and grow are likely to lead you deepest into the valley of requiring significant sums to return to break-even. In theory at least, the upside justifies the additional risk in the right hands, though in some sectors such as pharmaceuticals

Figure 20. Break-even point and fixed costs

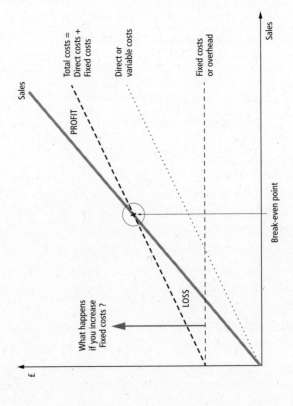

Figure 21. Financing
the journey

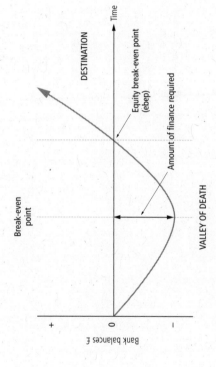

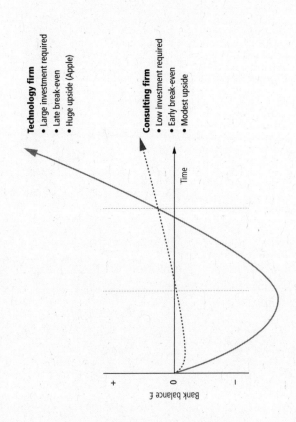

Figure 22. Different firms, different profiles…

increasingly large 'bets' are required in the hope of finding the next-generation blockbuster drug that will pay for dozens of projects costing eight-figure sums that do not make it past clinical trials.

Net present value (NPV)

Net present value is key for investors. Put simply, it is 'the value *today* of all outgoing and incoming cash flows over the life of the investment'.

To calculate NPV, you need to identify the appropriate *discount rate* to reflect the fact that '£10 today is worth more than £10 next year'. You may find it easier to think of this if you imagine yourself as a 'buyer' rather than a 'seller': if you were putting your savings in a really safe place (such as an old-fashioned, well-run bank), then taking account of other similar opportunities out there and the low level of risk, you might be happy with a 2 per cent interest rate on a one-year deposit.

On the other hand, if you were prepared to risk putting your savings in a small, offshore deposit-taker run by a team of MBAs from a famous business school, you may take the view that to justify the extra risk you need a margin of 8 per cent – and even then you might not put all your savings in one place. As the old saying goes, when the odds are good, the goods are odd. Are you buying or selling?

NPV formula

$$R_0 = \frac{R_t}{(1+i)^t}$$

R_0 = net cash flow *today*

t = time of the cash flow

i = discount rate

R_t = net cash flow(s) at time t (e.g. 1 year away)

NPV worked example

Alan's new job will involve driving considerable distances each year, so he proposes to buy a newer car. He is offered a decent nearly-new hatchback for £11,000. He only has £2,000 towards the deposit so he needs to borrow the balance of £9,000. The dealer offers him finance on the following terms:

Principal: £9,000
Term: 3 years
Interest rate: 10% on balance outstanding at the start
                   of the year

Alan wants to know what the loan will really cost him.

$$R_0 = \frac{3000 + 900}{(1 + 0.1)^1} + \frac{3000 + 600}{(1 + 0.1)^2} + \frac{3000 + 300}{(1 + 0.1)^3}$$
$$= 3545 + 2975 + 2480 = 9,000$$

The cash cost is £10,800 (the sum of the three top line sums) but taking account of the time value of money, the net present value of the loan is only £9,000.

Note that this example is heavily simplified for illustrative purposes. For instance, in consumer finance, interest is likely to be applied to the actual amount outstanding. But the interest rate would probably be closer to 18 per cent currently. Other real-world issues that might need confronting include: is the bank's interest rate the same as the opportunity cost or the real risk to Alan? Does he have savings? What interest rate does he earn on his savings – more or less than the interest on the bank loan?

Summary NPV calculations

In the example of Alan buying a new car, we only had three years' worth of discounted cash flows to take into account, so working out the NPV in stages was not unduly onerous. However, where numerous years need to be taken into account, the formula can be summarised as follows:

$$NPV = \sum_{t=0}^{N} \frac{R_t}{(1+i)^t}$$

Sum of payments today (t_0)

= payments throughout all periods (N) discounted for rate of return (i)

Return on investment (ROI)

ROI is a measure of performance used to assess the 'efficiency' of an investment or to compare the relative efficiency of two or more investments. If (a) the proposed investment does not have a positive ROI or (b) other current opportunities have higher ROI, then other things being equal investors should not proceed with the investment in question. It is popular because it is flexible, but flexibility can mean that the numbers input to the formula risk being easily manipulated.

ROI formula

$$ROI = \frac{\text{Ratio of money gained or lost}}{\text{Initial investment}}$$

$$ROI = \frac{\text{(Final value of investment – initial value)}}{\text{Initial value of investment}}$$

ROI worked example – and comparisons

Martin is planning a marketing campaign for his online music pay-per-play service. Since the business has been running for six years already, he has reliable analytical data showing the likely impact, in terms of increased sales, of various marketing initiatives. Budgets are tight, so he needs to be sure that the chosen medium will have maximum impact.

Option A is to give away free membership to the music service, which his analytical data show produces limited initial revenue in the short term but considerable added sales in years 3, 4 and 5. Option B is to run a BOGOF – buy one, get one free – campaign, which past experience reveals has a big hit up-front but with a tapering effect in later years. Option C is to sponsor the annual music awards of *The Music Chronicle*. Since the next awards ceremony is not until the following year, no additional sales are generated this year. And since followers of award ceremonies are a fickle crowd, the analytical data predicts limited impact in later years as well.

The impact of these three scenarios can be seen in Table 18.

Table 18. Comparison of ROI, NPV and IRR

Simple ROI vs NPV vs IRR	Today	Year 1	Year 2	Year 3	Year 4	Year 5	Total	ROI	Proceed?	NPV (@10%)	IRR
Cash flow A (£'000)	−10,000	2,000	4,000	5,000	6,000	7,000	14,000	40%	Yes	£6,659.16	31%
Cash flow B (£'000)	−10,000	7,000	6,000	4,000	3,000	2,000	14,000	20%	Depends	£6,925.87	45%
Cash flow C (£'000)	−10,000	–	5,000	3,000	2,000	1,000	1,000	−90%	No	−£1,478.98	3%

If Martin were simply analysing ROI as defined above ([final value minus initial value]/[initial value]), he would definitely proceed with Option A as it produces a 40 per cent ROI and is the highest performer of the three. He hesitates with Option B and decides to look at some other performance metrics. Using the cost of capital provided to him by Irene, the CFO, he works out that Option B is actually a better bet in terms of NPV, if only by a small margin. The reason for this is that, with Option B, the income is better in the earlier years.

Intrigued, he asks Irene how sure she is that 10 per cent is the right discount rate. She says that, when testing capital projects, company policy is to see what would happen if the cost of capital (a) rose to 20 per cent and (b) fell to 4 per cent. Running those numbers, he found the results shown in Table 19.

The higher the cost of capital, the more the NPV valuation favours 'the bird in the hand'. But with a low cost of capital, both the ROI and NPV metrics favour the better 'absolute' return of Option A to the discounted returns of Option B. Even though Option C produces £1,000 more cash over five years than the initial investment, it is a poor return on all three metrics – NPV, ROI and IRR.

A revealing trade-off is the difference between NPV and IRR.

Generally, NPV provides a more reliable guide to the merits of a project because it uses the 'known' cost of capital (derived from external sources, such as traded securities or what it costs you to borrow) in discounting cash flows, not a derived rate which ensures that NPV = 0. More complex project finance calculations assume that in either case – NPV or IRR – cash flows are reinvested at the discount rate used. If IRR is high compared with cost of capital, reinvestment at this elevated rate of return is unrealistic.

Finally, just to demonstrate that IRR is the cost of capital at which NPV = 0, we can recalculate inserting the derived IRR as the discount rate in the NPV formula. No additional insight is provided, but it provides a cross-check to show the limitations of the IRR method of project appraisal. Check out Table 20.

Table 19. Using ROI, NPV and IRR in financial decision-making

Simple ROI vs NPV vs IRR	Today	Year 1	Year 2	Year 3	Year 4	Year 5	Total	ROI	Proceed?	NPV (@20%)	IRR
Cash flow A (£'000)	−10,000	2,000	4,000	5,000	6,000	7,000	14,000	40%	Yes	£2,537.19	31%
Cash flow B (£'000)	−10,000	7,000	6,000	4,000	3,000	2,000	14,000	20%	Depends	£3,804.44	45%
Cash flow C (£'000)	−10,000	–	5,000	3,000	2,000	1,000	1,000	−90%	No	−£2,854.40	3%

Simple ROI vs NPV vs IRR	Today	Year 1	Year 2	Year 3	Year 4	Year 5	Total	ROI	Proceed?	NPV (@4%)	IRR
Cash flow A (£'000)	−10,000	2,000	4,000	5,000	6,000	7,000	14,000	40%	Yes	£10,527.50	31%
Cash flow B (£'000)	−10,000	7,000	6,000	4,000	3,000	2,000	14,000	20%	Depends	£9,656.11	45%
Cash flow C (£'000)	−10,000	–	5,000	3,000	2,000	1,000	1,000	−90%	No	−£171.82	3%

Table 20. Limitations of IRR in project appraisal

Simple ROI vs NPV vs IRR	Today	Year 1	Year 2	Year 3	Year 4	Year 5	Total	ROI	Proceed?	NPV =IRR	IRR
Cash flow A (£'000)	−10,000	2,000	4,000	5,000	6,000	7,000	14,000	40%	Yes	£0.00	31%
Cash flow B (£'000)	−10,000	7,000	6,000	4,000	3,000	2,000	14,000	20%	Depends	£0.00	45%
Cash flow C (£'000)	−10,000	–	5,000	3,000	2,000	1,000	1,000	−90%	No	£0.00	3%

Cost of capital

So far, we have treated cost of capital as a given, and in most cases for early-stage firms it will be just that. But if you are interested in undertaking some reverse-engineering to find out how investors might derive your cost of capital, we have set out below the conventional formula.

Formula for cost of capital

$$E_s = R_f + \beta_s (R_m - R_f)$$

E_s = expected rate of return for a security
R_f = risk-free return (e.g. bond of AAA-rated government)
β_s = sensitivity to market risk of the security
R_m = historical rate of return of the market
$(R_m - R_f)$ = risk premium over risk-free assets

The bottom line is this: 'the greater the risk premium of your stock and its correlation with market risk, the higher the cost of capital'.

As for the relationship between cost of equity and cost of debt, a good place to start is with the insight provided by two Nobel Prize-winning economists, Franco Modigliani and Merton Miller. Their theorem states that: 'in an efficient market, in the absence of taxes, bankruptcy costs or agency costs and asymmetric information, the value of a firm is unaffected by how that firm is financed'.

The fundamental point here is that the conditions Modigliani and Miller envisaged are extraordinarily unlikely to occur. Markets are of variable efficiency, information asymmetries are rampant (the used car salesman always knows more about his stock than you do), and in most countries tax law enshrines basic differences between debt and equity:

• Interest on loans tax deductible.
• Dividends on shares paid out of taxed profits.

This debt advantage (and collective amnesia about bankruptcy costs) was one reason why up until 2008 many financial transactions had a high level of debt to equity (or 'leverage').

Although it can be helpful to have an idea of how cost of capital is derived, because considerable amounts of data are required for accurate calculations (for instance, relating to the sensitivity to market risk of securities), formulae used in assessing established corporations will not 'read across' directly to the entrepreneurial world.

CASE STUDY
Boom and bust – greed and fear

During the period 1996–2000 the Western world saw an astonishing race by investors to pile money into companies without rational financial justification. This was 'dotcom boom and bust'. The advent of the World Wide Web and the birth and public share issues of Netscape and Amazon. com led to the manic race of very many 'dotcoms' to initial public offerings on public markets in the US and Europe, and early investors making fortunes. The dotcoms dragged technology stocks in general to giddy heights of value as 'technology' companies became grouped together with – and confused with – 'e-commerce' companies migrating to online businesses with pretty ordinary retail products.

During the boom IPO fever raged. Many companies were floated on public markets before they reached maturity. Something similar also happened in the biotechnology sector. If you want to understand how markets work and how investors drive them, you need to consider more than money; you need to take into account the driving forces of greed and fear. The boom was 'greed time' – so many investors leaping onto the apparent gravy train of dotcom and technology stock investing. Fortunes were made fast.

But the financial viability of so many of the 'boomers' was bad and along came the bust. Then fear became the driver – not greed – and the result was that venture capital in the technology sector disappeared almost entirely. There's nothing especially new in this story; the greed and fear drama has been re-enacted in the more recent sub-prime mortgage disaster. Thomas Jefferson, the third US president, actually warned about such circumstances in a public speech given in 1778!

Our narrative is included here to illustrate the fragile nature of investment markets and to counsel caution in funding businesses without due care and attention. You need an awareness of the motivating forces behind or in front of money market circumstances at a given point in time. One simple example shows just how values and valuations can swing – not as a result of changes in people's performance or behaviour in companies, but simply through market forces and the effects of greed and fear. Before its stock market debut in May 2012, Facebook's shares were expected by most analysts to be valued at around $28–35 per share, giving a maximum total market capitalisation of the company of $96 billion. So fevered did speculation about its launch share price become that the stock debuted at $38 a share ($104 billion) – for a company only eight years old! A week after the IPO, sobriety began to gain a small foothold, and shares closed at below $27, later dropping below $18 before trading fairly consistently in the $27–29 range early in 2013. Internal rate of return and net present value calculations have little to do with market considerations of value.

A funding fable

A brilliant young entrepreneur was running a fast-growing technology company. He discovered some outstanding new technology in two universities and managed to persuade some business angels to invest £250,000 in starting a new company and acquiring the intellectual property rights to it. At the height of the boom in technology stocks, our entrepreneur had found something new in the fastest-growing sector of them all – telecommunications. A talented team was hired to rapidly turn the technology into a business. Premises were rented. Equipment was bought. The money was spent. One year later – and the market was still booming – the company needed a further investment of £3.5 million.

Full of confidence (some might say arrogance), the company went to all the known venture capital firms, and the angel investors demanded the highest valuation they could get as the new money was raised. Worthy and friendly investors were told that their valuations were not high enough. Over a period of months, three venture firms offered various terms to the company – but without consummation of a deal. The third venture firm insisted that the company sign an exclusivity contract that would grant the fund 45 days to carry out due diligence during which time the company would not consort with any other investors. After 43 days the venture firm decided not to invest!

At this point, the company had three days' money in the bank, a £50,000 overdraft and a bank manager close to a nervous breakdown. Great technology, great team, huge market – no money! And now it's 2000 and technology and telecommunications shares are plummeting.

Surprisingly, the story does have a happy ending. The original business angels stepped back in like fairy godmothers and helped with short-term loan finance and to raise the £3.5 million. The technology was and is great. The lifeboat was launched in time and the company lives on today – having raised a great deal more of equity.

This funding fable hopefully illustrates the danger of basing fundraising purely or largely on valuation at a single point in time. The significant valuation of a company is that which is realised when a successful exit is achieved.

CHAPTER 7

'AFTER THE BALL IS OVER': APPLICATION OF FUNDS AND PLANNING THE FUTURE MONEY SUPPLY CHAIN

Overview

So, feelings of relief have replaced the euphoria which followed the period of stress and probably intense activity to secure necessary funding. The empty champagne bottles are in the recycling bin awaiting collection. It may all have 'gone to the wire'. It often does. And now there are new and different things to consider in addition to keeping the business running, if it has already been started, or getting it properly set up if it has not yet begun operations. Whatever the precise situation, the company now has a new shareholder agreement and new shareholders, probably articles of association, and new directors or at least new directors about to be appointed.

This section deals with six important topics for the newly funded company and the founding entrepreneurs, and provides real-life case studies illustrating what can go right and what can go wrong. The topics are:

- Investor relations
- Board structures and directorships
- The role of non-executive directors and investor directors
- Planning for and funding expansion
- Subsequent fundraising rounds and staying on future funders' radar screens
- Dealing with board conflicts

Investor relations

Most early-stage and smaller companies will have a small number of investors and new shareholders following the fundraising process. It is a very different situation when a company goes to the public markets to seek funds; it may have hundreds, or even thousands, of investors assuming ownership. Investor relations in public companies become a major preoccupation for the management, with the company literally 'in the public eye'. For the company successfully raising its first finance from private individuals such as business angels or from venture capital sources, typically between two and four new individuals or one or two syndicate groups will have invested.

When syndicates invest it is usual for one individual to be elected to represent them if a board seat has been part of the conditions of investment. Some investors do not demand or wish for board participation. By the time the money is in the bank, the founders will know that there are to be new directors nominated by those investors who made a board position a condition of investment. Such conditions will be reflected in the shareholder agreement. The names and detailed information about the new directors who are to be appointed may not be known immediately after the funding round is completed. The founders are likely to have limited influence over who investors nominate for board positions.

Investor relations extend beyond the new directors to be appointed, especially when investment has been made by a syndicate or business angel group. It is worth reflecting on some simple realities at this point:

- The founders will have retained a vision for the business and an agenda for forward actions.
- New investors will hopefully share or support the vision but will have varying agendas regarding future activities. They will also be thinking of eventual exit and securing a return for themselves or those they represent.
- The dynamics of the board will be about to change. A complete shake-up in decision and business dynamics may occur.
- Incoming investors may have preference shares, which means

they have greater influence in specific situations. Entrepreneurs will often see this situation as disadvantageous to them – which essentially is the case.

• Once outside investors become part owners of the business their power and influence will inevitably increase if the company fails to perform to plan and at the same time needs to raise more money.

Regardless of the number of shareholders (and some business angel syndicates can include multiple members – not all participating in the business but all interested in knowing how their money is being used), a key principle is to keep investors as fully informed about the progress of the company as possible. As the life of the company moves forward after new money has been invested, regular communications from the chief executive and board will prove helpful in keeping investors supportive as well as informed. Investor meetings can be arranged when there is something significant to communicate or discuss. In smaller companies, other than when investors are also board members and meet regularly at board meetings, meetings of all investors are uncommon.

Entrepreneur founders need to be prepared for a fresh start at this stage in the life of the company. They must understand that the rules have changed compared to what may have been a fairly free-wheeling existence with decisions taken on the hoof and without formalised justification or reference to others. For some entrepreneurs the transition proves to be very difficult.

In relation to the application of funds, from the time of an injection of new money, investors will be very keen to see that the funds are utilised as set out in the business plan which led to the investment decision. Seeing that this happens and reporting on it is one of the key roles of the board.

Board structures and directorships

It is likely that the board of an early-stage company comprises only small number of people. A newly funded company we helped start up and grow for just over a year raised £1.2 million and had only two directors, including the founder, for the first year of its life. There were no structured board meetings in the usual sense of these things and decisions were taken as needed. The founder worked full time and the supportive director part time. Bookkeeping and accountancy were outsourced. The product was a web portal and no significant assets were involved and no premises used. The company operated 'virtually'.

A condition of the investment was that each of two investor groups putting in £500,000 would have a seat on the board. A non-executive chairperson is to be appointed. Much of the young entrepreneur founder's time will now be taken up with regular board meetings and management reporting in addition to leading the product development and marketing efforts. Part of the money raised will be used to employ more software developers and business development specialists. The Chinese market has suddenly opened up to the company and the first Chinese employees are now being hired.

Many of the positive aspirations of the founding entrepreneur can now be realised with the money raised. But the change in focus, orientation, decision making and indeed lifestyle will be radical for a young person with a highly independent entrepreneurial nature who has never before engaged in formal company board activity. The positioning of founder entrepreneurs in these circumstances is a key consideration in seeking to build a balanced and well-structured board. Decisions on the structure will be partly, maybe largely, determined by the new investors, especially if they have secured a significant equity share and voting rights with their investment.

In Chapter 4 we dealt with the difficult issues involved in negotiating private equity, and hopefully our entrepreneur post-new money will have managed to emerge from negotiations with a fair and favourable deal. You may find it helpful to refer back to that chapter while you study this one.

In this example the founder entrepreneur has one other founder director in support. This director will be deemed 'non-executive'. According to the terms of the shareholder agreement, the founders have retained majority shareholding and control of voting rights so have some protection should disagreements and conflicts arise within the board. A key factor could be the selection of the chairperson and other non-executive directors deemed necessary as the board develops. Very often entrepreneurs find that, post raising investment finance, aspects of control, power and influence have suddenly changed dramatically in ways they had not fully appreciated would be the case. Figure 23 shows how bringing in outside money in exchange for equity dilutes the founders' 100 per cent shareholding and, with it, influence in the business – but the notional value at least may increase between investment rounds. The realities of life after equity investment need to be fully appreciated in advance.

Experience shows that having a highly experienced and knowledgeable non-executive chairperson and a committed non-executive director, both respected and supported by the founding entrepreneur and incoming investors, can make a very significant difference to the success of the company, starting with the establishment of a balanced board which is focused on strategic and key operational performance and avoids micromanagement. The operation of the board will also determine the way in which key executives and employees (likely to be growing in number in successful companies) are able to develop effectively and operate with inspiration and motivation.

Writing about the period after an injection of new money in the form of an equity stake assumes that some of the key issues dealt with here have been understood, explored and managed in advance. This is often not the case, and in any event there will always be unknowns and uncertainties. The 'brave new world' of the well-funded young company can be extremely challenging but also a place of great opportunity for personal development and fulfilment.

The frequency of board meetings varies; often they are held monthly or no less than every other month.

Board papers need to be made available in advance of meetings to enable sufficient time for study and analysis. The task of circulating board papers is most often undertaken by the finance director or

Figure 23. The early-stage business balance: what do investors look for and see?

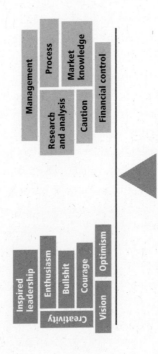

company secretary, if there is one. Minutes will be taken by the finance director or another appointed executive and must be circulated soon after board meetings. Keeping all board-related documents, including minutes, in an orderly and accessible fashion is essential for good governance. Investors considering later funding rounds will seek further information, and all documents relating to board meetings will be part of such due diligence.

Guidance on the conduct and documentation of board meetings can be downloaded from the Institute of Directors (IoD) website.[103] It is almost certain that incoming investors, the chairperson and non-executive directors will be well versed in the proper conduct of board meetings.

Founder CEOs and role changes

The founder of early-stage companies is often also the first chief executive officer (CEO). The founder may be a technical specialist rather than a manager when the company is formed. Some founders cling to the desire to remain the CEO. Some grow into the job and make the grade. Often, as outside money comes into the company, investors will argue that the start-up phase is over and the founder, who may retain a significant shareholding, must move over into a specialised role and an experienced CEO be imported to take the company through the next period of growth. This pattern has become increasingly common in technology-based companies and now often occurs without damage or disruption. The founder remains a member of the board and the CEO joins alongside to lead the executive team. The transition process needs sensitive handling and the mature non-executive chairperson can play a very important role at such times.

The finance director

In most small and early-stage companies, there is no need for a finance director and all financial matters are outsourced. Once serious money is injected into a business, however, investors will

---

103 www.iod.com.

usually expect an experienced finance director to be engaged, even if only on an initial part-time basis. The finance director might be employed prior to fundraising to enhance the prospect of gaining investment. In other cases incoming investors want to be involved in the selection and appointment of a head of finance, who will usually hold a board position.

The role of non-executive directors and investor directors

Company directors all share legal responsibilities as set out in company law. It is important for entrepreneurs to understand the legal responsibilities of company directors, and we recommend that you attend one of the many short courses available. The IoD offers free downloadable pamphlets on this subject on its website.

Much has been written about the difference between executive and non-executive directors in terms of their role and responsibilities. Both law and practice today have moved away from the historical distinction between them. All directors share the same legal responsibilities for the activities of the company. Therefore all share the responsibility for key strategic decisions taken by the board. The 'executive' is charged with implementation. When a new or restructured board starts work it is important to clearly define those areas where board decisions and approvals are needed and those where the executive has decision-making power and authority. In essence, the key roles of the board are to:

- Ensure there is a clear strategy and corporate plan which are in line with the stated objectives of the company as expressed in the articles of association.
- Ensure that the company operates at all times within the law and with appropriate governance applied to all aspects of company law and regulations. This extends to making sure the company is solvent and can be operated from a financial standpoint as 'a going concern'. This becomes particularly important at times of financial stress.
- Apply direction and influence to make sure the executive and company operate in line with the agreed corporate plan.

- Review and monitor results, including but not exclusively, financial performance, and redirect activities as necessary.
- Oversee and direct any material changes in the nature of the company and its operations requiring adjustment to core activities and the objectives of the company.
- Assess performance overall, including performance of the CEO and other key executives.
- Apply stewardship to the company's assets, including financial assets, and ensure that funds are applied in line with the plan which inspired investors to invest their money. To agree and approve changes in proposed direction of funds.
- Manage and monitor, usually through a remunerations committee (REMCO), the salary and other remuneration policies of the company and contractual arrangements with executives and staff. Also to approve any proposed share option schemes and other proposals, plans and actions related to employee share ownership.
- Support and engage in fundraising when additional external finance is required.
- Report to all shareholders on the performance of the company on a regular basis.

A company board should set out, with the approval of all members, a simple charter stating the responsibilities of that board. Although the board will review and contribute to adjustments in major operational matters, it will delegate responsibility for implementation to the executive and should not become engaged in micromanagement. A strong chairperson will ensure that the board operates in this way. Unfortunately, we often see a blurring of the distinctions between board and executive responsibilities, which leads to over-long and drawn-out board meetings and frustration for the executive.

The ideal chairperson is an individual with a track-record of success in the role, who is independent, that is, is not a significant shareholder. In some (probably rare but possible) circumstances the chairperson may have the casting vote on a key decision for the company.

Why non-executives are necessary

Non-executive chairpersons and directors, if carefully selected and well-qualified, will bring much more than lively discussions and perceptive assessments to board meetings. They can make a major contribution to the business and be strong supporters of the executive. Among the value-added elements provided by non-executives will be:

- Assistance with the continuing professional development of executives and employees – human resource management issues.
- Valuable network connections with prospective customers, sources of business information, sources of finance, government connections and eventually routes to disposition or exit.
- Bringing specialist expertise – for example, in marketing or market knowledge, technical knowledge, financial acumen and understanding of the law.
- Wisdom to take time to advise executives on specifics when needed.
- Promotion and representation of the company – at home and where appropriate internationally.

Non-executive directors may not have specific knowledge or experience of the company's products and markets. In some ways, having a non-executive director from an entirely different sector and background can assist 'out of the box' thinking and creativity. At the same time, some companies benefit from having an 'industry guru' as a non-executive director who knows the business and has connections of note which help the executive. There is no standard ideal non-executive director. Another key factor to consider when selecting and appointing non-executive directors is 'chemistry'.

The best-functioning boards are those which operate with coherence and understanding between the members. This does not mean continuous agreement on all matters. Managed contention can be very creative in a board or any team operating in an open style with freedom from restraint in raising key issues. The non-executive and investor directors are also in a good position to challenge the executive in constructive ways, which can result in new thinking and positive changes in direction. Challenge is part of their role and entrepreneurs should welcome it if the board environment is open and non-constrictive.

Creating a coherent and well-balanced board is never easy and, with the different agendas of the different players at work, efforts are necessary to keep things on the straight and narrow. This is the collective responsibility of the board. Case studies show, however, that such balance is not always managed or maintained.

Investor directors

Why is there a separate note on investor directors? Are they not non-executive directors?

The answer to the second question is 'yes'. But they are not independent, having been nominated by a fund or having invested their own money and that of others. Often investor directors bring to the company many of the same benefits as those supplied by non-executive directors. However, their agenda will also take into account their responsibility to the funds or investors they represent. This responsibility may come to outweigh general responsibilities during periods when the company is under stress, particularly related to the ultimate aim of the investor – to make an acceptable return on the investment within a manageable timeframe. Many investors look for a return in two, three or five years. Venture funds operate in ways that place limits on the exit point.

It is important for the entrepreneur to understand that the dynamics influencing director behaviour and therefore that of the board can become determined by the interests and driving forces behind investor directors. And if there are two or more investor directors on a board they may have conflicting interests, which can become disruptive. All of which brings us back to the need for a strong non-executive and independent chairperson.

Planning for and funding expansion

Here we look ahead, beyond the first fundraising to a company that is seriously 'on the move' with motivated investors. Success is indicated by the impending need for more finance to sustain growth. The board should have been anticipating well in advance the likely need for additional finance, knowing that it will take time to raise more funds. By this stage the company should have reliable and detailed financial accounts, including cash flow projections.

The business or corporate plan will (or should) have been regularly updated and the strategic intentions of the company should be clear for a period of two or three years ahead. It may well be that opportunities in new domestic or overseas markets have been identified and/or that new customers and unanticipated new product opportunities have emerged which will need finance to develop and bring to market. You can imagine a whole range of scenarios in which more cash is required. Fact is – your company is growing fast and sustaining growth requires more money coming into the business.

Just as with the initial funding activity, the board and executive need to develop a new business plan for external consumption. All of the processes described in Chapter 3 need to be repeated. The company is preparing for fundraising again. But this time there is a track-record and more complete market knowledge, so the story needs to be framed accordingly.

The value of the company will need to be reassessed. The position and likely attitude of existing investors – some of whom will be investor directors – will also need to be taken into account. This time round it will not be the lone or small group entrepreneur/s making the plan and the pitch and deciding upon target investors. Now the company has an able and connected board to mobilise to make the plan collectively and participate in fundraising activities, including presentations to investors.

Ideally, the board will nominate a leader for the fundraising planning and effort and a team that will be the front end of the activity. All board members can input target investor details and review the proposed presentation material.

Existing investors may well have pre-emptive rights to invest in new rounds and to avoid dilution of their shareholding. In some instances new lead investors will be sought to set the new valuation and co-ordinate the new round. There is no set pattern. Investor directors on the board may seek to take a lead depending on circumstances.

In the event the company has not performed well and not met planned targets, it may be difficult to attract new investors. In such circumstances the existing investors may agree to invest further funds only at a valuation of the company below that attained at the previous investment round. This will mean the dilution of the share value of the entrepreneur founders unless they can invest more. If such trends continue, the ownership of the company will pass progressively to outside investors.

When the value of the company falls between rounds, it is termed 'down rounds'. Following boom and bust periods such as that experienced by dotcom companies between 1996 and 2000, there may only be down rounds as valuations often over-inflated unrealistically in the good times move rapidly downwards in markets in general. All those considering and working with equity capital investments in young companies need to be aware of the pitfalls. Markets can move fast from boom to bust!

Subsequent fundraising rounds and staying on future funders' radar screens

The need for additional funding to finance growth can often become obvious without long-term notice. New opportunities may arise. Just as with investor relations, maintaining connections with prospective future funders will be valuable. If the longer-term plan foresees future funding rounds this will be particularly important. Some companies will do well enough to consider eventual offerings on public stock exchanges, but not many. The growth and financial strategies of companies need to be closely aligned at all times. Good public relations and keeping the name and identity of the company in view of prospective future investors is always a positive strategy.

Dealing with board conflicts

Given the varying agendas of board members – founders, investor directors and independent non-executive directors – and if the number of investor directors grows beyond one or two, conflicts may arise regarding future strategy and operations. We know of a company with one founder, two angel investors and three venture investors that experienced a serious board conflict. One of the venture investors insisted that it was their normal practice to change the CEO when seeking stage-two investments. The other investor directors and the founder objected. The investor insisting on changing the management refused to invest in the next round unless his demands were met. This hiatus resulted in the resignation of some of the directors, the eventual departure of the founding CEO and a period of instability which proved a serious setback for the company.

Conflict resolution requires strong and independent non-executive chairpersons and directors acting in the best interests of the company. Serious board conflicts and the disruption they cause can unsettle all investors and deter prospective new funders. There are no complete answers to such problems. The ideal board comprises directors with common values, a shared vision for the company and an ability to work together. The founding entrepreneur, however, often has little influence on board structure beyond a certain point. Securing a chairperson with the right philosophy is something the entrepreneur should seek to influence if they can.

The two examples below demonstrate the success or failure that can result from board structure:

- *Success achieved by importing a CEO and chairperson prior to public issue of shares.* In this case the entrepreneurial founder, an engineer, as he prepared to list his company on the stock exchange, took the advice of the investment bank running the share issue and instated a full-time chief executive, exiting this position himself but remaining a board member with a focus on creativity and invention, a mature non-executive chairperson with knowledge of the industry and one additional non-executive director. The other board members were finance director and operations director – both executive positions.
- This balanced board was well regarded by investors, and the company raised substantial funds through a successful share

issue on the London Stock Exchange. It then experienced five years of substantial growth. The decision of the founder to step aside within the management team took courage and resolve. It paid off. The founder retained a major part of the equity and realised a handsome reward when shares were sold over time.

• *Failure as a result of non-performance.* This company was full of promise and was developing an excellent new technology. However, it failed to move this technology from the laboratory to the marketplace in time to prevent running out of money. The journey from founder to founder plus two business angels to venture capital funding and the introduction of a CEO to replace the founder CEO changed the ownership and dynamics of the company. The inventive founding entrepreneur lost his influence in the company, which ultimately went into receivership.

Last word: keeping the flame alive

Because of the amount of information to be conveyed, this last chapter has erred on the side of being somewhat didactic rather than inspirational. But ultimately being an entrepreneur *is* inspiring. It is your opportunity to put into practice – for your own benefit and for the benefit of many others – the vision you had when solving some of life's conundrums, big and small.

For ambitious entrepreneurs the early months and years of fundraising can seem like trench warfare. But after a while, as you make progress, you may find that the unpredictable nature of taking a vision to market has a positive, productive quality very much like the 'negative capability' of the artist's creative process that the poet John Keats described in 1817 in a letter to his brothers; a state in which you can transcend and alter the context in which you live and work: 'capable of being in uncertainties, mysteries, doubts, without any irritable reaching after fact and reason'.

So after you've studied the details of planning and pitching and funding, lean back to stay in touch with your inner artist.

Good luck!

INDEX